THE PROMISE OF MARTIN LUTHER'S
POLITICAL THEOLOGY

T&T Clark Enquiries in Theological Ethics

Series editors
Brian Brock
Susan F. Parsons

THE PROMISE OF MARTIN LUTHER'S POLITICAL THEOLOGY

Freeing Luther from the Modern Political Narrative

Michael Laffin

Bloomsbury T&T Clark
An imprint of Bloomsbury Publishing Plc

BLOOMSBURY
LONDON • OXFORD • NEW YORK • NEW DELHI • SYDNEY

Bloomsbury T&T Clark
An imprint of Bloomsbury Publishing Plc

Imprint previously known as T&T Clark

50 Bedford Square	1385 Broadway
London	New York
WC1B 3DPNY	10018
UK	USA

www.bloomsbury.com

BLOOMSBURY, T&T CLARK and the Diana logo are trademarks of Bloomsbury Publishing Plc

First published 2016

© Michael Laffin, 2016

Michael Laffin has asserted his right under the Copyright, Designs and Patents Act, 1988, to be identified as Author of this work.

All rights reserved. No part of this publication may be reproduced or transmitted in any form or by any means, electronic or mechanical, including photocopying, recording, or any information storage or retrieval system, without prior permission in writing from the publishers.

No responsibility for loss caused to any individual or organization acting on or refraining from action as a result of the material in this publication can be accepted by Bloomsbury or the author.

British Library Cataloguing-in-Publication Data
A catalogue record for this book is available from the British Library.

ISBN: HB: 978-0-5676-6989-6
ePDF: 978-0-5676-6990-2
ePub: 978-0-5676-6991-9

Library of Congress Cataloging-in-Publication Data
A catalog record for this book is available from the Library of Congress

Series: T&T Clark Enquiries in Theological Ethics

Typeset by Newgen Knowledge Works (P) Ltd., Chennai, India
Printed and bound in Great Britain

Dedicated to the memory of Steve Holtrust (1956–2011). He lived his life in faithful service to the gospel of our Lord Jesus Christ and ultimately gave his life in service to it. I hope in my lifetime to be at least half the disciple of Jesus that Steve was in his.

CONTENTS

Acknowledgments	ix
List of Abbreviations	xiii

INTRODUCTION: LUTHER, THEOLOGY, AND THE DIGNITY OF
THE POLITICAL 1
    A Portrait of Luther in the History of Political Philosophy 9
    Luther and Contemporary Political Theology 16
    Content and Structure of the Book 21
    Luther's Theological Contribution to a Contemporary
    Understanding of Politics 26

Chapter 1
ONTOLOGY AND POLITICS: LUTHER'S ROLE IN JOHN MILBANK'S
CRITIQUE OF SECULAR MODERNITY 29
    Milbank's Interpretation of Luther 31
    Luther, Nominalism, and "the Finnish" Interpretation 38
    Union with Christ and Luther's Grammar of Faith 42

Chapter 2
THE WORD OF GOD IN LUTHER'S POLITICAL THEOLOGY 57
    Luther's Theology of the Word of God 61
    The Word of God in Scripture and in the Church 70
    The Word of God and the Eucharist 76
    Conclusion 85

Chapter 3
"THE TWO" IN MILBANK AND LUTHER: *CIVITATES* OR *ECCLESIAE*? . . 87
    The Doctrine of "the Two" in Milbank 88
    Violence and Politics: Hannah Arendt 93
    The Construal of "the Two" in Luther 98
    Conclusion: On the Need for a Doctrine of the Two *Ecclesiae*
    and the Two Regiments 110

Chapter 4
VIRTUE AND AGENCY: JENNIFER HERDT'S CRITIQUE OF LUTHER . . 113
    Herdt's Narrative of Virtue Acquisition 115
    Response to Herdt 129

Concluding Reflections on the Importance of Luther's Account of the New Creation for Political Theology	150

Chapter 5
THE THREE INSTITUTIONS: A POLITICS FORMED BY GOD'S STORY
WITH US   153
Criticism of the Institutions as Orders of Creation (*Schöpfungsordnungen*): Karl Barth	155
The Commandments of God as an Invitation to Formed Creaturely Life: The Three Institutions	161
Luther's Description of the Three Institutions	175
Conclusion: A Politics of Remaining in the Good Will of God	188

Bibliography	195
Index	211

ACKNOWLEDGMENTS

In undertaking a project like this, which began as a doctoral thesis at the University of Aberdeen, one spends a great deal of time alone working in quiet seclusion from the rest of the world. However, it has been during this time that I have realized, more than ever before, my deep dependence on all of the people who make up my life. While my name is on the title page, I could not have done this work without the generosity of so many people who have so profoundly shaped my life.

First, I would like to thank the people at North Hills Community Church for teaching me something about what it means to belong to the body of Christ. Jacob and Melody Fredricks, without your insistence that I could, indeed, move my family across the ocean and pursue theological work that might one day serve the church, I would not have had the faith or courage to pursue this book. Early on, when I did not think a PhD program was a realistic possibility, you not only convinced me otherwise, but also initiated and pursued the actions that made it a reality. Your support has enabled this project in more ways than I can name. Others at North Hills have likewise generously provided the financial and other support that, quite literally, made this book possible. I would like to especially thank Mike and Lisa Duran, Bobby and Stephanie Gibson, Debbie Holtrust, Jim and Terri Mann, Chris and Krystal Nunez, and Gary and Yvonne Oltmanns. I am also thankful to other brothers and sisters in Christ outside of North Hills who have also given support to our family during the time of this project, namely, my grandfather, Chet Bennett, my grandmother, Shari Duran, Lorraine Berg, Jeremy and Kim Canell, Bob and Teresa Erickson, Matthew and Cassie Erickson, my aunt Mary Laffin, my uncle and aunt Mike and Kathy Laffin, Matt and Harvest Riggio, and Bryan and Natalie Taylor. Of course, the support you have all given us goes far beyond just our time in the United Kingdom. Most of you have been a part of my life since a young age and have shaped me more than I likely recognize. Please know how much all of you mean to our family and how humbled and awed we have been by your amazing generosity. I will have to accept all that you have given me as the grace that it is, because I will never be able to live up to it.

Next, I thank those who have had a role in my academic development and in this specific project. First, I would like to thank Bernd Wannenwetsch. I began this project under your supervision, and it was your book, *Political Worship*, that set the trajectory for my interest in the project's themes well before I met you in person. Thank you for the insight, guidance and encouragement you have given throughout. Next, I would like to thank Brian Brock. Your excellent supervision of my thesis was a tremendous blessing, and I am grateful for the generosity you displayed to my family and me during our years in Aberdeen. I will always look back at Wednesday morning prayer and breakfast as one of the defining experiences of my time in Scotland. To Mike Mawson, thank you for all of the advice and guidance you have given me along the way. You too have displayed tremendous generosity towards me with your time, and I am so pleased that my arrival at Aberdeen overlapped with yours. Next, I would like to thank Rob Price of Talbot School of Theology. You encouraged me in my applications to PhD programs, and your guidance has been crucial, both then and now. Thank you for the mentor that you have been to me. Finally, I would like to thank Hans Ulrich for time spent in conversation and for the influence of his work on my own thinking.

Gerald McKenny and Stanley Hauerwas served as examiners for the thesis phase of the project, and they made my viva a truly enjoyable and instructive experience. It was an honor to have two deservedly renowned theologians take time to discuss my work. I greatly appreciate the care with which they examined the thesis and their generosity with comments and feedback.

The people we met in Aberdeen made for a rich postgraduate experience. To my former colleagues at the University, particularly Tyler Atkinson, Josh Carroll, B. J. Hutto, Andrew Keuer, Lieve Orye and Johnny Ramirez, thank you for great conversations and meaningful friendship. To those at Trinity Church, Aberdeen, thank you for opening up your lives to my family and me even though you knew we would be there only for a short time. We are so grateful to you for being our 'home' church while we were away from home. Thank you especially to Peter and Eleanor Dickson and to David and Angela Gibson.

A special note of acknowledgment goes out to Steve Holtrust. Although he, tragically, was not able to see the completion of this book, his early support and encouragement when I thought a PhD program was out of the question proved crucial. Beyond this project, Steve was a man I admired from my earliest childhood and is still someone I strive to imitate. I had the honor of writing the first draft of the final chapter of this book from Steve's old desk, and I only hope I have in some way returned the favor by honoring his memory with this work. It is to him that I dedicate this book.

Last, though certainly not least, I want to acknowledge my family. To my brothers, Scott and Philip, thank you for the innumerable ways in which you have shaped my life. To my parents, Richard and Vicki Laffin, thank you for showing me from an early age what it means to follow Christ. I only hope I can pass on whatever faithfulness you have taught me to my own children. Thank you for giving us a place to live before we moved to the British Isles and for providing a place to which we could return. Your love and support is one of the great joys of my life.

To my young sons, Luke and Cole, time spent with the two of you is one of the purest and simple satisfactions of my life. I hope that now that the project is finished, I will have even more time to simply be with you guys and delight in being your 'daddy'. Thank you for what you have given for me to complete this work, even if you are not yet aware that you have done so. I love you both.

Finally, and most importantly, I want to express my gratitude to my wife Bria. I still cannot even begin to understand your love for me, but I continue to receive it in grateful wonder. You have sacrificed more than anyone in order for me to pursue my academic dreams. I am continually awed by your selflessness, compassion and quiet strength as we have moved homes and countries (twice!) to pursue this project. There really is nothing adequate that I can say except thank you. I love you and will always.

ABBREVIATIONS

Full bibliographic details for each reference are found in the Bibliography.

All Bible quotations are taken from the New Revised Standard Version unless otherwise noted.

BoC	*The Book of Concord: The Confessions of the Evangelical Luthera Church*. Edited by Robert Kolb and Timothy J. Wengert.
BSLK	*Die Bekenntnisschriften der evangelisch-lutherischen Kirche*. Edited by Deutscher Evangelischer Kirchenausschuß.
BSO	*Beyond Secular Order: The Representation of Being and the Representation of the People*. John Milbank.
CH	*Church History*
CurTm	*Currents in Theology and Mission*
FR	*Freedom in Response: Lutheran Ethics: Sources and Controversies*. Oswald Bayer.
HeyJ	*Heythrop Journal*
HTR	*Harvard Theological Review*
JRE	*Journal of Religious Ethics*
LQ	*Lutheran Quarterly*
LW	*Luther's Works*. 55 vols. Martin Luther. Edited by Jaroslav Pelikan and Helmut Lehman.
MLT	*Martin Luther's Theology: A Contemporary Interpretation*. Oswald Bayer.
PV	*Putting on Virtue: The Legacy of the Splendid Vices*. Jennifer Herdt.
SJT	*Scottish Journal of Theology*
TLW	*Theology the Lutheran Way*. Oswald Bayer.
TST	*Theology and Social Theory: Beyond Secular Reason*. John Milbank.
TynBul	*Tyndale Bulletin*
WA	*D. Martin Luthers Werke: Kritische Gesamtausgabe*. Martin Luther.
WATR	*D. Martin Luthers Werke: Kritische Gesamtausgabe. Tischreden*. Martin Luther.
WMS	*The Word Made Strange: Theology, Language, Culture*. John Milbank.
WTJ	*Westminster Theological Journal*
WW	*Word and World*

INTRODUCTION: LUTHER, THEOLOGY, AND THE DIGNITY OF THE POLITICAL

Already in early modernity political thinkers commonly criticized Christianity for having an "otherworldly" nature that undermines the possibility of a genuinely *political* human life. In his *Discourses on Livy*, Niccolo Machiavelli makes a comparison between ancient religion and Christianity. He argues that the ancients had greater love of freedom than his contemporaries because of the ancient religion, which esteemed the honor of the world and refused "to beatify men if they were not full of worldly glory." Such a religion encouraged greatness of spirit. In contrast, Christianity "placed the highest good in humility, abjectness, and contempt of things human." It praised not the life of action, but rather that of contemplation.[1] Machiavelli suggests that Christianity might be reinterpreted according to virtue rather than "idleness," but in his contemporary context it had served only to encourage tyranny by promoting political passivity among the majority.[2] As he puts it, "[T]he collectivity of men, so as to go to paradise, think more of enduring their beatings than of avenging them."[3] This leads not only to political, but also ecclesial subjection. Machiavelli suggests that Christianity would have become extinct due to the corruption of the ecclesiastical authorities had it not been for the rise of the Franciscan and Dominican movements, which taught Christians "not to say evil of evil, and that it is good to live under obedience [to the corrupt clergy and ecclesial hierarchy] and, if they make an error, to leave them for God to punish."[4] We can already see here in the sixteenth century a version of Friedrich Nietzsche's later criticism of Christian slave morality.[5]

---

1. Niccolo Machiavelli, *Discourses on Livy*, trans. Harvey C. Mansfield and Nathan Tarcov (Chicago: University of Chicago Press, 1996), 131.
2. Ibid., 132.
3. Ibid., 131.
4. Ibid., 212. Like Machiavelli, Luther seeks political freedom as well as freedom from ecclesial tyranny. However, their grounding for such freedom could not be more different. To perhaps oversimplify, one could say that whereas Machiavelli sought a pagan solution to the abuses of his day, Luther sought a Christian solution.
5. Friedrich Nietzsche, *On the Genealogy of Morality*, ed. Keith Ansell-Pearson, trans. Carol Diethe (Cambridge: Cambridge University Press, 1997).

In his famous discourse on civil religion in *On the Social Contract*, Jean-Jacques Rousseau likewise criticizes Christianity for its antipolitical nature. He speaks of Jesus's establishment of "an otherworldly kingdom" that detaches humans from commitment to their political communities. Of this Rousseau writes, "I know of nothing more contrary to the social spirit."[6] As adherents of "a totally spiritual religion," Christians display a "profound indifference" to political matters. "If the State is flourishing," so argues Rousseau, "[the Christian] barely dares to enjoy the public felicity for fear of becoming proud of his country's glory. If the State declines, he blesses the hand of God that weighs heavily on his people."[7] According to Rousseau, this attitude leads to servitude and an acceptance of tyranny. In other words, the spirit of Christianity is an antipolitical one, fit for subjects of despots, but not for citizens of republics. Beyond the effects of this "otherworldliness," Rousseau further argues that Christianity has led to a division between temporal and churchly authority with dire practical consequence. In dividing loyalties, historically Christianity has meant antagonism between jurisdictions and the impossibility of good political order.[8]

Friedrich Nietzsche puts criticism of Christianity on behalf of a greater embrace of this world in particularly sharp terms when he writes:

> Christianity was from the beginning, essentially and fundamentally, life's nausea and disgust with life, merely concealed behind, masked by, dressed up as, faith in "another" or "better" life. Hatred of "the world," condemnations of the passions, fear of beauty and sensuality, a beyond invented the better to slander this life, at bottom a craving for the nothing, for the end, for respite, for "the sabbath of sabbaths."[9]

Hence Christianity is understood as an escape from mundane sensuous reality into a sort of beatific nothingness. There is no space here for the full-blooded civic ties that give meaning to human life and make possible human excellence. Instead, cowardly renunciation is called virtuous faith.

In contrast to Nietzsche, Dietrich Bonhoeffer saw Christianity in completely opposite terms as a necessary embrace of life in this world. In a letter to Eberhard Bethge, he wrote, "In the last few years I have come to know and understand

---

6. Jean-Jacques Rousseau, *On the Social Contract with Geneva Manuscript and Political Economy*, ed. Roger D. Masters, trans. Judith R. Masters (Boston: Bedford/St. Martins, 1978), 128.

7. Ibid., 129.

8. Ibid., 126. I say here "historically," because Rousseau makes a distinction between the true Gospel and "the religion of the priest." The former is characterized by "otherworldliness," while the latter divides the world into two, which leads to "a type of mixed and unsocial right that has no name" (128).

9. Friedrich Nietzsche, *The Birth of Tragedy*, trans. Walter Kaufmann (New York: Vintage Books, 1967), 23.

more and more the profound this-worldliness of Christianity. The Christian is not a *homo religious* but simply a human being . . . I think Luther lived in this kind of this-worldliness . . . one only learns to have faith by living in the full this-worldliness of life."[10] In many ways, this book can be seen as an attempt, against the political criticisms leveled at Christianity, to grasp what Bonhoeffer saw as its "profound this-worldliness." Particularly, it is concerned with the hero of Bonhoeffer's citation, Martin Luther, and his understanding of the simply human life. Not the life of a *homo religious*, but of the human being placed by God within the institutions of God's good creation, the life of a human being who responds to the Word of God as it encounters her in the community of fellow believers and the preaching and sacraments at the center of their shared ecclesial life, in the life of the household and its connectedness to the larger economy, and, of particular interest for the purposes of this book, in the political life of the human being who speaks and acts in concert with her fellow human creatures. Of course, such a life is lived under the conditions of a fallen humanity, which has implicated all of creation in its fallenness, and therefore such a life cannot be focused in a backward glance to an idealized creation setting the pattern for life today, but rather also always looks forward to the consummation of creation in the judgment of God and the resurrection of the new creation, a reality that is always breaking in on a dying world. In other words, such a life is lived in the middle, it is a life in the midst of death[11] and therefore is centered on the one whose death and resurrection is the key to the whole. As a political life, the Christian life does not fail to recognize God's good work in sustaining and preserving human life with God's own provision and government, yet it is not forgetful that such life is lived under the judgment of God against the principalities and powers that seek to destroy creation and pridefully enthrone other false gods. Such a life remains attentive to God's judgment against the sin that would disembed the human from the webs and networks that sustain life and drive her instead into her own "self" and her own self-constituted cosmos.

To put all that has been said into more traditional terms, a this-worldly life as understood by Luther is one lived always in response to the unified but manifold work of God the Creator and Redeemer, the God who has been revealed to us in Jesus Christ. It is the conviction of this book that Luther's theology holds together these themes in such way that it proves to be a uniquely political theology, that is, a theology that understands the Christian life as fundamentally political, because it is truly human. Furthermore, his politics is genuinely theological, in that it is a politics lived out of faith in the God who alone judges and justifies, thus placing necessary restrictions on the tendency of politics to absorb all of human life, as would be the case in the thinking of the aforementioned critics of Christianity,

---

10. Dietrich Bonhoeffer, *Letters and Papers from Prison*, ed. John W. De Gruchy, trans. Isabel Best, Lisa E. Dahill, Reinhard Krauss, and Nancy Lukens, in Dietrich Bonhoeffer Works 8 (Minneapolis: Fortress Press, 2010), 485.

11. Luther, "Lectures on Genesis, Chapters 21–25 (1538–42)," LW 4:116.

who seek in place of full-blooded Christianity a civil religion.[12] However, to see this, it is essential that Luther's political thought be understood always within the grammar of his larger theology. It is my contention that most treatments of Luther's political thought, especially in the English-speaking world, fail to make the connection between his politics and the deeper structures of his theology, and hence misinterpret Luther in nominalistic, individualistic, inward focused terms, which is to say that he is interpreted as being *a*political and essentially quietistic at best or antipolitical and authoritarian at worst (of course, the two typically go together). In reading Luther this way, the criticisms of Machiavelli and Rousseau regarding Christianity are largely granted from the outset, and he is not read closely enough to bring to light the contours of his thought as he presents it. The burden of this book is to show the life affirming this-worldliness of Christianity as articulated in exemplary fashion in the theologically saturated politics of Luther. Importantly, however, while avoiding a turn away from the world by affirming its creaturely goodness, Luther does not fall into the trap of either a totalization of politics or an overly suspicious disdain for politics in the way that the trajectory of the politics of the modern state all too often has by forcing theology into a private realm and lowering the moral expectation of politics to more "realistic" standards. Rather, Luther's theology can give room to both the posture of the good citizen and the subversive rebel as appropriate when discerned in response to the Word of God at a particular time and place. For Luther, politics is a good within creaturely limits. As such, it cannot demand undue sacrifices or offer ultimate justification to human life. Rather, politics rightly serves as a location for God's loving provision communicated to creatures through creatures and a place (but not the only place) where God's Word can be heard and responded to faithfully. When it becomes more or less than this, politics becomes an inflated anti-institution, a false god, or is wrongly subjected to another false god, another anti-institution. But where faith in the one true God is confessed, there, and there alone, can an articulation of a genuine politics, a politics as a form of creaturely response to the divine initiative, be found. In Luther's theology, particularly in his teachings on the two *ecclesiae* and the three estates (or institutions),[13] flesh will be given to the bare bones laid out here.

---

12. Ronald Beiner, "Machiavelli, Hobbes and Rousseau on Civil Religion," *The Review of Politics* 55.4 (September 1993), 617–38. Beiner interprets all three thinkers named in his title as belonging to "the civil religion tradition," with Machiavelli and Hobbes seeking to "de-Christianize Christianity" and Rousseau having no solution to the problem of a political life in the wake of Christianity (624). He argues that this tradition could be extended further to include Nietzsche. In identifying an early modern "civil religion" tradition, Beiner draws on the work of Leszek Kolakowski, who identifies, in addition to these three, Marsilius of Padua, Spinoza, and Montesquieu. See Kolakowski, *Modernity on Endless Trial* (Chicago: University of Chicago Press, 1990).

13. I use "estates" and "institutions" interchangeably throughout the book. A discussion of the terminology for this aspect of Luther's teaching is given in Chapter 5.

I am aware, of course, that this has not been the standard way of reading Luther, at least in the English-speaking world following the Second World War. It is undoubted that Luther's theology plays a significant role in the development of modern Western political thought. However, the nature of that significance is highly disputed, and in the English-speaking world, especially the world of political science and political history, Luther's contribution is often viewed in largely negative terms. If Luther's place in the history of political thought bears any resemblance to the descriptions in many accounts of the development of Western political and ethical philosophy, he would seem to be a proponent of an inward social atomism and the sort of "otherworldly" Christianity that Nietzsche rails against, anything but a champion of "profound this-worldliness." While he is recognized for stressing the importance of secular rule, he views it, according to these interpreters, in absolutist fashion giving rise to an autonomous secular sphere. Theology is strictly separated from politics—the infamous "two kingdoms." This misreading is particularly the case in genealogical accounts aimed at telling the story of the development of the Western political mind.[14] In fact, when such accounts take the form of modernity criticism in the mode of overarching narrative, Luther is continually cast in the role of a great villain.

In his early work *A Short History of Ethics*, Alasdair MacIntyre provides a fairly standard and representative account of Luther's role in contributing to "the acids of individualism which for four centuries have eaten into our moral structures."[15] He argues that in the work of Luther (along with Machiavelli), there appears for the first time the modern figure of the "individual."[16] According to MacIntyre, Luther structures his ethics around an "Ockhamist" divine command theory in which "the events that matter all occur in the psychological transformation of the faithful individual."[17] Communal life is no longer the context for the moral life, but rather what is of significance is the individual who stands alone before God. These ethical positions have the political implication that the individual likewise stands immediately before the state, which is itself now understood as distinct from society. The dense web of social relations that once characterized one's political standing is now replaced by the mere status "subject." Here, MacIntyre follows the famous argument regarding mediating institutions that had earlier been set forth by J. N. Figgis. In fact, MacIntyre quotes from Figgis, "For the first time [i.e., in the Reformation period], the Absolute Individual confronts the Absolute State."[18] Further, given what MacIntyre calls Luther's "bifurcated morality," the

---

14. It should be said that such misreading is easy to understand in light of some of the ways in which Luther's thought was misinterpreted and abused in the twentieth century.

15. Alasdair MacIntyre, *A Short History of Ethics: A History of Moral Philosophy from the Homeric Age to the Twentieth Century*, 2nd ed. (London: Routledge, 1998), 266.

16. Ibid., 121.

17. Ibid., 122.

18. J. N. Figgis, *Studies of Political Thought: From Gerson to Grotius, 1414–1625* (Cambridge: Cambridge University Press, 1907).

political order is left to its own separate secular realm subject to its own norms and justification. Included in the presumption of this separate realm is provision for the "the absolute rights of the secular authority" and a "handing over of the secular world to its own devices." It is this separation of realms that MacIntyre identifies as Luther's particular contribution to the history of moral philosophy.[19]

Another influential critic of Luther's role in the history of Western political thought is the political philosopher Eric Voegelin, who calls Luther the "prototypical" modern type.[20] By this, Voegelin means that Luther looked in an inward direction for truth, but ultimately sought to project this truth outward. He writes, "Luther was fundamentally concerned with nothing but the promulgation of his peculiar, personal experience and its imposition as an order of existence on mankind at large. The shadow of egoistical obscurantism, this strongest force of the modern world, begins to close in."[21] The human heart alone will tell one whether what one has done is good. Traditions and institutions are no longer required, because the decision of the individual conscience is free to decide all things. In this sense, so Voegelin argues, Luther's modernity shows itself as that of the self-willed individual who fights against the world to impose upon it his own particular vision of order. He argues that Luther's tendency toward radical individualism derives from his *sola scriptura* doctrine and emphasis on the priesthood of all believers. In overturning the *magisterium* of the church, Voegelin argues that Luther "made every Christian his own infallible pope—with the inevitable consequence of opening an anarchy of conflicting interpretation."[22]

In her *Public Man, Private Woman*, Jean Bethke Elshtain likewise views Luther as a harbinger of modernity in his turn against the world and into the self. In a world falling apart socially and politically, so Elshtain argues, Luther turned to the tiniest point of order for stability. Rather than constructing a community, he turned to the individual. She writes, "Clinging to the anchor of the Self, the Christian subject, male or female, dramatically turned inward, for there Luther said, the Kingdom of God was truly to be found . . . this world of externals is inessential to the faith of the Christian. The true epicenter of his existence is a pietistic, ever-scrutinized *vie intérieur*."[23] Again, like Voegelin, she insists that "Luther is a prototypical modern in many recognizable ways, though that ambiguous accolade usually goes to his

---

19. MacIntyre, *Short History of Ethics*, 122.

20. Eric Voegelin, *History of Political Ideas, Vol. IV: Renaissance and Reformation*, ed. David L. Morse and William M. Thompson, in The Collected Works of Eric Voegelin 22 (Columbia: University of Missouri Press, 1998), 268.

21. Ibid., 259.

22. Ibid., 235.

23. Jean Bethke Elshtain, *Public Man, Private Woman: Women in Social and Political Thought* (Oxford: Robertson, 1981), 81. At this point in her argument, Elshtain draws from MacIntyre's *Short History of Ethics*. She compares Luther's turn with Augustine's retreat into himself to contemplate the City of God. However, she writes, "Unlike Augustine, Luther's city lay primarily within his own being" (84).

Italian contemporary, Machiavelli."[24] Included in Luther's fledgling modernity, she argues, is a disdain for politics and "the dignity and purposes accorded secular rule by St. Thomas."[25] Luther's Christian is free in a totally negative sense, which is to say the Christian has "no need of institutions and offices," but stands in a private, interior, individual relationship immediately before the naked Word of God. "Reduce the Christian life to its irreducible dimensions," claims Elshtain's Luther, "and keep one's distance from all institutional forms of rule."[26] The external sphere of politics is characterized for Luther by coercion and force and has nothing essential to do with the life of Christian faith. In this reading, Elshtain insists, Luther hands politics over to the devil and gives us a glimpse into the Hobbesian Leviathan that would shortly follow.[27]

A major task of this book will be disentangling Luther from the political trajectories (particularly the Machiavellian and Hobbesian) to which he is typically tied by the modernity critics and other interpreters of the Western political tradition, while showing that his understanding of Christianity meets the criticism of the early modern defenders of politics who found that Christianity had become characterized by a false "otherworldliness" by many strands of the faith in the late medieval period. Like Machiavelli and Rousseau, Luther seeks for a genuine politics. Unlike the trajectory to which they are said to belong, he resists the drift toward an amoral realism or the tendency of the political to absorb all of earthly human life. He does so by his stress on God's rule in institutions, not just in the *politia*, but also in the *ecclesia* and *oeconomia*. I will show that Luther's political thought stands in a much more sharp and critical connection to modernity than is supposed by the modernity critics and that his theological reading of politics provides for more nuanced discernment than are attainable by the stark polarities of "liberalism–communitarianism," "Augustinianism–Aristotelianism," and "modernism–pre/postmodernism" that often characterize such accounts.

In his "Introduction" to Machiavelli's *Discourses on Livy*, Harvey Mansfield shows that Machiavelli seeks a return to virtue, but does not mean by this that he wants simply to return to the ancients. Rather, he argues that for Machiavelli, both the ancients and Christians "find the highest type—philosopher or saint—in one

---

24. Ibid., 91. We have already seen MacIntyre's grouping of Luther and Machiavelli together. In fact, we can see by the title of Chapter 10 of his *A Short History of Ethics*, that is, "Luther, Machiavelli, Hobbes, and Spinoza," the trajectory to which Luther belongs in his genealogy. Quentin Skinner argues that the "familiar coupling" of Luther and Machiavelli began in the polemical works of the early Jesuits, who saw them "as the two founding fathers of the impious modern State." Skinner, *The Foundations of Modern Political Thought, Vol. 2: The Age of Reformation* (Cambridge: Cambridge University Press, 1978), 143.

25. Elshtain, *Public Man, Private Woman*.

26. Ibid., 80–1.

27. Ibid., 84. To this negative account of Luther, one should note in Elshtain an acknowledgment of one positive feature of Luther's "modernity," namely, "his enlightened attitude on sexuality in general and female sexuality in particular" (88).

who puts the contemplative life over politics."[28] As was the case for certain strands of monasticism against which Luther reacted, so for Aristotle, the leisure necessary for contemplation was the condition required for the acquisition of virtue. One of the presuppositions of this book is that Luther shows a way forward beyond the contemplative–active divide and in this way seeks something revolutionary like Machiavelli in that he is highly critical both of ancient pagan and late-medieval Christian virtue. However, unlike Machiavelli, Luther's eschatological openness refuses a totalization of politics or a simple pragmatic realism. Put another way, necessity does not place the kind of pressure on Luther's politics that it does on Machiavelli's. Rather, Luther's politics truly is a politics of freedom. As it reconciles the divide between the contemplative and active forms of life, it also goes beyond the polarity "necessity–freedom." In this way, politics does not feed parasitically off of the other spheres of life, as one could argue the *politia* does in Machiavelli (as well as in classical political philosophy) or as the *ecclesia* does in late-medieval monastic and ecclesiastical abuses.[29] Again, the aim is a genuinely theological politics, which pushes against the tendency of ancient politics to subsume all of life to politics (the gods are the gods of the particular city), and the modern tendency to divorce politics from religion, usually to the denigration of both. However, for present purposes, the remainder of this introduction aims at four things. First, I give an account of the role assigned to Luther in predominant accounts of the rise of modern Western political thought in the work of two leading contemporary scholars. This will fill out in more detail the brief criticisms summarily stated earlier and provide the necessary background for the more explicitly theologically driven discussions to follow. Second, I argue that these readings are paralleled in contemporary theological accounts of Luther's place in the Western canon, although these accounts get more to the theological questions that are at the heart Luther's thought. The narratives underlying these theological works are derivative from the work of contemporary political philosophers and historians of political thought. I will argue that these theological accounts need to be nuanced with greater attention to Luther's works themselves, which show a surprising degree of relevance to discussions in contemporary political theology. Interaction with these theological accounts will be a major component of the book, and so I here explain and justify the choice of John Milbank and Jennifer Herdt as primary interlocutors who each, in their own way, either contribute to or build from the contributions of the modernity critics, although in opposite directions. Third, I set out the overall structure of the book and lay out the broad outlines of the content that forms each of its chapters. Finally, I briefly suggest the contours of the constructive contribution of Luther's theology to contemporary understandings of politics, a contribution I spell out more fully in the body of the chapters to follow.

28. Mansfield, "Introduction," in Machiavelli, *Discourses on Livy*, xxxv–xxxvi.
29. On this point, see Bernd Wannenwetsch, *Political Worship*, especially Chapter 6, "The Surmounting of Political Antinomies in Worship," trans. Margaret Kohl (Oxford: Oxford University Press, 2004).

A Portrait of Luther in the History of Political Philosophy

The average American undergraduate studying political science is likely to first encounter Luther's political thought in sources like Quentin Skinner's *The Foundations of Modern Political Thought* and Sheldon Wolin's *Politics and Vision*.[30] The stories they tell about the development of modern political philosophy are highly influential.[31] We see that the same themes noted in the works discussed earlier, themes such as nominalism, voluntarism, inwardness, and anti-institutionalism, crop up in Skinner and Wolin's renderings of Luther's political significance. Further, many English-speaking theological accounts of politics, that

---

30. Quentin Skinner, *The Foundations of Modern Political Thought, Vol. 1: The Renaissance* (Cambridge: Cambridge University Press, 1978) and *Vol. 2: The Age of Reformation*; Sheldon Wolin, *Politics and Vision: Continuity and Innovation in Western Political Thought*, Expanded Edition (Princeton: Princeton University Press, 2004).

31. In his recent *On Politics: A History of Political Thought from Herodotus to the Present* (London: Penguin, 2012), Alan Ryan recommends Wolin to his readers for "illumination" on Luther and calls Skinner "indispensable" (1043). Harro Höpfl, in his *Luther and Calvin on Secular Authority* (Cambridge: Cambridge University Press, 1991) in the well-regarded series *Cambridge Texts in the History of Political Thought*, likewise acknowledges both authors. He states, "No bibliography of Luther could pretend to adequacy even at an introductory level unless it referred readers to Q. Skinner." His recommendation of Wolin is more guarded. He views Wolin's work on Luther as "worth considering for its magisterial sway and seductive oversimplifications" (xlv). Nonetheless, Wolin's influence cannot be underestimated. William Connolly, himself an influential political theorist, writes of Wolin's *Politics and Vision*, "One mark of its significance is that for at least three decades after its publication a horde of graduate students studying for comprehensive examinations in political theory used it as a primary source of guidance and inspiration. And who knows how many assistant professors have modelled their introductory theory courses on it? I could name one, at least. Others can confess on their own time." Connolly, "Politics and Vision," in *Democracy and Vision: Sheldon Wolin and the Vicissitudes of the Political* (Princeton: Princeton University Press, 2001), 6. Further, Wolin's influence on theological ethics and politics should not be overlooked, especially his criticism of liberalism, which, along with the work of the modernity critic Alasdair MacIntrye, has proved influential to Stanley Hauerwas. Hauerwas suggests that "one of the reasons I found Yoder so compelling is he offered me an account of ecclesial existence I thought required if Wolin's criticisms of liberalism were correct." Hauerwas, "Democratic Time: Lessons Learned from Yoder and Wolin," *Cross Currents* 55.4 (Winter 2006), 543. Additionally, Jeffery Stout, in discussing the significance of Wolin to him, writes, "While I do not discuss Wolin explicitly in *Democracy and Tradition*, I did intend my book to be viewed as a complementary corrective to his conception of fugitive democracy." Stout, "The Spirit of Democracy and the Rhetoric of Excess," in *JRE* 35.1 (March 2007), 16. For another recent account of Wolin's importance to political theology, see Chad Pecknold, "Migrations of the Host: Fugitive Democracy and the *Corpus Mysticum*," *Political Theology* 11.1 (January 2010), 77–101.

is, works by theologians with political questions in mind, tend to follow the stories told by Skinner and Wolin, holding to the same assumptions about Luther.[32] In both cases, it becomes evident that the key to understanding Luther's political thought is the manner in which one construes his theology generally.

The Disappearing Jurisdiction of the Church: Quentin Skinner on Luther

In his two-volume *The Foundations of Modern Political Thought*, Quentin Skinner places Luther's political thought within the larger contextual framework of a narrative of the rise of the modern concept of the State. He focuses on the transition from medieval to modern political theory, arguing that from the late thirteenth to the end of the sixteenth century the modern idea of the State arises in its recognizably Weberian form, according to which it is "the sole source of law and legitimate force within its own territory" and "the sole appropriate object of its citizens 'allegiances.'"[33] Luther looms large in Skinner's account, with approximately one-third of the second volume devoted to Luther and Lutheranism, presented under the title "Absolutism and the Lutheran Reformation."[34] The broad sweep of the argument is "that the main influence of Lutheran political theory in early modern Europe lay in the direction of encouraging and legitimating the emergence of unified and absolutist monarchies."[35] However, Skinner begins his account of Luther's thought by first laying out in summary fashion his broader theology, before turning more specifically to the political implications of Luther's teaching.

Skinner locates Luther's theology relative to two late-medieval movements, the *devotio moderna* and the *via moderna*. The former, exemplified by figures such as Meister Eckhart and Johannes Tauler, emphasized God's absolute freedom and the necessity of human passivity before the grace of God. Skinner argues that the element in their thought that had primary influence on Luther was their emphasis, following Augustine, on the fallen nature of humanity and consequent need for faith in God's gracious redemption. The *via moderna* was reactionary against Thomism and drove a wedge between faith and reason. Among its influential exponents were Duns Scotus and William of Ockham, and later Robert Holcot, Gregory of Rimini, Pierre d'Ailly, and Jean Gerson. These thinkers, according to Skinner, excised reason from questions of ethics, instead focusing on the divine commands. Their influence was strongly felt in German lands through the

---

32. See for a very recent example, Rustin E. Brian, *Covering Up Luther: How Barth's Christology Challenged the Deus Absconditus That Haunts Modernity* (Eugene, OR: Cascade Books, 2013). Following closely the narrative told by John Milbank, which I set out in Chapter 1, Brian puts Luther's purported nominalism at the center of his treatment of the Reformer and finds here the stage being set for the arbitrary, all-powerful God of modernity.

33. Skinner, *The Renaissance*, x.

34. Skinner, *The Age of Reformation*, 3–110.

35. Ibid., 113.

nominalism of Gregory Biel in the late fifteenth century. Biel and his followers stressed the importance of faith over reason in understanding God and the priority of grace over nature in salvation. Skinner writes, "Luther was unquestionably a product of both these traditions of thought."[36] However, he called for an even greater human passivity before the grace of God than the *devotio moderna* and likewise went beyond the *via moderna* "in his despairing sense that it is absolutely impossible for a man to act in such a way as to make himself worthy of being saved."[37] We will see later in the work of contemporary theologians that a recurring point of criticism is Luther's connection to these two groups of thinkers, especially to Scotus and Ockham, and also his indebtedness to late-medieval nominalism. This theme is especially prominent in the work of John Milbank.

In treating Luther's writings themselves, Skinner highlights two of the theological themes prominent in the two traditions just mentioned, namely, the unworthiness of human beings and a voluntaristic understanding of the divine commands. Skinner explicates these two themes in terms of Luther's anthropology and ecclesiology, the latter of which proved to have significant political implications. Anthropologically, Luther rejected the more optimistic views of human nature held by the Thomists and turned instead "to the earlier and more pessimistic Augustinian emphasis on man's fallen nature."[38] However, this was a break not only with Thomism, but also with the humanists, who had begun to recover and disseminate a high view of human virtue. In stressing human bondage to sin, Skinner argues, Luther's anthropology was "anti-humanist" and "ultra-Augustinian."[39] Crucial in this move is a denial of reason's capacity to understand God's will for humans. God's commands do not follow a rational order, as in accounts positing a natural good, but rather are good simply because God wills them. As such, humans can only know God as he reveals Himself in His Word, whereas his hidden will, the will of the *Deus absconditus*, the omnipotent will ordaining the happenings of the world, remains entirely beyond our understanding and comprehension. When this is combined with a corrupt human nature, unable to achieve anything towards its salvation, Luther is left with a doctrine of justification that proclaims faith alone (*sola fide*).[40] Again, we will see that this movement toward a strong doctrine of original sin and away from the discourses of virtue, coupled with a perceived voluntarism and the idea of an arbitrary hidden God, are prominent in theological criticism of Luther. These themes are central in Jennifer Herdt's treatment of Luther.

Skinner argues that Luther's "*solafideism*" results in an individualism that undermines the importance of the visible church. It is in this aspect of Luther's theology that Skinner finds its most important political significance. Given that

---

36. Ibid., 25.
37. Ibid.
38. Ibid., 4.
39. Ibid. Charges of "hyper-Augustinianism" are common in criticism of Luther. See Chapter 4.
40. Skinner, *The Age of Reformation*, 5–8.

there are no mediators between the individual and God, the church is reduced to a "*congregatio fidelium*" without any "real existence except in the hearts of its faithful members."[41] Ecclesiastically, this meant an attack on the priesthood and on the clerical estate as such. The "spiritual" kingdom, to which the church belongs, possesses "a purely inward form of government," entirely separate from the concerns of the temporal realm, and focused solely on the otherworldly salvation of the faithful. According to this view, the church is not authorized to regulate the lives of Christians. In fact, in relation to the temporal authorities, Skinner reads Luther as saying, "It cannot properly be said to possess any separate jurisdiction at all."[42] By dissolving the jurisdictional power and authority of the church, which had earlier been acknowledged during the *regnum/sacerdotium* battles of the Middle Ages, Luther left behind a power vacuum that he filled by extending the jurisdiction of the temporal authorities. He transferred "the sole right to exercise all coercive powers, including powers over the Church," to the secular authorities.[43] Practically, this meant that the church visible would be placed under the control of earthly princes.

Luther's transfer of power to the secular authorities was derived theologically, Skinner argues, from his grounding all political authority in the providence of God, using Romans 13 as his key text. "His key theological belief," Skinner writes, is "that the whole of the existing framework of social and political order is a direct reflection of God's will and providence."[44] On the one hand, this view has the effect of tempering the exercise of secular power, in that the rulers are merely masks (*larvae*) of God, who must be disobeyed when they command contrary to God (Acts 5:29). On the other hand, it leads to Luther's harsh opposition to the peasant uprising, since to resist the ruler is tantamount to resisting God. We find here, Skinner argues, a dangerous two kingdoms theology, which is grounded in Luther's distinction between immediate justification and a later to follow sanctification of the faithful sinner who is *simul iustus et peccator*. According to this distinction, all Christians live simultaneously in two kingdoms. The first kingdom, the kingdom of the justified belonging to the church, is ruled by Christ alone by means of "entirely spiritual" powers, given that true Christians need not be subjected to coercion. God likewise ordains the temporal authorities, but in contrast to the spiritual kingdom, the worldly kingdom is ruled by coercion, or in Luther's favored terminology, "the sword." The purpose of the latter kingdom is maintaining the peace among sinful humanity, a community to which Christians continue to belong given that they remain sinners. This concern over Luther's "two kingdoms" doctrine is central to early- and mid-twentieth-century criticisms of his political thought, which is exemplified especially in Barthian criticisms of Luther, but which also recurs in Milbank's criticism.

41. Ibid., 10–11. Skinner argues that in Luther's ecclesiology, the reader is continually led back to "the central figure of the individual Christian" (12).
42. Ibid., 14.
43. Ibid., 15.
44. Ibid., 18.

As can be seen, then, Skinner reads Luther politically in Augustinian terms, according to which politics is merely a postlapsum necessity required to curb the disorder and chaos of sin. Politics does not have a positive purpose relating to the nature of humanity as originally created, nor does it point in any way to eschatological fulfillment. It is merely a means to be used by the church sojourning through this world on the way to the next one. In the long term, Skinner argues that the historical influence of this understanding, as transmitted through Luther's political writings, was that it provided "two guiding principles" to subsequent Western European political thought.[45] First is the insistence that the New Testament, particularly the Pauline writings, is authoritative for social and political questions. Second is the principle derived from this that the New Testament prescribes "complete Christian submission to the secular authorities, the range of whose powers he crucially extends, grounding them in such a way that their rule can never in any circumstances be legitimately resisted." In sum, Skinner concludes, Luther bequeaths to the Western political tradition the resources for what would later become the doctrine of the divine right of kings.[46]

The Loss of Institutions: Sheldon Wolin's Luther

In his *Politics and Vision*, Sheldon Wolin argues that the Protestant Reformation "began, with Luther, as an attempt to depoliticize religious thought, and ended, with Calvin, in the readmission of political elements into religion."[47] In accordance with the common pattern of coupling them, Wolin claims that Luther depoliticized religion while Machiavelli detheologized politics, both to the advantage of national particularism.[48] In his fight against hierarchical church structures and a church too closely involved in secular affairs, Wolin argues, Luther sought an antiauthoritarian and antipolitical church. He provides two examples of what he takes to be Luther's tendency to depoliticize the church. First, he argues that in the Thomist conception of the sacraments, the political character of the church and the priesthood was brought to the fore, whereas in Luther's sacramental theology the political elements are "practically eliminated."[49] In the former understanding, the sacraments conveyed justifying grace, while in Luther's account grace is relocated into the inward realm of faith, individualizing the conception of justification.[50] Second, Wolin finds depoliticizing tendencies

---

45. Ibid., 19.
46. Ibid., 113.
47. Wolin, *Politics and Vision*, 126.
48. Ibid., 128.
49. Ibid., 135.
50. I treat the political nature of the sacraments in Luther in Chapter 2, in conversation with William Cavanaugh, who, like Wolin, argues that Luther's view of the Eucharist depoliticizes the church and undermines medieval conceptions of organic political community.

in Luther's two kingdoms teaching. The spiritual kingdom, which is ruled by Christ, is deprived of all the important qualities normally associated with politics. Christ's kingdom is apolitical, as He rules not by His power but by His Word alone. Meanwhile, all political attributes, such as "repressive power, law backed by coercion, and all the other elements of governance" were relocated to the temporal kingdom alone.[51] The ultimate outcome of these moves was that Luther "succeeded in creating a religious vocabulary largely devoid of political categories."[52] Luther stripped his conception of the church of all its political elements and invested them solely in the temporal authorities. The result was autonomy for political thought "rid of the enclosing framework of mediaeval theology and philosophy," thus providing justification for authoritarian secular powers.[53] In Wolin's account, "as Luther's Church became less political in concept, it became increasingly political in its dependency on secular authority."[54] Under this arrangement, the role of the Christian is merely to obey. Practically, Wolin says, "the end-product was the territorial Church (*Landeskirche*)."[55]

Like Figgis and MacIntyre, Wolin argues that Luther's purported inward form of religion is accompanied by an anti-institutionalism with far-reaching political consequences. "If we are to look for the fundamental weakness in Luther's thinking, it is to be sought in his failure to appreciate the importance of institutions."[56] For Luther, the Kingdom of God is apolitical and stands in direct dialectical contrast to the kingdom of the world. Unlike the necessary authoritarianism that characterizes secular government, the church is organized according to the doctrine of the priesthood of all believers. There is no mediation between humans and God (save Christ and Scripture), and every person stands inwardly before God alone. Therefore, there is no visible church with accompanying hierarchical institutions. The church is a society of true voluntary fellowship without need of government. Luther's penchant for simplicity and enmity toward institutions is reflected, suggests Wolin, not just in his ecclesiology, but also in his treatment of secular authority. Wolin writes:

No provision was made for the other complex relationships in a political order. The political relationship, like the religious, was a personalized rather than an institutionalized one . . . These ideas marked the eclipse of the mediaeval

---

51. Ibid., 136. The agonistic and coercive understanding of politics and the Weberian conception of power should be noted here. In Chapter 3, I will propose a more Arendtian and positive understanding of power, which I find also in Luther, and which shows that Luther does not "depoliticize" the church, but rather understands politics in a quite different manner, a manner consistent with his highly political understanding of the church.
52. Ibid., 129.
53. Ibid., 130.
54. Ibid., 133.
55. Ibid.
56. Ibid., 145.

conception of a political society with all of its rich suggestion of a corporate whole knit together in a common involvement.[57]

The relationship is strictly between a divinely authorized ruler and a subject under divine command to obey. Complex community, in which institutions act as benign mediators, are replaced in Luther by individuals starkly confronting one another (whether it be rulers and subjects, or God and the individual believer). What disappears from view is a shared public space providing for joint action. As we will see, a defense of complex community is one of the core elements in John Milbank's political theology.

A final point worthy of note in Wolin's account of Luther is the latter's concept of order. In Augustine's understanding of order, according to Wolin, the political order was part of the larger order of creation, giving it "a rooted stability, a sustenance drawn from the nature of creation itself." Although it only served a purpose in the *saeculum* and was destined to disappear in the *eschaton*, until that time, the political order "participated in the perfection written into the very essence of things." For Luther, on the other hand, order became a formal principle rather than one immanent to the creation as a whole. Rather than "a sustaining principle within a larger pattern of meaning," Luther's conception of order meant that he saw the political order as inherently unstable and vulnerable, easily given to collapse. Luther did not see the political order itself as upheld by divine providence. Rather, the secular powers upholding the political order were divinely ordained. A "powerful, repressive authority" was required to impress order onto a fundamentally disordered and chaotic human social world. In such a conception, the need for authoritarian government and passively obedient subjects is evident.[58]

Notably absent in both Skinner's and Wolin's treatment of Luther's political thought is any discussion of Luther's teaching on the two *ecclesiae*, which Luther clearly states he carries out with Augustine's teaching on the two *civitates* in mind, or of his teaching on the three institutions, which is present throughout Luther's theology, especially in his biblical, ecclesiastical, and sacramental writings. The primary writings of Luther treated by Skinner prove instructive here. He focuses on "Two Kinds of Righteousness (1519),"[59] "The Freedom of a Christian (1520),"[60] "To the Christian Nobility (1520),"[61] "Temporal Authority: To What Extent It Should be Obeyed (1523),"[62] "The Bondage of the Will (1526),"[63] as well as a brief treatment of the writings surrounding the peasant's revolt[64] and "Whether Soldiers Too Can

---

57. Ibid., 146.
58. Ibid., 141.
59. LW 31:293–306.
60. Ibid., 327–77.
61. LW 44:115–217.
62. LW 45:75–129.
63. LW 33.
64. These writings can all be found in LW 46.

be Saved (1526)."[65] I cite Skinner's sources as his use of them is representative of treatments of Luther's political thinking, which tend to neglect Luther's works concerning Scripture (sermons, lectures, commentaries, prefaces) even though these prove central to understanding Luther's theology and politics. The first thirty volumes of the fifty-five-volume American edition of *Luther's Works*[66] comprise his lectures and sermons on Scripture, with an additional volume devoted to his sermons.[67] Additionally, there is little attention given to Luther's writings on the sacraments, which I will likewise show to be crucial for understanding his political theology. However, while not ignoring these writings, in this book additional focus is placed on his later writings, as well as his Scriptural, ecclesiological, and sacramental writings, which give a very different picture of his politics.[68] It does not negate the earlier writings, but rather casts them in a different and broader theological light. Further, the focus on Scriptural, sacramental, and ecclesial writings brings to light the teaching on the two *ecclesiae* and the three institutions, with an interpretation of Luther on the two regiments included as this teaching is related explicitly to these other two relatively neglected doctrines. I will argue that these teachings do not merely serve to correct historical interpretation of Luther's political thought, but more importantly point to its critical and constructive potential for the contemporary task of understanding the Christian life in relation to politics, and for a theological affirmation of political forms of life. However, before laying out how I approach this task in the structure of this book, it is first necessary to consider the more straightforwardly theological criticisms of Luther that will prove crucial for explicating his theological politics.

Luther and Contemporary Political Theology

In the main body of the book, the primary critics of Luther's political thought whom I will engage will be John Milbank and Jennifer Herdt. I chose Milbank given the relevance of his work to political theology and his founding influence on "Radical Orthodoxy," a movement whose authors have likewise engaged regularly in political theology largely within an Augustinian framework as set forth and

---

65. LW 46:87–137.

66. The series is expanding as new volumes continue to be released.

67. In addition to the "Lectures on Genesis, Chapters 1–5 (1535–36)," I also give a good deal of attention to Luther's commentaries on Psalm 82 (1530), Psalm 101 (1534–35), and Psalm 127 (1524). James Estes notes that "Luther's commentaries on Psalms 82 and 101, particularly the latter, have only recently begun to emerge from almost complete neglect." Estes, *Peace, Order and the Glory of God: Secular Authority and the Church in the Thought of Luther and Melanchthon, 1518–1559* (Boston: Brill, 2005), 181.

68. For the importance of genre in interpreting Luther, see Christine Helmer, *The Trinity and Martin Luther: A Study on the Relationship between Genre, Language and the Trinity in Luther's Works (1523–1546)* (Mainz: Verlag Philip von Zabern, 1999).

interpreted by Milbank in his *Theology and Social Theory* and more recently in *Beyond Secular Order: The Representation of Being and the Representation of the People*.[69] As have many of the critics discussed earlier, Milbank presents his argument in genealogical form, and like them he takes aim at modernity and its spawn, liberalism. In the case of Milbank, however, he is concerned particularly with deconstructing modern Western secularism. As I will show in Chapter 1, Luther plays a villainous role in the story. I interact with Herdt because she can be said to be representative of a larger movement propounding a reading of Augustine that has proved highly influential in contemporary English-speaking political theology. Specifically, she calls for an "engaged Christian particularism" that stands in contrast to "exclusive particularism" characterized by "antiliberal rhetoric."[70] Her specific concern is with telling the fortunes of the virtue tradition in the history of Western Christianity, and again, Luther plays a negative role. I focus specifically on Herdt, rather than the more explicitly "political" theologians in the "Augustinian" tradition she gestures toward given her comparatively extensive engagement with Luther and the centrality of his place in her narrative. In the case of both Milbank and Herdt, I will treat of their engagement and criticism of Luther in further detail in chapters to come. For the purposes of this introduction, I simply want to set out the constructive elements in their political proposals and briefly indicate where they see Luther to be inimical to their projects.

69. John Milbank, *Theology and Social Theory: Beyond Secular Reason*, 2nd ed. (Oxford: Blackwell Publishing, 2006); Milbank, *Beyond Secular Order: The Representation of Being and the Representation of the People* (Chichester: Wiley Blackwell, 2014). For those who have followed in Milbank's wake, see William Cavanaugh, *Theopolitical Imagination* (London: T&T Clark, 2002); *Migrations of the Holy: God, State, and the Political Meaning of the Church* (Grand Rapids, MI: Eerdmans, 2011); and Graham Ward, *Cities of the Good* (London: Routledge, 2000). In the book, I have intentionally avoided, as much as possible, the terminology "Radical Orthodoxy," as I recognize it to be loosely organized around the works of several authors whose contributions vary in numerous ways from Milbank's own. When I do reference these authors, it is because I see the particular work under consideration to be an explicit development of previous work by Milbank, which helps illumine his relationship to Luther.

70. Herdt points to the work of Luke Bretherton, Charles Mathewes, and Eric Gregory as exemplary in their treatments of Christian particularism. Herdt, "Hauerwas among the Virtues," *JRE* 40.2 (June 2012), 223. See Bretherton, *Christianity and Contemporary Politics: The Conditions and Possibilities of Faithful Witness* (Chichester: Wiley-Blackwell, 2010); Mathewes, *A Theology of Public Life* (Cambridge: Cambridge University Press, 2007); Gregory, *Politics and the Order of Love: An Augustinian Ethic of Democratic Citizenship* (Chicago: The University of Chicago Press, 2008). In terms of moral philosophers, Herdt is particularly concerned to see theological ethics move in the direction of Jeffrey Stout, *Democracy and Tradition* (Princeton: Princeton University Press, 2004).

John Milbank's Confrontational Metaphysical Politics

As in the case of many of the authors cited earlier, Milbank seeks a politics that challenges the regnant liberalism of the modern West. He claims, "The 'modernity' of liberalism has only delivered mass poverty, inequality, erosion of freely associating bodies beneath the level of the state and ecological dereliction of the earth," together with abolishing worker's rights, destabilizing the family, and enslaving women.[71] A bit more specifically, he argues that liberal democracy has devolved into tyranny following upon its positing the ontological priority of violence. In this view, the beginning, or state of nature, is imagined as that of the "threatened individual, piece of property, or racial terrain."[72] The power of liberalism therefore lies in its promise to protect these threatened atomized entities from the danger of the alien other. As such, it places ultimate value on "individual security and freedom of choice," suspending all else should it prove "necessary" for the protection of these "rights." According to this logic, all mediating institutions between the individual and the state are dissolved leaving behind only "the free market along with the nation-state as a competitive unit."[73]

Milbank asserts that the church alone has the theoretical and practical resources necessary to address the challenges presented by late-modern liberalism and "the global hegemony of capital."[74] The Anglo-Catholic tradition in particular, Milbank argues, is theoretically resourced by a participatory ontology (to be spelled out in more detail in Chapter 1) drawn from the ideal of the Trinitarian God, which provides the transcendent notion necessary for a universality grounded in reconciled differences. Further, in this tradition, one finds a nonstatist socialism capable of challenging the global market economy without falling into a discourse of nominal individualism.[75] Luther falls far without this tradition, as Milbank finds him implicated in the voluntarist theology responsible for the sphere of politics coming to be understood as an autonomous secular realm associated with sheer formal power rather than understood as a participation in the divine economy.

Practically, the church as envisioned by Milbank is able to bring forth the conceptuality that makes the politics he is after possible. Never lacking ambition, Milbank argues that "in the Europe and the World of the future," we need a new conception of the economy as gift exchange. As a mode of both economy and politics, gift exchange makes possible both an economics and a politics that sees

---

71. Milbank, "Liberality versus Liberalism," in *The Future of Love: Essays in Political Theology* (London: SCM Press, 2009), 249–50.

72. Ibid., 243.

73. Ibid., 244.

74. Milbank, "Preface," in *The Future of Love*, xi. For more on this theme, see also *Being Reconciled: Ontology and Pardon* (Abingdon: Routledge, 2003), 162–86.

75. Specifically, Milbank states his preference for a Blue Socialism, which is to say a socialism with a "Burkean twinge." Milbank, "Preface," in *The Future of Love*, xvii. In his most recent work, Milbank calls for a new politics "which fuses Christian socialism with a new sense of what is valid in the 'conservative' critique of modernity." *BSO*, 268.

generosity, rather than contract, as foundational for society. The church serves as a model of such economy, Milbank argues, which itself has its life in the exchange of gifts understood as the "talents and insights" of the people. Just as in the church the people give their gifts to the head, Christ, so in "like manner the people should give their gifts of insight and talent to the sovereign representative who acts in their name."[76] A return to a gift-exchange economy and politics requires a turn back before the late Middle Ages when the metaphysical conceptions making it possible were undone by a theological insistence that divine and human agency be understood as standing in competitive relationship to one another.[77]

In addition to a gift-exchange economy, Milbank calls on Catholic Christianity to draw from its classical resources for two further purposes. First, he urges it to once again assert the need for a mixed form of government, where democracy, aristocracy, and monarchy are all blended together into a harmonious whole. This conception stands in opposition to both the right and the left, which either focus on "the One" or "the Many" and construe them nominalistically.[78] We will see in Chapter 1 the centrality of nominalism in Milbank's rejection of Luther's theology, which he sees as giving rise to the Hobbesian state.

Mediating institutions constitute the second classical resource that Milbank calls Christianity to draw upon. He argues for a "gothic" notion of complex space, such as was promoted by Catholic socialism prior to 1848, after which the notion began to be associated with conservative and reactionary elements.[79] Again, he sees this political insight deriving from a prior ecclesiology, "ultimately the Pauline concept of the church as 'body of Christ.'" Here the focus is less on the ratio between the part and the whole and more on the "*unit of relation* (taken as essential to the identity of its components) whether between persons, or different groups of persons regarded as possessing collective identity."[80] This is offered in opposition to the simple space of the Enlightenment, whereby individuals stand directly before other individuals and the state, mediated in their relationships only by contract, ordered either as atomic individuals under an absolute sovereign, or regulated by the "providential co-ordination of individual desires and choices in the agonistic harmony of a market economy."[81] Here too Milbank reads Luther

---

76. Milbank, "Liberality versus Liberalism," in *The Future of Love*, 245.

77. In the second chapter, I will explore this theme in Milbank in more detail, and consider how Luther's understanding of the Eucharist contributes to the "gift" discussion. I will do this in particular with reference to William Cavanaugh, who builds upon Milbank's writings on gift-exchange while engaging extensively with Luther.

78. Milbank, "Preface," in *Future of Love*, xii; cf. *BSO*, 137–41, 211–14.

79. Milbank, *The Word Made Strange* (Oxford: Blackwell Publishers, 1997), 272. We have already noted the importance of mediating institutions in the thought of MacIntyre, and in Wolin following Figgis. Milbank acknowledges that his essay on the theme is written in the spirit of Figgis and his teacher, Otto von Gierke (276). Cf. *BSO*, 214–18.

80. Milbank, *WMS*, 276.

81. Ibid., 275.

in terms quite similar to Wolin, arguing that Luther undermines the possibility of mediating institutions and starkly divides the sacred and secular realms in accordance with an ontology of simple space.

Jennifer Herdt's Engaged Virtuous Politics

While seeing herself as standing within the Augustinian tradition, Herdt argues that contemporary Christian ethicists and political theologians should move beyond the suspicions concerning pagan virtue that have plagued the tradition in order to more fruitfully engage with contemporary moral philosophers and find common ground in virtue ethics. Her project can perhaps be seen as taking a mediating position between Stanley Hauerwas and his criticism of liberalism on the one hand, and Jeffrey Stout and his defense of the "liberal tradition" on the other. On the whole, Herdt finds that Christian ethics has moved in the right direction toward virtue ethics in the past few decades. In light of these developments, Herdt is hopeful that a genuinely Augustinian account of habituation into virtue can be provided, absent Augustine's suspicions about pagan virtue.

As does Herdt, those she instances as moving Christian political theology in the right direction share with Milbank a general Augustinian framework, yet construe the relationship between the church and politics much more in terms of encounter rather than confrontation. I already mentioned earlier her pointing toward Luke Bretherton, Eric Gregory, and Charles Mathewes as noteworthy in this respect.[82] Bretherton advocates for a "post-liberal, theological politics" that "presumes a liberal constitutional order."[83] Following Augustine's two *civtates* framework and Jeremiah 29 ("seek the welfare of the city where I have sent you into exile"), he seeks the possibility of forming a common life between "pagans" and Christians.[84] Mathewes sees political engagement as a means of spiritual formation and calls for an eschatological engagement that eschews apocalyptic escapism. His version of Augustinianism may sound a bit more like Aquinas, although he clearly reads Augustine as having a "postlapsarian vision of politics" that avoids the problematic "nature/supernature" distinction of Thomas.[85] Gregory describes his project as a reconstruction of Augustinian liberalism into an "Augustinian civil liberalism." He includes in this trajectory Jean Bethke Elshtain and Oliver O'Donovan.[86] Crucial for his account, as for Herdt, is an emphasis on the virtues.

Despite these hopeful new directions, Herdt still discerns too many traces of the hyper-Augustinian legacy in contemporary Christian ethics. She suggests that Christian ethicists have made an overly sharp distinction between Christian

---

82. See earlier, n. 70.
83. Bretherton, *Christianity and Contemporary Politics*, 48.
84. Ibid., 3–6.
85. Mathewes, *A Theology of Public Life* (Cambridge: Cambridge University Press, 2007), 21–2.
86. Gregory, *Politics and the Order of Love*, 107–25.

and non-Christian habituation. The result has been similar to what she views as Luther's relinquishing of all agency to God, but in this case agency is surrendered to the church and its processes of habituation and moral development. Instead of an overly strong God–human dualism as in the former case, in the latter there is an overly strong church–world dualism. The result is an idealization of the church and its practices coupled with a demonization of "liberalism," secular modernity, and the current political order that does not allow place for God's providence in the modern world. In response she calls for a focus on habituation, an affirmation of the porous nature of the Christian self, and "a *chastened* account of Christian distinctiveness." On such an account, the virtues would be understood as allowing humans a fuller participation in the divine life. The development of such virtue would also not be limited to the practices of the church, but would extend to "ordinary inclinations and social relationships."[87] Therefore, humans can transform their character through action, and this does not exclude divine agency, even absent recognition of human action's dependency on God. Since divine grace is front and center, and since recognition of dependency on grace is not required, there is no need to make careful distinctions about identity. All this, Herdt argues, stands in strong contrast to Luther's account of the Christian life and the pagan virtues, largely owning to what she sees as his competitive understanding of the relation between divine and human agency. The result, according to Herdt, is that Luther sees no possibility of genuine Christian engagement in politics given that politics is simply authoritarian imposition of order on an otherwise chaotic world.

Content and Structure of the Book

Materially, the content of this book consists in bringing together the political theology of Luther as informed by the work of several important recent interpreters of Luther's theology with what I take to be two of the most influential strands in contemporary political theology in the English-speaking academy. The latter include the work associated with the Radical Orthodoxy movement and its "founder," John Milbank, as described earlier, as well as the work focusing on virtue formation that has evolved from earlier work by Alasdair MacIntyre and Stanley Hauerwas, and which finds a new and influential expression in the recent work of Jennifer Herdt, also described earlier. As far as interpreters of Luther, I draw extensively from Oswald Bayer, whose writings have recently largely become available to an English-speaking readership, as well as the work of Hans Ulrich and several of his students (namely, Bernd Wannenwetsch, Brian Brock, and Reinhard Hütter), in addition to the work of David Yeago. What holds all of these seemingly diverse accounts together is an interest in pursuing a genuinely theological

---

87. Herdt, *Putting on Virtue: The Legacy of the Splendid Vices* (Chicago: The University of Chicago Press, 2008), 344.

politics.[88] Milbank and Herdt both aim to criticize the excesses of modern prejudices that would limit or even dissolve the place of politics in accounts of a fully human life. For both, a recovery of a genuinely theological account of politics means an overcoming of Luther's unhelpful contributions to modern Western understandings of politics. However, I will argue that these supposed contributions are a caricature of Luther's theology, and that when the political implications of Luther's theology as understood by Bayer and the other authors mentioned earlier are brought to the surface, what we find is that Luther is a resource for the modernity critics rather than a hindrance to be overcome. More importantly, I argue that Luther provides a more radical criticism of modern politics than does either Milbank or Herdt precisely because his account remains theological to the core, whereas both Milbank and Herdt bring in philosophical assumptions concerning politics that are at cross-purposes with the theological elements in their accounts. Specifically, Milbank's interpretation and reappropriation of Augustine's two *civitates* framework in an attempt to overcome modern political understanding ironically understand politics as grounded and generated by human desire, whereas Luther's two regiments framework speaks of the differentiated but unified rule of God, according to which politics is understood as instituted by the Word of God in loving provision for God's creation. Herdt's virtue-driven account, while rightfully concerned with univocal accounts of divine and human agency, which problematically put the two into a competitive relationship with one another, nonetheless overextends the reach of human agency in politics at the expense of neglecting the biblical language of "principalities and powers." She underestimates the extent of human enslavement to such principalities, an enslavement from which humans can only be freed by a deliverer, and not by the acquisition of proper virtue. Luther's theology, in contrast, with his focus on trust in the deliverer, results in a freedom from concern for one's "self" and therefore freedom for one's neighbor in carrying out the properly creaturely good works that God has prepared beforehand (Eph. 2:10). The carrying out of such works is central to Luther's account of sanctification, and thus to his account of the three estates (or institutions), which I will argue provides a more theologically rooted account of Christian good works in the political realm than does a virtue-driven account. Therefore, in addition to responding to and correcting common criticisms of Luther's political thought, the primary contribution of this book will be to show the critical potential of Luther's theology in engaging leading contemporary theological conceptions of politics and the constructive ways forward that a reflection on his theology suggests. However, given that so much of this critical potential lies in

---

88. By the term "theological politics" is meant an interpretation of politics that is determined by theological considerations, rather than a theology that tries to appeal to a neutral public sphere or that seeks to locate theology within a larger task of political philosophy. For a typology of contemporary approaches to political theology, see Eric Gregory, "Christianity and the Rise of the Democratic State," in *Political Theology for a Plural Age*, ed. Michael Jon Kessler (Oxford: Oxford University Press, 2013), 99–101.

aspects of Luther's theology largely neglected in English-speaking accounts of his theology and political thought, it will be necessary first to bring out these elements and situate them within the more general thrust of his theology. This will not be done in abstraction, however, but rather will be carried out as I engage with both the constructive and critical arguments presented by Milbank and Herdt. This will not only sharpen my account of Luther's contribution, but will also help to show how his thought provides a genuine alternative to these two more dominant streams of thought that attempt to relate theology and politics. I am not seeking a repristination of Luther, or merely a correction of interpretations of Luther in the interest of a "more" historical Luther, however important historical research is for our present understanding of Luther. Rather, I seek to bring more fully to the surface trajectories in Luther's thought that make him a far more interesting and penetrating interlocutor, with many critical and constructive insights, in the conversations currently forming the quickly ascendant field of political theology in the English-speaking world.

Of particular importance is the argument, which I will make in Chapter 2, that the grammar of Luther's theology resists easy systematization or assumption under broader conceptual categories. While I speak of his theology as a "theology of the Word," it is clear that for Luther the Word of God is not static, but living and active and never cemented to a single, simple referent. Rather, it is densely layered and allows Luther to speak of Trinity, creation, redemption, Scripture, history, and other theological and philosophical *loci* without ever hardening into a static conceptual schema. Luther's attentiveness to the living Word means that Luther's theology is likewise lively and continually transgresses standard categories and spills out beyond the boundaries necessary for maintaining neat systems. Given this character of Luther's theology, it becomes highly difficult (probably impossible) to locate him within a larger genealogical narrative, such as those standard in most accounts of Western political thought and theology. Luther can only be made to "fit" these stories by blocking the logic inherent in his theology from category transgression and redirecting the flow of his thought so that it does not break the dams holding up the systems into which he is placed. That Luther's theology has this character follows from the centrality of the living and active Word of God, the real presence of the risen and ascended Christ, in his understanding of the world. Rather than seeking an overarching conceptuality allowing for the circumscription of God, humans, and the rest of creation, and their interactions across space and time, Luther's theology instead seeks to be always responsive and attentive to the *viva vox* of its Lord. As such, its critical and heuristic potential is massive when it is not blunted by the attempt to place Luther under predetermined categories.

The book is divided into five chapters. In Chapter 1, I consider Milbank's criticism of Luther for moving theology in the direction of a privatized and spiritualized Christianity and dividing the world into a transcendental spiritual realm and an autonomous sphere of nature, humanity, and society characterized by "sheerly formal power."[89] A shift from a participatory ontology toward a univocal

---

89. Milbank, *TST*, 9.

and nominal view of God with a voluntaristic emphasis, prioritizing faith and imputation at the expense of love, is central to this new conception of religion and society. Additionally, Milbank accuses Luther of fanning the flames of modernism with his *sola scriptura* doctrine, which would be put to use by Hobbes and Spinoza in order to evacuate Scripture of all political consequences and further privatize Christianity.

Chapter 1 responds to Milbank's charges relative to Luther's ontology and stress on faith, reserving his criticism of Luther's *sola scriptura* for Chapter 2. My response begins by showing the importance of union with Christ in Luther's conception of justification that goes beyond a merely extrinsic imputationism, but rather is organically related to the process of sanctification. I argue that this account of justification and sanctification follows the grammar of faith and love, which is accentuated in the metaphor that Luther most commonly uses for describing this union, namely, the martial metaphor.[90] In such union, the Christian has the free confidence to turn toward the neighbor and bear fruit in season.[91]

Chapter 2 responds to Milbank's criticism of Luther's *sola scriptura* and its political consequences. Additionally, I use the question of Luther's relationship to Scripture to develop an account of his theology of the Word, which I take to be crucial in coming to grasp the grammar of Luther's theology. I show that this grammar is itself highly political, and that Luther's theology, focused as it is on the Word, moves strongly against the modern tendencies attributed to Luther's thought by the modernity critics. However, a criticism of modern liberal political understandings based in Luther's thought is grounded more in the concrete reality of Jesus Christ and his presence to the church, particularly in preaching and the sacraments, than it is in an account of opposing ontologies or of an ecclesiology generally conceived. While not framed in an ontological register, I show that Luther's account of the sacraments, especially, works against a nominalistic conception of reality, while his account of the life of the church, as itself political, works strongly against voluntarism and individualism. In spelling out the way in which the Word of God is understood by Luther, and its centrality to the rest of his theology, this chapter provides a basis for understanding Luther's theological grammar, allowing for a more nuanced discussion of the more specifically political elements in his thought in the chapters to follow.

In Chapter 3, rather than seeking the commonality between Luther and Milbank, or showing how Luther's theology can achieve much of the modernity criticism Milbank is after without requiring an ontological register, I instead elaborate the constructive differences between the political theologies of the two. Specifically, I argue that Luther is better able to hold together what might be termed the Augustinian and the Thomist (i.e., Aristotelian, Arendtian) conceptions of

---

90. Gerhard Sauter argues, "Justification is itself a metaphorical occurrence . . . It insists on being expressed in its own way. At the same time it evades every effort at conceptual realization." Sauter, "God Creating Faith. The Doctrine of Justification from the Reformation to the Present," *LQ* 11.1 (Spring 1997), 17.

91. Luther, "Treatise on Good Works, 1520," LW 44:26.

politics than is Milbank. This is accomplished by Luther's teaching on the "two *ecclesiae*," which retains the critical edge found in Milbank's understanding of the two *civitates*, but in such fashion that the *politia* does not have to be resisted and opposed outright in the way that the false *ecclesia* does. In this framework, Christians can go beyond merely using the peace of the earthly city and instead more fully participate in exploration of a common good that all humans (Christian or not) share together as creatures of the same God, exploration that the *politia* as creature together with humankind (and not merely an outcome of human generational loves or ontologies) serves. Luther can speak of such a common good because he sees all reality as under the one rule of God, whether God is ruling in the church or in the politics of the world. Luther describes the differentiated, but unified rule of God in his teaching on the "two regiments," which I briefly explicate at the end of the chapter.

In Chapter 4, and the one to follow, I continue to consider the theme of the relationship between the church and the political, which was central to Chapter 3, in this case restricting the question not to the meaning of power or the status of the political relative to sin and the Fall, but rather by focusing on God's present and ongoing work in the *politia* among both Christians and non-Christians. Simultaneously, I continue the project of responding to criticisms of Luther that would make him an unhelpful conversation partner for discussions in theological ethics and political theology. My interlocutor for this section is Jennifer Herdt, who finds problematic what she sees as Luther's focus on complete human passivity in response to an acknowledged utter dependence on divine activity. Besides complicating an account of sanctification (by separating it too sharply from justification), Herdt charges that Luther's call for passivity and acknowledgment means there is no room for true pagan virtue, thus rendering politics nothing but the imposition of order by an authoritarian state. As in the criticisms set forth thus far, Herdt traces Luther's shortcomings back to his relation to nominalism and voluntarism, especially the construal of divine and human agency on a competitive and contractual basis.

I respond to Herdt, first by addressing her question regarding pagan virtue, showing that God's gracious activity among "pagans," especially in political matters, is highly evident for Luther. However, he distinguishes, without separating, redemption and providence such that the particularity of the Christian confession is not elided and the imagining human heart is confronted. Significantly, Luther remains faithful to the Scriptural witness to human enslavement to principalities and powers, and therefore for the need for a deliverer, which is lacking in Herdt's virtue-driven account.

In Chapter 5, I explicate Luther's understanding of sanctification. Contra Herdt, I argue that Luther holds justification and sanctification organically together, while still making the proper distinctions that prevent a tendency toward Pelagianism, as is seen in Herdt's protagonist Erasmus. More significantly, in this chapter I name the "three estates" as institutionally naming sanctification, as the estates are the places for Luther where humans can expect to encounter the promised presence of God and receive and hand on God's goodness from and to one's neighbors. It is in bringing the teaching on the two "*ecclesiae*" and the three "estates" to the forefront of an interpretation of Luther's political thought, themes largely neglected in treatments of Luther, that a true picture of the constructive value of his political theology comes to view. Chapter 5, and the book as a whole, thus concludes with an account of Luther's contribution to a contemporary understanding of politics. I give a foretaste of this conclusion in the section that follows.

Luther's Theological Contribution to a Contemporary Understanding of Politics

What all the critics of Luther described earlier share in common is a concern for preserving or regaining politics in the midst of circumstances that threaten to eclipse political forms of life. In this book, I argue that this same concern is central in interpreting Luther's political thinking. However, in order to see this, the common prejudices regarding Luther's theology must be overcome. Having done that, it is possible to find in Luther clues to what a theologically driven attempt at overcoming the depoliticization of human life in our own times might look like. In other words, Luther gives us insight into the grammar that enables a creaturely form of political life, the shape of its contours, and a heuristic for recognizing and criticizing the many forms of antipolitics that threaten such forms of life.

Specifically, I describe the critical purchase to be gained by Luther's concepts of the two *ecclesiae* and the three estates (or institutions), both of which provide the larger frame within which to understand the much better-known concept of the two regiments.[92] Each serves to give place for both human and divine agency in politics, to preserve an account of the positive good of politics, and yet critically interrogate any given political formation by sensitivity to the real possibility of antipolitics in the form of the principalities and powers and their false construction of anti-institutions. These themes tend to be underplayed, if not neglected outright, in accounts of Luther's politics. Instead, most accounts of his theology center on justification and the relationship of God to the individual

---

92. Further, as I will argue in chapter 3, focusing on Luther's language of two *ecclesiae* in his later "Lectures on Genesis," rather than the language of "two kingdoms" as found in his earlier occasional writings, makes clear the eschatological distinction between the kingdom of God and the kingdom of Satan and the more creation-oriented distinction between God's singular rule in twofold form ("two regiments") in the *ecclesia* and in the *politia*. All three teachings must be stressed together if one is to avoid interpretations of Luther that result in a quietistic positing of an autonomous secular realm. William Lazareth argues that "much of traditional Lutheranism . . . frequently became socially quietistic by virtually identifying Luther's later Christ *and* Caesar dialectic ('twofold reign') with his earlier God *or* Satan dualism ('two kingdoms')." Lazareth, "Response to Antti Raunio, 'Natural Law and Faith,'" in *Union with Christ: The New Finnish Interpretation of Luther*, ed. Carl E. Braaten and Robert W. Jenson (Grand Rapids, MI: Eerdmans, 1998), 128; emphases in the original.

believer. While I do not challenge the centrality of justification in Luther's theology, I argue that it must be understood within the larger picture of his theology of the Word of God and what this reveals about creation and eschaton. It is particularly in these relations that Luther discusses the estates and the regiments, such that a neglect of either creation or eschatology necessarily reduces Luther's theology and neglects its political import. It is in his account of creation that Luther provides a more theologically fruitful account of politics than does Milbank. Further, it is in his eschatology that Luther provides a more theologically fruitful account than Herdt. It is the elements of each that allow his theology to have both a positive and negative account of politics. Put another way, the two regiments teaching avoids a separation of the world into secular and sacred spheres, without either collapsing the church into the world or the world into the church. The "three estates (institutions)" teaching is a more "Aristotelian" (or "Herdtian") moment in Luther's thought, whereby he gives an account of the goodness of politics as one of the places where humans can concretely encounter God's promises and provision, but in such a manner that a critical sensitivity for false or demonic anti-institutions is not undermined. The two *ecclesiae* teaching is a more "Augustinian" (or "Milbankian") moment in Luther's thought, whereby the *ecclesia* and *polis* can confront one another in critical interaction, but in such a way that politics is not rendered as little more than tragic response to the Fall. However, unlike Milbank, Luther does not give us new ideas to then implement, nor like Herdt, practices to put in play in the quest for virtue, but rather he directs us to the place of divine promise where humans are freed in faith for responsiveness to life in communion with God and neighbor.

In this theology, the properly biblical emphasis on the centrality of faith expects that believers who hear this Word are given a new heart and thereby freed for political life. Further, it is a faith that expects to find this Word continually speaking to the church in its worship, subjecting both the church and the world to a saving criticism that follows the baptismal pattern of death and resurrection. This is in opposition to views that would put at the center of the Christian contribution to political life either a new theory (change in thinking through change in ontology), or that would locate the Christian contribution at the level of behavior or action (through the development of virtue). So rather than theory or practice, Luther gives us the concept of the passive life (*vita passiva*), which is a life of faith. Both of the former postures (theory and practice) suggest that something is lacking that can be obtained or provided for by human initiative and agency. However, for Luther, it is not the heroic efforts of the theologian, nor imitation of the heroically virtuous, that is needed, but rather recognition of, and trust in, what has always already been given. A theological politics following Luther thus clings to the promise of Christ that "I am with you always, to the end of the age" (Matt. 28:20). As such, Luther's contribution to a contemporary understanding of politics is an explorative discernment in humble, yet assured response to the Spirit's work of reconciliation and to God's promise to govern and provide for human life, a promise that is encountered concretely in what Luther refers to as the institutions of the *ecclesia*, *oeconomia*, and *politia*. In this sense, Luther does not give us a blueprint for enacting political constitution or reform, but rather a heuristic and hermeneutic by which to read Scripture[93] and the constitutive forms of human life within which the divine Word is addressed to us here and now. Luther's theology thus postures us in such a manner as to be responsive to God's rule over human political life and to be alert and attentive to the in-breaking of the Word that is continually making all things new in opposition to the false schemas and orders that would undermine creaturely life. These false schemas can take the form of both political theories or of political practices, which become static and closed rather than attentive to the always new divine address. It is a theology of waiting on the Spirit, of expectation of encountering the living Word, and is therefore fundamentally responsive and forward-looking rather than passive and reactionary.

---

93. "The Bible speaks and teaches about the works of God . . . These works are divided into three hierarchies: the household, the government, the church. If a verse does not fit the church, we should let it stay in the government or the household, whichever it is best suited to." "Table Talk," in LW 54:446.

Chapter 1

ONTOLOGY AND POLITICS: LUTHER'S ROLE IN JOHN MILBANK'S CRITIQUE OF SECULAR MODERNITY

In his well-known *Theology and Social Theory: Beyond Secular Reason*, as well as in numerous subsequent articles and publications, including most recently his *Beyond Secular Order: The Representation of Being and the Representation of the People*, John Milbank puts forward a narrative claiming to lay bare the root of modern social science and the secularization of reason. This root, he argues, proves to be an ontology of violence in which competitive struggle is central. Milbank opposes the narrative of modern social science with the narrative told by the "Christian mythos," which has an ontology of peace at its core.[1] According to Milbank, several "contingent" theological decisions made possible the ontology at the heart of modern social science and its attendant conception of secularity. Much of Milbank's narrative consists in an articulation of these theological decisions and the fruit they eventually bore. Rather than summarizing his entire narrative, in this chapter I will focus specifically on Milbank's interpretation of the role played by Luther's theology in helping to lay the groundwork for modern sociology and secular universalized reason. The points Milbank raises are all major theological themes underlying Luther's understanding of politics. Crucial to my criticism of most contemporary treatments of Luther's political thinking is that they fail to clearly take into account the overall theological grammar within which his more obviously political thought is located. Too often, Luther's politics is not understood because his basic theological convictions are misunderstood. Milbank's account gives us occasion for clarifying these convictions in providing a theologically astute interlocutor with a real sense for the theological issues at stake, but who nonetheless reads Luther along the same lines as the political thinkers and historians mentioned in the introduction. After setting out the broad frame of Luther's theology in this chapter in response to Milbank, the following chapter, while continuing to respond to Milbank, will more specifically name the leading theme of all of Luther's thinking as "the Word of God" and give articulation to its importance for Luther's treatment of politics. In this way, Chapters 1 and 2 can be viewed as more broad overviews of Luther's theology with special reference

1. *TST*, 383.

to his political thought taken up, not abstractly, but in explicit conversation with Milbank's work, while Chapter 3 makes the political thought central and explicit.

At the core of his criticism, Milbank sees Luther as positing a nominalist and univocal ontology discernible especially in his Christology and soteriology (i.e., in Luther's doctrine of justification). Closely related to Luther's treatment of justification, Milbank argues, is a replacement of love with faith at the center of Christianity. I also present here Milbank's more obviously political critiques of Luther to show the way in which he ties Luther's understanding of metaphysics to his account of politics. Having set forth Milbank's account, this chapter will then offer a response to Milbank's metaphysical–ontological case against Luther in the form of a consideration of what has been called "the Finnish school" of Luther interpretation, a school of thought originating at the University of Helsinki with Tuomo Mannermaa and his students in dialogue with the Eastern Orthodox Church. While helpfully reminding students of Luther of the centrality of union with Christ for Luther's understanding of justification, I argue that the focus of the Finnish interpreters on deification and a participatory ontology is historically questionable, and theologically it is unnecessary for my response to Milbank's criticisms of Luther. As such, I develop a response to Milbank by giving particular attention to Luther's use of the imagery of marital union in describing justification. As will become evident, Luther's treatment is tied closely to his understanding of faith and its relation especially to love, a relation of particular importance for Luther's political theology.

My aim in this chapter is rather modest as I seek to show that Luther's thought is not as anathema to much of Milbank's critical project as might appear from his use of Luther. Attention is given particularly to Milbank's assumption that Luther's thought is basically grounded in a metaphysical nominalism. This charge merits response given that it plays an important role in other treatments of Luther's political thought, including those we have already examined (especially in the treatment of Quentin Skinner).[2] In the two chapters that follow I will pursue a more constructive engagement with Milbank. First, in Chapter 2, I will set forth the political implications of Luther's theology of the Word in contrast to Milbank's "ontology of peace." Then, in Chapter 3, I will offer an interpretation of Luther's teaching on the two *ecclesiae*, which allows for greater engagement in and with the world than does Milbank's insistence on a "postmodern critical Augustinian" two cities approach to politics.[3] Overall, I show that a political theology grounded in Luther's thought can at the same time both hold to the critical force of Milbank's work, yet more fully engage the life of politics as a positive good.

---

2. The role of nominalism is likewise given an important place in Charles Taylor's story of the rise of modern self-understanding. See his *Sources of the Self: The Making of the Modern Identity* (Cambridge: Harvard University Press, 1989), 82–3, and for a nonparticipatory ontology, see 186–91.

3. Milbank, "Postmodern Critical Augustinianism: A Short *Summa* in Forty-Two Responses to Unasked Questions," in *The Future of Love*, 337–51.

Milbank's Interpretation of Luther

Before discussing Milbank's critique of Luther, it is helpful to bear in mind his assertion that "the main historical target of Radical Orthodoxy [i.e., the movement inspired by Milbank's work] is not the Reformation but rather late Scholasticism,"[4] and his view that "the Reformation can be seen as a partial though imperfect critique of the later Middle Ages."[5] These statements are important in demonstrating that Milbank's primary criticism of Luther's theology, and the theology of the Reformation generally, is its failure to break completely with the late medieval scholastic tradition of voluntarism, nominalism, and univocal ontologism, represented by such figures as Duns Scotus, William of Ockham, and Gabriel Biel.[6] However, Milbank's criticism of Luther extends to the charge of a fideistic positing of trust and hope as the essence of Christianity, rather than the centrality accorded to love prior to the Reformation. In replacing love with "a loveless trust in an inscrutable deity," Milbank argues, the Magisterial Reformers abolished gift by compromising charity as a principle of organizing society, giving way to capitalist contractual conceptions.[7] Therefore, despite the fact that the Reformation is not the primary mark of Radical Orthodox polemic, the Reformers, and particularly Luther, fare poorly in Milbank's overall treatment. In that any serious attempt at political theology today must reckon with Milbank, a political theology based in Luther's teaching must address Milbank's criticisms. More importantly, in delineating the fundamental differences (and agreement) between Luther and Milbank, we acquire a much better sense of Luther's theology and its relation to the highly significant challenges to modernity that Milbank's project represents.

Ontology

Milbank's critique of Luther fits into the broader sweep of his narration of a Christianity that has shifted away from its origins. He argues that modern sociology fails to see that the secular had to be positively instituted because sociology assumes that humanism and "human autonomous freedom" are genetic to the Judeo-Christian tradition. However, Milbank writes:

> In this respect [sociology] is doomed to repeat the self-understanding of Christianity arrived at in late-medieval nominalism, the Protestant reformation

---

4. Milbank, "Alternative Protestantism: Radical Orthodoxy and the Reformed Tradition," in *Radical Orthodoxy and the Reformed Tradition* (Grand Rapids, MI: Baker Academic, 2005), 26.
5. Ibid., 27.
6. *TST*, 15–17, and idem, "Radical Orthodoxy: A Conversation," ed. Rupert Shortt in *The Radical Orthodoxy Reader*, ed. John Milbank and Simon Oliver (London: Routledge, 2009), 33.
7. *BSO*, 63.

and seventeenth-century Augustinianism, which completely privatized, spiritualized and transcendentalized the sacred, and concurrently reimagined nature, human action and society as a sphere of autonomous, sheerly formal power.[8]

In this view, the Protestant Reformation is part of an early modern movement away from original Christianity that had the dual effect of driving Christianity itself radically inward and upward while surrendering the public domain to the guidance of the autonomous human will. Hence, we have the institution of the secular heavily barricaded against the influence of the sacred. Religion is of private concern; the public sphere can only be concerned with the decisions of human beings guided by a universalized rationality or by the exercise of their willful autonomy. Milbank argues that this self-understanding of Christianity was carried forward in the past century by, among others, Ernst Troeltsch and Max Weber, who failed "to see individualism, voluntarism, fideism, and Kantian ethicization as contingent changes in Christian doctrine and ethos" rather than part of Christianity's original self-understanding.[9]

At the root of this new conception of society and religion is a theological move away from a participatory ontology toward a univocal and nominal view of God, a move for which Luther shares responsibility. While acknowledging that Luther's early treatment of justification tended toward a patristic understanding of "participation" in Christ when compared with the treatment of justification by Ockham, Pierre d'Ailly, and other late-medieval theologians, Luther was still too indebted to their ontology, according to Milbank, leading more to a fusion of the redeemed with Christ rather than a participation. In Milbank's narrative, Luther's metaphysics, which "was a specifically univocalist and nominalist metaphysics," is essential to his theological failings.[10] Milbank demonstrates what he takes to be the failure of Luther's metaphysic in comparing Luther's Christology with that of Calvin's as it relates to the question of justification. In the early Luther, Milbank argues, the univocalist aspects of his metaphysics require him to understand the hypostatic union "in a fashion that is more or less monophysite."[11] In the fusion of God and man in Christ, there is "a reduced or else suspended human kenotic possession of the divine attributes."[12] In the incarnation, God enters creation "as a

8. *TST*, 9.
9. Ibid., 95.
10. Milbank, "Alternative Protestantism," 28. See also Milbank's "Knowledge," in *Radical Orthodoxy: A New Theology*, ed. John Milbank, Catherine Pickstock, and Graham Ward (London: Routledge, 1998), 23, where Milbank argues that Luther followed Duns Scotus in his univocal understanding of being and "broadly accepted the framework of late medieval nominalist philosophy."
11. Milbank, "Alternative Protestantism," 28. Elsewhere, Milbank writes, "Actually Luther was *more* monophysite than the formal monophysitism of the 'monophysites.'" *Being Reconciled*, 111 (emphasis in the original).
12. Milbank, "Alternative Protestantism," 33.

kind of alien place or locality" and the humanity is "more or less fused" with the divinity, given that being can only be predicated of atomic individuals according to nominalism. Further, the Christian's "participation" in Christ is conceived as a fusion, tending toward an absolute fusion, rather than a sharing, because on a univocalist account there can be no allowance of a sharing that falls between identity and difference, but instead "participation" in Christ "edges too closely towards mere identity and subsumption."[13] This leads Milbank to conclude that the "danger of the early Lutheran view is that the sharing in Christ is simply imputation taken in a physicalist mode and, moreover, a mode so all-complete as to downgrade the importance of later sanctification."[14]

In contrast to Luther, Calvin, by Milbank's interpretation, proposes a Christology that initially appears more amenable to a participatory ontology. Calvin could be read to begin "with the relation of the human nature to the divine nature in Christ," which allows our participation in Christ to occur through his human nature. In so participating, our finite nature shares in Christ's human nature, which in turn shares in his infinite divine nature. In other words, in Calvin's Christology, the possibility remains for positing a human participation in divine being. As opposed to Luther's account, Calvin does not go the route of "absolute fusion," but allows somewhat for a "partaking" and "imitating" of Christ that allows that "justification immediately opens upon sanctification."[15] Nonetheless, Milbank argues, Calvin goes too far in the opposite direction from Luther. Rather than the Lutheran tendency toward monophysitism, Calvin succumbs to a drift toward a schizophrenic Nestorianism.[16] According to Milbank, this drift results from Calvin's failure "to truly grasp a participatory ontology" and "the difference between nature on the one hand and hypostasis or substantive personality on the other." The human nature in Christ does not fully participate in the divine, for example, in the infinity of God (the idea that the finite cannot bear the infinite), which Milbank notes "the famous *extra-calvinisticum*" asserts. Like Scotus, Calvin with his inadequate participatory ontology does not see the necessity for the deification of the humanity of Christ in the incarnation. In the end, then, Milbank views Calvin's Christology and ontology, like Luther's, as tending too much toward univocalism and hence to the idea of justification as imputation. The important point for Milbank is the inadequacy of a univocal ontology to

---

13. Milbank, *Being Reconciled*, 111.
14. Milbank, "Alternative Protestantism," 28.
15. Ibid., 27–9. Milbank argues that the relative openness to a participatory metaphysic in Calvin as opposed to Luther is also evident in their theology of the Eucharist: "if God is not in the elements by local spatial presence, as in Luther's doctrine of consubstantiation, but nonetheless the Eucharist conveys a spiritual sharing in Christ's body in heaven [as it does in Calvin's doctrine], then is not this also a kind of participation of the finite in the infinite?"
16. Milbank, "The Grandeur of Reason and the Perversity of Rationalism: Radical Orthodoxy's First Decade," in *The Radical Orthodoxy Reader*, 373.

account for participation in Christ. Again, there is no space between identity and difference where beings could participate or share in and imitate being as such. In Luther, the believer is fused or absorbed into Christ such that there is too great an identity between the two. For Calvin, on the other hand, the humanity does not really participate in the divinity such that there is too great a difference between the two.[17]

Milbank argues that the limitations of his ontology eventually led Luther to an extrinsicist imputational account of justification. In contrast, for example, to Aquinas's realist and analogical ontology, Milbank argues, "Luther's nominalism will not really admit the Thomist paradox of a righteousness that is entirely supernatural, yet also entirely ours since it is deification." In his earlier, participatory attempts, "Luther is in fact developing the consequences of an almost monophysite Ockhamist and nominalist Christology which cannot really think two universal 'natures' in a single personal reality, nor think this reality other than on the model of a single finite thing 'within which' God has somehow entered."[18] In this account, the Christian is justified, not because she participates in Christ, but because Christ's righteousness has been imputed to her. All that remains is to believe. On this reading, faith understood as mere acknowledgment, is justificatory faith. For Milbank, a *sola fide* of this sort is a misreading of Paul. He writes, in a comment on Hegel's interpretation of atonement:

> Hegel shows himself to be perhaps a still profounder reader of the Pauline epistles than Martin Luther. For if there is a "centre" to Paul's theology, then it is surely not "justification by faith," but rather "participation in atonement," the "filling up what is lacking in the sufferings of Christ for the sake of his body, the Church" (Col. 1:24). This is especially enunciated in the first chapter of the second epistle to the Corinthians (2 Cor. 1:3–12). Not only does this passage make clear that every Christian must personally pass through, *and not merely acknowledge*, the cross, it also indicates that these sufferings are of 'consolatory' or atoning value to the community.[19]

This understanding of faith and justification gives rise to Milbank's charge that Luther (and the magisterial Reformers generally, "even if Luther is far more guilty") posit trust and hope as the essence of Christianity, rather than the centrality accorded to love prior to the Reformation, a change he calls "in many ways, the

---

17. See also *BSO*, 80.

18. Milbank, *Being Reconciled*, 111. Elsewhere, Milbank argues, "Both Luther and Calvin attempted to restore, against the later Middle Ages, a participatory vision to Christology, if not more generally, and the treatment of grace and faith was made once again more Christ-centered, compared with later scholasticism. Calvin, in particular, can be read in different ways. Unlike Luther, who remains basically a nominalist thinker, Calvin doesn't really have much of an ontology or a philosophy." Milbank, "Radical Orthodoxy: A Conversation," 39.

19. *WMS*, 184 (emphasis mine). In *TST*, Milbank argues that the proper Pauline emphasis is participation in Christ's body, not justification by faith (122, cf., 401).

gravest imaginable heresy."[20] When love is moved from the center of theology, Milbank argues, it becomes "moralised, sentimentalized and marginalised." In the case of Luther, whose view on these matters "had a long later echo," Milbank argues that "erotic, preferential and friendly love" is confined to "the natural and trivial" cut off from divine love.[21] Luther "fails to see that faith is from the outset received and enacted charity or a *habitus*," that it is "from the outset the work of charity, our work only in so far as it is God's."[22] Instead of infused habit directing the Christian life, the Reformation emphasizes grace in the context of arbitrary election, with love being simply a consequence of justification, and therefore belonging properly to sanctification. Human love in this conception, Milbank argues, follows divine love in that it is purely disinterested, having more the character of arbitrary election than of divine gift. Most importantly for our purposes, Milbank holds that

> charity comes to be something that need not inform the public sphere, since the community of Charity, the Church, is now more thought of as merely a collection of individual believers, and the political arm is seen as concerned with either the prudential policing of sins (Luther) or the enforcing of the moral law of the Old Testament (Calvin), now less seen as subject to the equitable revisions of charitable insight.[23]

Voluntarism

In addition to the danger posed to "orthodox" theology by the conceptions of Christ and justification noted earlier, Milbank also sees Luther's theology as having other dire consequences for political conceptuality. This takes the form of an antipolitical church that, nonetheless, requires the force of the external state. To understand what he refers to as Luther's antipolitical church, one must again follow Milbank's narrative back to late medieval nominalist–voluntarist theology, which viewed human essence in terms of power (*dominium*) that lay at the center of the divine essence. Human dominion, reflecting that of the willful Creator, was defined "as power, property, active right, and absolute sovereignty."[24] Tied to this was an extreme account of divine simplicity making possible both imperialistic and papist claims for a connection between monotheism and monarchic unity. As Milbank describes it:

> The Trinity loses its significance as a prime location for discussing will and understanding in God and the relationship of God to the world. No longer is the world participatorily enfolded within the divine expressive *logos*, but instead

20. Milbank, "Alternative Protestantism," 33.
21. *BSO*, 227.
22. *WMS*, 230, 228.
23. *BSO*, 225.
24. *TST*, 13.

a bare divine unity starkly confronts the other distinct unities which he has ordained.[25]

This nominalistic and voluntaristic conception is eventually translated by Hobbes into the absolute sovereignty of the individual, a sovereignty that she willfully transfers absolutely to the artificial state in the interest of self-preservation. The state absolutely fills up the newly imagined spaces called "the secular," which is the domain of humans absent God (i.e., the domain "created" by the assertion of human autonomy). Because the absolute secular state cannot share space with a "political" church, Milbank argues that it was necessary for Luther, still in the infancy of this new conception prior to Hobbes, "to produce the paradox of a purely 'suasive' Church which must yet involve external state coercion for its self-government."[26] Luther, through his doctrine of the two kingdoms, assisted in the formation of the secular by separating the concerns of the state from those of the church. The separation was made possible by "the Protestant view" of the church, which "understands it as an association of individual believers who possess outside the social context, their own direct relationship to God."[27] It was then left to Hobbes to make sure that this "private" religion with its asocial relation to God maintained such asociality with respect to the claims of the political realm.

Sola Scriptura

In separating church and state, Milbank argues, it would be impossible for Hobbes simply to exclude scriptural authority from public deliberation. Therefore, he (as did Spinoza) attached a biblical hermeneutics to his work of political science built upon the foundation laid by Luther's own hermeneutic. Milbank argues that it was Luther's *sola scriptura* that helped make possible the modern concepts of science and politics devoid of "religious" influence. By denying that the authoritative interpretation of Scripture lies within the tradition of the Catholic Church, Luther prepared the way for a distinctly modern biblical hermeneutic

---

25. Ibid., 15. Although Milbank centers his account of a harmonious peaceful ontology in the Trinity, Todd Breyfogle argues that Augustine centers harmony in the Incarnation, not the Trinity. In fact, like Luther, Augustine foregrounds the imagery of the bride and bridegroom. I discuss Luther's use of this imagery later. Breyfogle, "Is There Room for Political Philosophy in Postmodern Critical Augustinianism?" in *Deconstructing Radical Orthodoxy: Postmodern Theology, Rhetoric and Truth*, ed. Wayne J. Hankey and Douglas Hedley (Hants: Ashgate, 2005), 31–48. For an argument that social and political thought is better served by focusing on Christology rather than the Trinity, see Kathryn Tanner's chapter, "Politics," in her *Christ the Key* (Cambridge: Cambridge University Press, 2010).

26. TST, 19.

27. TST, 403. On this reading, the church really has very little importance. It is excluded from the political (public–social) realm and is, in the most important sense, unnecessary for the individual's relationship to God.

in which Scripture interprets Scripture. As Milbank argues, such biblical self-authorization "is bound, in the end, to arrive at either voluntarist-formalist or rationalist solutions, or else a mixture of both." The primary end for Hobbes and Spinoza in their interpretive method was to ensure that Scripture authorized obedience to the sovereign will and limited all possible disputes over the meaning of Scripture to matters concerning the private sphere alone. In order to achieve this end, it was necessary that revelation be seen as a directly private positivistic interruption of "the normal self-sufficiency of reason," and that this revelation always be subject to a sort of scientific objectivity that methodologically ensures correct interpretation.[28] In order to achieve such objectivity, "charisma" must not be allowed "to attach to transmission, other than the formal circumstance of continuity." This meant, especially, that the traditional "fourfold" interpretation of Scripture be banished because it "implied an uncontrollable proliferation of Christocentric meaning which inserted divine communication into the process of human historical becoming and must forever escape from sovereign mastery."[29] Hence, the necessity that revelation be private in nature, or if public, that it be attached to miracles, which according to the Reformers had ceased with the apostolic age. In other words, according to Milbank, Hobbes and Spinoza used Reformation hermeneutics, particularly the "Lutheran *sola scriptura*," to evacuate Scripture of political consequence, or at least to subordinate Scripture's meaning to political authority. Milbank argues, "It is the destiny of the *sola scriptura* to be so deconstructed as to come to mean that we must believe the Scriptures because they are politically authorized."[30]

In summary, Milbank finds resources for modern secularism in several aspects of Luther's theology. First, in his nominalistic and univocalistic metaphysics, which Milbank claims can be discerned in Luther's Christology and ultimately imputational understanding of justification, in which faith as mere belief replaces participation and Christianity becomes interiorized and personalized. Second, Luther's "secular modernism" is evident in his remaining under the sway of the late medieval voluntaristic view of God that privileges *dominium* and makes possible a depoliticized church, allowing Luther to conceive of autonomous individuals operating under a two kingdoms principle grounding a separation of church and state. A third aspect is Luther's *sola scriptura* principle, which, Milbank argues, lays the groundwork for the privatization of the Bible and the relocation of religion as private conviction that does not contaminate politics.[31]

---

28. On the relation of positivism and the Reformation, Milbank writes, "In the case of hermeneutics ... positivism is finally traceable to the exigencies of the Protestant *sola scriptura*, which, instead of a traditional accumulation of meanings, requires methodological guarantees that it can reproduce 'the original' and untrammelled word of God." *TST*, 79.
29. TST, 22.
30. *TST*, 21.
31. *WMS*, 95.

Luther, Nominalism, and "the Finnish" Interpretation

As can be seen, Milbank's core criticism of Luther is his overdependence on the univocal ontology characteristic of late medieval nominalism. However, the relation of Luther to nominalism is highly complex, and has been disputed in much recent scholarship.[32] Although the present consensus seems to lie with the idea that Luther was a nominalist, on the self-understanding of the Reformers, as articulated by Melanchthon in defense of Luther, whereas the Paris theologians aligned themselves with Ockham, Scotus, and Biel, Luther aligned himself with the Fathers, including Augustine, Cyprian, and Chrysostom.[33] However, this does not necessarily imply a break with nominalism, for, as Heiko Oberman argues, even "nominalism was fully involved in the ongoing medieval search for the proper *interpretation* of Augustine."[34] However, as early as the 1517 "Disputation against Scholastic Theology," Luther had broken with the nominalist *facere quod in se est*.[35] In opposing this doctrine, Luther points out that he is challenging Scotus and Biel specifically.[36] In light of these considerations, Oberman argues, "The wholesale identification of Ockham and nominalism with Luther's theology as articulated in the tradition from Denfile to Lortz is gradually disappearing."[37] As such, perhaps the most cautious approach is to view Luther's early training and career as influenced by numerous, largely inseparable elements, including not only nominalism, but also Augustinianism, humanism, and even mysticism.[38]

Rather than attempt an account of Luther's relation to nominalism as a whole, I restrict myself to Milbank's specific criticism of Luther's alleged nominalism as

---

32. See Graham White's *Luther as Nominalist: A Study of the Logical Methods Used in Martin Luther's Disputations in the Light of Their Medieval Background* (Helsinki: Luther-Agricola-Society, 1994), which argues for Luther's dependence. Heiko Oberman identifies Jüngel as a proponent of the view that Luther completely rejected the nominalist heritage. See Oberman, *The Two Reformations: The Journey from the Last Days to the New World*, ed. Donald Weinstein (New Haven: Yale University Press, 2003), 24, 179n. 15.

33. Heiko Oberman, *Forerunners of the Reformation: The Shape of Late Medieval Thought*, trans. Paul L. Nyhus (Cambridge: James Clarke, 2002), 28–9.

34. Oberman, "The Catholicity of the Nominalism," in *The Harvest of Medieval Theology: Gabriel Biel and Late Medieval Nominalism* (Cambridge: Harvard University Press, 1963), 427; see also idem, "Headwaters of the Reformation: *Initia lutherie-Initia Reformationis*," in *The Dawn of the Reformation: Essays in Late Medieval and Early Reformation Thought* (Edinburgh: T&T Clark, 1986), 58. Oberman notes that the influence of nominalism had already been reduced by the sixteenth century with the rise of "rejuvenated Thomism" and the spread of religious humanism (57–8).

35. Oberman, "*Facientibus Quod in se est Deus non Denegat Gratiam*: Robert Holcot O.P. and the Beginnings of Luther's Theology," in *Dawn of the Reformation*, 97.

36. "Disputation against Scholastic Theology, 1517," LW 31:3–16.

37. Oberman, "Headwaters of the Reformation," 59.

38. Oberman, "Preface" to *The Dawn of the Reformation*.

it bears on his account of Christology and justification. In turning to the work carried out by Tuomo Mannermaa and his students (what has come to be called the "Finnish" interpretation), as well as to Luther's writings, particularly his "Lectures on Galatians 1535," a case can be made for the centrality of union with Christ in Luther's soteriology and a conception of justification that goes beyond a merely extrinsic imputationism and is organically related to the process of sanctification. As such, at least on the question of justification and participation in Christ, it seems questionable to describe Luther as a nominalist.

Sammeli Juntunen describes Luther's metaphysics in his contribution to a collection of essays by Mannermaa and his students.[39] Juntunen begins by acknowledging that to raise the question of metaphysics in Luther "is very daring, maybe even reckless."[40] It is often viewed as inappropriate to discuss Luther's thought in metaphysical terms. Juntunen notes a certain "antimetaphysical" element in Luther, but this is not due to his refusal to think of the question of being. Rather, it is because the role of philosophical metaphysics is kept within limits. "His understanding of the structure of being is above all *theological*—it is a matter about which one knows something through the Scriptures and through the intellect, which assumes (*apprehensio*) the divine Word."[41] Nonetheless, Luther "does not deny the analogy of being and goodness between God and the world."[42] Instead, Luther is skeptical of its spiritual usefulness given that philosophy is driven by *amor hominis*, the natural human love that aims at the good of the lover rather than the beloved herself. This is not to deny that God is humankind's highest good—the *summum bonum* or *summum ens*—but that *amor hominis* prevents the metaphysical attainment of God.[43] In light of these considerable qualifications, Juntunen argues, Luther still leaves a limited role for philosophical metaphysics. However, philosophical language has to be bathed, to become a "*nova vocabula*," to be of use to theology.

In discerning realism in Luther, Juntunen is in accord with Mannermaa, who writes, "Whatever Luther's stance on nominalism may be, in his theology, at least, he follows [the] classical [realist] epistemology quite explicitly from beginning to end . . . according to which knowledge brings about a real participation in the object that is known."[44] Juntunen points further to Luther's emphasis on God's

---

39. Sammeli Juntunen, "Luther and Metaphysics: What Is the Structure of Being according to Luther?" in *Union with Christ*, 129-60.

40. Ibid., 129.

41. Ibid., 135.

42. Ibid., 132.

43. Bayer argues against metaphysics as rooted in the desire to attain identity. In so doing, he makes more explicit that it is an attempt at human self-justification. See "The Being of Christ in Faith," *LQ* 10.2 (Summer 1996), 145; cf. Bayer, *Living by Faith: Justification and Sanctification* (Grand Rapids,MI: Eerdmans, 2003), 21.

44. Mannermaa, "Why Is Luther So Fascinating?" in *Union with Christ*, 6. Cf. Allen G. Jorgenson, "Luther on Ubiquity and a Theology of the Public," *International Journal of Systematic Theology* 6.4 (October 2004), 353-5.

omnipresence, such that at the basis of each being's existence is God's presence. In holding this position, Juntunen argues, Luther distances himself from late-medieval "textbook" nominalism, which held, for example, that human being is *ens per se*. Instead, Luther sees all being as existing only through God, in continuance of "an old tradition, which leads all the way (through, e.g., Staupitz, Tauler, Eckhart, Bonaventure, and Bernhard) back to Augustine and in some sense even to Plato."[45] On this point, the Finnish interpreters provide their distinctive voice to Luther research and challenge Milbank's too-easy ascription of nominalism to Luther where Milbank most particularly directs it.[46]

The Finnish interpretation of Luther argues for a corrected understanding of Luther on justification that emphasizes Christ's presence in faith. Central to the argument is a rejection of the separation of justification and sanctification. Here the Finns' understanding is similar to Oswald Bayer's, who argues that for Luther the alternative of "forensic" or "effective" justification is a false alternative. Rather, when Luther speaks of sanctification, he speaks in terms of justification. The unity of the two is found in the unity of speech and deed in God. "What God says, God does . . . God's work is God's speech."[47] While Milbank is correct to note Luther's lack of stress on sanctification, the Finns would reply that this is because

45. Juntunen, "Luther and Metaphysics," in *Union with Christ*, 138n. 37. In the more general context of Luther's doctrine of creation, Robert Jenson argues that Luther rejects his nominalist heritage in his understanding of creation and the Word: "The nominalists continued the understanding of creation as an imminent act of intellect and will; they merely made the divine act of will contingent over against the divine intellect, and so arbitrary. Luther understands creation as effected not by an imminent act of will but by an uttered public word and so as effected by a word with rational content." Robert W. Jenson, *Systematic Theology*, Vol. 2 (Oxford: Oxford University Press, 1999), 8n. 35.

46. Of course, the Finns have not carried out their research in response to Milbank. Rather, their research began in the context of Eastern Orthodox–Lutheran dialogue.

47. Bayer, *Living by Faith*, 43. This can be compared to Milbank's statement that the idea of justification as imputation is inadequate for this very reason. "If God is simple and omnipotent, then his decision to treat us as just immediately makes us just, because the divine action cannot be ineffective. If the creation is not univocally 'alongside' God, as if God and creation were both individual entities, then there is no ontological limbo in which the divine decree of justification can hover. When it reaches us it is already created grace, and as freely accepting us it must make us really again just and with persistence." Milbank, "Alternative Protestantism," 32–3. However, in an earlier statement, Milbank seems to have a different understanding of the way God's Word is what it says. He writes concerning the "Joint Declaration on Justification": "An Aquinas-Luther consensus has been exaggerated . . . and the 'Joint Declaration' is ambivalent regarding imputation: both playing down its Protestant role, and yet seeming (paras 23–4) to leave (unlike Newman or Küng) the possibility that the forensic declaration of righteousness rather than its consequent effectiveness is what renders us 'just.'" Milbank, *Being Reconciled*, 223n. 4. It might be pointed out here that Milbank's quotation from "Alternative Protestantism" is more consistent with Luther's understanding of the creative Word than is the latter statement

Luther does not view sanctification as a reality outside or alongside of justification, but one related in a single whole—the whole being Christ present in faith. The important point here is that the relation is not one of cause and effect, but personal indwelling. Luther is not thinking in terms of substance or *habitus*, but rather in terms of persons. In justification, persons are really brought into communion with the person of Christ, and sanctification names what this being brought into communion looks like in outward form.

The Finns view the justification and sanctification separation as a subsequent development in Lutheran theology arising from Melanchthon's narrowing of justification down to its forensic and imputational aspect, which was codified in the Formula of Concord.[48] In Luther himself, they argue, the two are kept organically together in the emphasis that in faith Christ is both grace (*favor*) and gift (*donum*) and is really present—in both his person and his work, which are inseparable—in the believer through faith. Hence, Luther's statement: *in ipsa fide Christus adest*.[49] By grace (*favor, gratia*) is meant an external good wherein the believer receives the forgiveness of sins and the removal of God's wrath. "Grace is God's mercy (*misericordia Dei*) and favor (*favor Dei*)."[50] This corresponds to what is typically referred to as the "forensic" aspect of justification. By gift (*donum*) is meant an internal good opposing the corruption in human nature wherein God is Himself present in the fullness of His person in the believer. This corresponds to what is typically referred to as the "effective" aspect of justification. Both grace and gift are received in faith, because both are united in Christ and in faith the believer is united with Christ. Christ himself is the Christian's righteousness.[51]

---

from *Being Reconciled*. "Consequent effectiveness" seems to separate out too greatly the creative activity of the Word from the creation that the Word brings into being.

48. Simo Peura, "Christ as Favor and Gift (donum): The Challenge of Luther's Understanding of Justification," in *Union with Christ*, 45; Mannermaa, *Christ Present in Faith: Luther's View of Justification* (Minneapolis: Fortress Press, 2005), 3, 49; cf. Bernhard Lohse, who writes, "For a long time, the fact that for Luther justification involved not merely forgiveness of sins or acquittal but also renewal has not been sufficiently appreciated. Melanchthon restricted the doctrine entirely to the imputation of Christ's righteousness. Following him, Lutheran theology long advocated merely the 'forensic' view of justification." Lohse, *Martin Luther's Theology: Its Historical and Systematic Development* (Edinburgh: T&T Clark, 1999), 262. However, Lohse argues that Melanchthon held to a broader view of justification at times (262n. 18).

49. Mannermaa, *Christ Present in Faith*, 2; cf. "Lectures on Galatians 1535, Chapters 1-4," in LW 26:129-30.

50. Peura, "Christ as Favor and Gift," in *Union with Christ*, 43-4.

51. Mannerma, *Christ Present in Faith*, 3-5. For Bayer on the "joyful exchange" and the communication of attributes to the believer in relation to the salvation event, see his "Justification as the Basis and Boundary of Theology," *LQ* 15.3 (Autumn 2001), 283; cf. "The Freedom of a Christian, 1520," LW 31:351-2. Stephen Chester writes: "Christ himself is the gift received by the believer. It is therefore clear that imputation of Christ's righteousness to the believer is not defined over and against, or even in indifference to, participation in Christ."

Union with Christ and Luther's Grammar of Faith

Having established the propriety of speaking of the union of the believer with Christ as a highly important theme in Luther's theology, it is now necessary to consider what this "union" precisely means. The Finnish interpreters prefer to describe the "union" in terms of "participation" in God, but they tend to be rather inexplicit on what is meant by the latter term. Mannermaa describes this "participation" as a relational community of being with God, whose being is itself relational.[52] He says that the union with Christ (*unio cum Christi*) is a "real ontological presence," a *unio personalis*,[53] and is so strong that Luther can write, following 2 Peter 1:4: "faith makes a [person] God."[54] In faith, Christ and the believer are one, such that the believer participates in the divine life.[55] Robert Jenson likewise argues that the Finns understanding of "participation," while not always clear, tends in the direction of a relational ontology.[56] However, what I would like to suggest is that rather than focusing too much on the manner of the believer's union with Christ from the starting point of ontology, perhaps it will prove fruitful to begin with a focus on the question of faith and its relation to love in Luther's thought. This move could be seen as getting to Milbank's criticism from the opposite direction in which he

---

The presence of Christ in faith secures an intimate relationship between imputation and the participation of the believer in Christ. God imputes because the Christian believes, but the faith of the Christian is itself a divine gift in which Christ is present. This christocentric conception of faith means that, for Luther, imputation itself involves participation in Christ!" Chester, "It Is No Longer I Who Live: Justification by Faith and Participation in Christ in Martin Luther's Exegesis of Galatians," *New Testament Studies* 55 (2009), 322. For the question of Luther on justification and the new perspective on Paul generally, see Stephen Chester, "Paul and the Introspective Conscience of Martin Luther: The Impact of Luther's *Anfechtungen* on his Interpretation of Paul," in *Biblical Interpretation* 14.5 (2006), 508–36. Cf. Gerhard Ebeling, *Word and Faith* (Philadelphia: Fortress, 1963), 203ff. The centrality of Christology in Luther's doctrine of justification stands in sharp contrast to the assessment of Richard B. Hays, "Πίστις and Pauline Christology: What Is at Stake?" in *The Faith of Jesus Christ: The Narrative Substructure of Galatians 3:1–4:11*, 2nd ed. (Grand Rapids, MI: Eerdmans, 2002), 293.

52. Mannermaa, "Why Is Luther so Fascinating?" in *Union with Christ*, 11–12.

53. Mannerma, *Christ Present in Faith*, 40–1; cf. "Lectures on Galatians 1535, Chapters 1–4," LW 26:366, 404–407. Peura uses this terminology to summarize the Finnish interpretation: "Luther's understanding that God the Father is favorable to a sinner (*favor Dei*) and that Christ renews a sinner (*donum Dei*) is based on the idea of *unio cum Christo*." Peura, "Christ as Favor and Gift," in *Union with Christ*, 56.

54. Mannerma, *Christ Present in Faith*, 43, quotation from "Lectures on Galatians 1535, Chapters 1–4," LW 26:100.

55. Ibid., 39–40; "Lectures on Galatians 1535, Chapters 1–4," LW 26: 406–407.

56. Jenson, "Response to Mark Seifrid, Paul Metzger, and Carl Trueman on Finnish Luther Research," *WTJ* 65 (2003), 245–50.

poses it. He argues that Luther's ontology leads him into an extrinsic imputational account of justification in which faith becomes central to Christianity, displacing earlier Christianity's focus on love. However, I propose to begin with Luther's account of justification as union with Christ, and then explicate the grammar of faith and love that it presupposes, which proves very different from that described by Milbank. The difference in the starting point accords well with Luther's own approach. Faith prioritizes the question of man *coram Deo*, rather than prioritizing the question of being or "human nature" generally. This would also accord well with Bayer's claim that "justification by faith" is tied by Luther explicitly to the doctrine of *creatio ex nihilo*, and therefore, that faith is not only anthropologically significant, but also speaks of creation and itself has ontological significance. It seems to me that a promising way to explicate Luther's understanding of union with Christ is to look at his use of marital imagery as illuminating the union between Christ and the believer and his explication of the meaning of faith as he challenges the "scholastic" formula *fides caritate formata*.

Before turning to Luther's utilization of marital imagery, however, I briefly note an important difference between the Finnish interpretation of Luther and my own reading. While agreeing with the Finnish interpreters that greater emphasis should be placed on the centrality of union with Christ in Luther's teaching, this does not require an ontological deification even if one does grant that Luther uses realist language at times in describing the union.[57] As Carl Trueman argues, Luther also uses realist language in describing the presence of Christ in the Lord's Supper, but even the real presence in the sacraments does not mean that the bread and wine are deified. The leap from Christ's presence to deification is not necessitated by the logic of Luther's argument.[58] On the other hand, it is important to stress with the Finnish interpreters that justification cannot be restricted to a merely forensic or imputational sense given Luther's understanding of the Word of God as an effective Word that also accomplishes what it says.[59]

Marital Imagery as Illuminating Union with Christ in Faith

When speaking of the union of Christ and the believer in faith, the typically bold Luther shows considerable caution. He has no hesitation acknowledging that "faith

---

57. Carl Trueman, "Is the Finnish Line a New Beginning? A Critical Assessment of the Reading of Luther offered by the Helsinki Circle," *WTJ* 65 (2003), 231–44.

58. Ibid., 239. Cf. Karl Barth: "Neither in Augustine nor in Luther is there anything about a deification in faith in the sense of a changing of man's nature into the divine nature. What makes the expressions possible is the *apprehension Christi* or *habitatio Christi in nobis* or *unio hominis cum Christo* that takes place in real faith according to the teaching of Gal. 2²⁰." Barth, *Church Dogmatics* I.1, 240.

59. On the use of *imputatio* in Luther, see Sibylle Rolf, "Luther's Understanding of Imputation in the Context of his Doctrine of Justification and its Implication for the Preaching of the Gospel," *International Journal of Systematic Theology* 12.4 (October 2010), 435–51.

justifies because it takes hold of and possesses this treasure, the present Christ." Yet, Luther hesitates to go beyond this, stating, "But *how* He is present—this is beyond our thought; for there is darkness, as I have said. Where the confidence of the heart is present, therefore, there Christ is present, in that very cloud and faith."[60] He says that the Christ whom faith takes hold of is sitting in darkness in the same way that God sat in darkness on Mount Sinai and in the temple. Paradoxically, His presence is there especially when He cannot be seen—that is, He is there in faith. An acknowledgment of the deep mystery and darkness surrounding what actually occurs in the believers' union with Christ in faith must caution against too strong an ontological reading of the union.

Characteristically, Luther describes the presence of Christ to the believer in faith in terms of marital union. This imagery allows Luther to maintain adherence to the darkness that necessarily surrounds justification in that it is first and foremost a divine creative work[61]—specifically the creation of faith in the heart of the believer.

> By faith we are in Him, and He is in us (John 6:56). This Bridegroom, Christ, must be alone with His bride in His private chamber, and all the family and household must be shunted away. But later on, when the Bridegroom opens the door and comes out, then let the servants return to take care of them and serve them food and drink. Then let works and love begin.[62]

The creation of faith in the heart is not visible to human eyes, but the works of such a heart—works of love—are visible to the eyes of faith. In that way, to gain a clearer picture of what Luther means by union with Christ, we will have to look to the activity of faith as it works in love. However, it will be useful first to examine further the imagery of marital union.

In "The Freedom of a Christian (1520)," drawing on Ephesians 5, Luther calls faith the power that "unites the soul with Christ as a bride is united with her bridegroom."[63] Christ and the believer are, by "this mystery," one flesh and exist in a true marriage, "indeed the most perfect of all marriages, since human marriages are but poor examples of this one true marriage." In marital union with Christ, Christ and the believer hold all that they have together in common. As the bridegroom, Christ takes the "sins, death, and damnation," which belong to the bride, while the believer (the bride) takes "grace, life and salvation," in short, "all things" that are Christ's.[64] "Who," Luther asks, "can fully appreciate what this royal marriage means? Who can understand the riches of

---

60. "Lectures on Galatians 1535, Chapters 1–4," LW 26:129 (emphasis mine).
61. "We do not do anything, but we let ourselves be made and formed as a new creation through faith in the Word." Ibid., 392.
62. "Lectures on Galatians 1535, Chapters 1–4," LW 26:137–8.
63. "The Freedom of a Christian, 1520," LW 31:351.
64. Ibid.

the glory of this grace? Here this rich and divine bridegroom Christ marries this poor, wicked harlot, redeems her from all her evil, and adorns her with all his goodness."[65]

In commenting on Galatians 2:20: "Nevertheless, I live, yet not I, but Christ lives in me," Luther takes up again the language of marital union.[66] He says that Paul rejects the "I" as a person distinct from Christ. "Christ is my 'form,' which adorns my faith as colour or light adorns a wall. (This fact has to be expounded in this crude way, for there is no spiritual way for us to grasp the idea that Christ clings and dwells in us as closely and intimately as light or whiteness clings to a wall). 'Christ,' [Paul] says, 'is fixed and cemented to me and abides in me.'"[67] In our attachment to Christ through faith "we become as one body in the Spirit."[68] The imagery of marital union is decisive here in that, just as in the marital union, the two become one, but in such manner that their difference is not abolished. Union is not absorption. Further, the union is not ontological, but rather is consistent with Luther's understanding of a man and woman coming together in one flesh as being "figurative."[69] The consummation of the union in marriage is also the moment when the distinction between the spouses is most apparent. Again, the point is that there is a unity that does not abolish difference. As Leinhard puts it, in his employment of marital imagery Luther upholds the ontological distinction between God and human beings such that the two are not simply identified. Rather, "Christ is simultaneously exterior to persons, to whom he offers himself through the Word, and interior in the framework of faith, until there is a very real communion of life and destiny between Christ and the believer."[70] The persons in a marital union are not fused, but constitute a community of persons and an exchange of goods.[71]

Luther's description of the "fortunate exchange" closely parallels his description of marital union. In discussing the exchange in the "Lectures on Galatians 1535," Luther speaks specifically in the context of the atonement or the cross, and the

---

65. Ibid., 352. In "A Brief Instruction on What to Look for and Expect in the Gospels, 1521," Luther speaks of the gospel as "a book of divine promises in which God promises, offers, and gives us all of his benefits and possessions in Christ." LW 35:120.

66. Marc Leinhard points out that in the commentary on Galatians 2:16-21, Luther relies heavily on the language of marriage: "Christ and the believer are united intimately (*conjunctissimmi*), they adhere (*conglutinatio*) to one another, they cleave (*inhaesio*) to one another, they 'become one body and one spirit.'" He notes that in describing the union of Christ and the believer with the terms of marriage Luther is joining in a long Christian tradition including Ephesians 5 and medieval mysticism. Leinhard, *Luther: Witness to Jesus Christ* (Minneapolis: Augsburg Publishing, 1982), 287.

67. "Lectures on Galatians 1535, Chapters 1-4," LW 26:167.

68. Ibid., 168.

69. "Lectures on Romans (1515-16)," LW 25:332.

70. Leinhard, *Witness to Jesus Christ*, 34.

71. Ibid., 132.

victory that occurred there, which is where he directs his hearers' attention in coming to terms with the *communicatio idiomatum* between Christ and the believer that occurs in faith. Faith makes possible the believer's participation in the Christ-event by the believer's grasping Christ. Faith is Luther's way of speaking about the presence of Christ. To lose the emphasis on faith is to lose Christ Himself. But "how" faith ties us to Christ and His blessings remains largely in darkness. The union of the believer with Christ stands in the same mystery as the "stumbling block" and "foolishness" of the God-man on the cross. In this union we passively receive Christ's righteousness, which is beyond human capacity and ability, but is rather "a righteousness hidden in a mystery," which one cannot work toward or merit, but which "we only receive and permit someone else to work in us, namely, God."[72] Perhaps one could say that to inquire too far after "how" it happens is the error of a theology of glory. However, it is possible to describe the life that is created anew because of its happening. "Hence it is evident that faith alone justifies. But once we have been justified by faith, we enter the active life."[73] In describing such a life, we will be describing the relation of faith and love. Therefore, in the final subsection, I will turn my attention specifically to Luther's exposition of this relationship.

The Work of Faith: Faith Active in Love against Fides Caritate Formata

Despite the range of what has been included in the concept "faith" for Luther as explicated thus far (gift, Christ present, forgiveness of sin, participation, fortunate exchange), we can still say in a certain sense that we have only yet begun to scratch the surface of this reality. This is because up to this point we have limited our attention primarily to the "passive" elements in Luther's account of the *vita passiva*. However, for Luther faith is always active, it always works. And it is in this that we begin to see more fully the scope of "faith" as conceived by Luther and the way that it opens out to politics.

For the present discussion, it is especially important to show how, for Luther, the renewal of the heart—or more specifically, the renewal of the affections—relates love to faith, if a response is to be given to Milbank's concern that Luther "displaces the centrality of love." What Luther means by "faith" will show itself to be perhaps much closer to what Milbank might mean by "love"—or at least to

---

72. "Lectures on Galatians 1535, Chapters 1–4," LW 26:5. The use of the *communicatio idiomatum* in this fashion can be found earlier in Luther's career in his "Lectures on Romans (1515–16)," LW 25: 332.

73. "Lectures on Galatians 1535, Chapters 1–4," LW 26:287. Note that here again at the end of this statement the activity of faith follows immediately upon the receptivity. The contemplative life for Luther always opens immediately into the active life, because each are but descriptions of the unified life of faith and love. Bayer points out that Luther called such a life the "vita passiva." See Oswald Bayer, *Martin Luther's Theology: A Contemporary Interpretation*, trans. Thomas H. Trapp (Grand Rapids, MI: Eerdmans, 2008), 42–3.

what Augustine, Milbank's great protagonist, means by love.[74] I will show this by examining how Luther distinguishes his position from the *fides caritate formata* common at his time.

Concern with this important element in Luther's thought is not unique to Milbank. Further, the way this basic theological grammar is understood is crucial for the way in which one will understand Luther's treatment of politics. It will determine whether one interprets Luther as arguing that the Christian takes a passive, quietistic stance toward an authoritarian state, or whether the Christian life is characterized by deep engagement in political life directed particularly at one's neighbor (i.e., at the local level). In his rendering of Luther's place in the history of political philosophy, the political philosopher Eric Voegelin notes the centrality of the question of faith and love for one's account of Luther and of its centrality to the question of the relation of Christianity and politics generally. Voegelin argues that Luther destroyed Christian spiritual culture through his attack on the *fides caritate formata* doctrine and its attendant concept of *amicitia*

---

74. See Bernd Wannenwetsch, "*Caritas fide formata*. 'Herz und Affekte' als Schlüssel zu 'Glaube und Liebe,'" *Kerygma and Dogma* 45 (2000), 205-24. I am deeply indebted to Wannenwetsch's article for my arguments in this section. Milbank, perhaps to a degree, recognizes that Augustine's love and Luther's faith may not be so far apart when he writes, "Essentially [Luther's] message is that of Augustine: without the virtue of worship there can be no other virtue." However, Milbank makes this statement in the context of emphasizing the priority of love to faith for a proper understanding of Christian theology. *WMS*, 230. The centrality of worship for the whole of the Christian life can be discerned in Luther's treatment of the First Commandment: "A 'god' is the term for that to which we are to look for all good and in which we are to find refuge in all need. Therefore, to have a god is nothing else than to trust and believe in that one with your whole heart . . . If your faith and trust are right, then your God is the true one. Conversely, where your trust is false and wrong, there you do not have the true God. For these two belong together, faith and God. Anything on which your heart relies and depends, I say, this is really your God." The Large Catechism, I, 2-3, in *The Book of Concord: The Confessions of the Evangelical Lutheran Church*, ed. Robert Kolb and Timothy J. Wengert (Minneapolis: Fortress Press), 386. For Luther, a rightly ordered love can only come from rightly worshipping the true God, that is, love can only be rightly ordered if one's heart clings to the God who is love. Augustine, in an interesting passage in the *City of God* (XXII.6), describes the relation of faith and love in the Christian life in a manner quite similar to Luther: "Rome believed Romulus to be a god because she loved him; the Heavenly City loved Christ because she believed Him to be God." Augustine, *The City of God against the Pagans*, trans. R. W. Dyson (Cambridge: Cambridge University Press, 1998), 1116. For the priority of worship in Augustine, see his own "catechism," *The Enchiridion on Faith, Hope and Charity*, trans. Bruce Harbert, ed. Boniface Ramsey (Hyde Park, New York: New City Press, 1999), 32. On the danger of distinguishing too sharply between faith and love in general, see Jenson, *Systematic Theology*, Vol. 2, 68-9. Mannermaa argues that for Luther, faith is part of the actual definition of pure love for God, *Two Kinds of Love: Martin Luther's Religious World*, trans. Krisi I. Stjerna (Minneapolis: Fortress Press, 2010), 81.

with God in the name of his *sola fide* doctrine. His interpretation of faith and love in Luther is based on the latter's 1520 "The Freedom of a Christian." He argues that the faith proposed by Luther is no more than a certainty of salvation, "it does not redeem the fallen nature itself and raise man through the imprint of grace into the *amicitia* with God."[75] The soul of the person is saved, but her empirical sinful self, the old Adam, remains. And nothing that she does in the natural world can affect her salvation. However, as Voegelin argues, Luther sees the danger of licentiousness in such an interpretation. In order to avoid such an outcome, Luther must find a place for good works. The motivation for these good works is love of God, but a love of God based on gratitude following upon faith and justification. (At this point one notes Voegelin's assumption of a mechanical cause–effect logic operative in Luther's account.) But, on Voegelin's interpretation of Luther, love of God is a work of the law. So, if love of God were to form our faith, then our faith and justification would in part be due to our works, which violates the principle of *sola fide*. In this way, then, Voegelin argues that Luther really does not allow for love of God. The scholastic *fides caritate formata* posited that faith is formed by the prior "penetration of the person, through infusion of grace, with the love of God as the spiritually orienting center of existence."[76] However, Voegelin argues that Luther insists that faith precedes love, and in doing so pushes *amicitia* out of the picture. Ultimately, then, our relationship to God is not one of love, but of faith. Where love does come in however is in our social obligations to our neighbors. This love compels Christians to perform good works. "Faith is for God, love for the neighbor."[77] The result of this move is a "world-immanentising" of love. It only serves the purposes of social order in the natural world, while a person's righteousness before God remains untouched by her works, no matter how evil they may be, since faith alone justifies. In fact, if done in faith, all works are good works. It follows, then, that all earthly occupations are equalized in faith. The only work left for the Christian person is to carry out her particular occupation in faith toward God and love toward the neighbor. "This," Voegelin argues, "is the doctrine that, especially after its intensification through Calvin, became the great driving force of Protestant societies in their realization of the progressive paradise." Love remains earthbound and its energy directed accordingly. In modern times, the focus on faith will fall away, with the practical consequence that love of the neighbor "will degenerate in practice into the aggressive, utilitarian welfare society without culture of intellect and spirit that we know all too well" and the theoretical consequence that "world-immanent love will become the altruism of Comte and his positivist successors."[78]

Luther takes up the questions we have raised here with reference to Voegelin regarding the relation of faith and love in his commentary on Galatians 5:6: "For

---

75. Voegelin, *History of Political Ideas*, Vol. IV, 253.
76. Ibid., 250.
77. Ibid., 258.
78. Ibid., 259.

in Christ Jesus neither circumcision nor uncircumcision is of any avail, *but faith working through love.*" He begins by stating his perception of his opponent's position.

> For they say that even when faith has been divinely infused—and I am not even speaking of faith that is merely acquired—it does not justify unless it has been formed by love . . . In fact, they even declare that an infused faith can coexist with mortal sin. In this manner they completely transfer justification from faith and attribute it solely to love.[79]

Luther responds to this opinion, that is, that faith can coexist with mortal sin, as a sign that those proposing it understand nothing at all about faith. It also shows that they are "uneducated" grammarians who cannot discern Paul's clear and plain meaning: "faith *working* through love."[80] Faith is not unformed "as though it were a shapeless chaos without the power to be or to do anything." Rather, it is an effective and active thing (*efficax et operosa quidditas*), a substantial form (*forma substantialis*). In fact, Paul "makes love the tool through which faith works."[81]

Luther inverts the "sophistic" argument. Rather than love forming faith, it is faith that forms love.[82] It is faith that is active in love—love is faith's tool. Importantly, Luther notes that in this passage Paul is speaking of the whole of Christian life, which can be described as faith toward God and love and works toward neighbor.[83] This, of course, does not mean that we have faith, not love toward God. Rather, it means that without faith we cannot love God. "For we must receive the Holy Spirit; illumined and renewed by Him, we begin to . . . love God and our neighbor."[84] In this discussion, it is important to emphasize once again the organic nature of the relationship between faith and love. It is not that faith is the cause of love the effect. Rather, loves flows forth from a heart transformed by faith. In other words, the love of the Christian is the love of Christ, the very Christ present in faith.[85] Luther uses the organic imagery of a plant and its fruit to describe this relationship. One who possesses Christ by faith "will certainly not be idle but, like a sound tree, will bear good fruit (Matt. 7:17)."[86]

79. "Lectures on Galatians 1535, Chapters 1–4," LW 27:28.
80. The italics are from the American Edition, whose editor notes that Luther's original put "working" in capitals. "Lectures on Galatians 1535, Chapters 5–6," LW 27:28n. 24.
81. Ibid., 29.
82. "But this love or the works that follow faith do not form or adorn my faith, but my faith forms and adorns love." "Lectures on Galatians 1535, Chapters 1–4," LW 26:161.
83. "Lectures on Galatians 1535, Chapters 5–6," LW 27:30.
84. "Lectures on Galatians 1535, Chapters 1–4," LW 26:255.
85. Velli-Matti Kärkkäinen, "'The Christian as Christ to the Neighbor': On Luther's Theology of Love," *International Journal of Systematic Theology* 6.2 (April 2004), 101–17.
86. "Lectures on Galatians 1535, Chapters 1–4," LW 26:154. As a result, Luther can say that "faith without works is worthless and useless . . . But faith without works—that, a fantastic idea and mere vanity and dream of the heart—is a false faith and does not justify."

The indwelling of Christ in faith means that all of His "goods" are held in common with the believer. "From Christ the good things have flowed and are flowing into us." It is at this point that the grammar of "faith" begins to open out into the grammar of "love" and their intimate union is revealed. The grammar of faith and love only begins to makes sense in light of the relationship God–believer–neighbor. Faith and love is the organic unity, a simultaneity, that binds the three together.[87] This unity is reflected in Luther's famous formulation in his "The Freedom of a Christian (1520)":

> A Christian lives not in himself, but in Christ and in his neighbor. Otherwise he is not a Christian. He lives in Christ through faith, in his neighbor through love. By faith he is caught up beyond himself into God. By love he descends beneath himself into his neighbor. Yet he always remains in God and in his love.[88]

The believer is not grounded in herself, nor in any qualities (whether received from God or otherwise), but is instead always placed in a relationship to God and neighbor, a relationship oriented always by the organic unity of faith and love. Elsewhere, Luther highlights the unity and centrality of both faith and love for his understanding of the Christian life. He writes:

> The whole of Christian doctrine, all works, and life in its entirety are included briefly, clearly and overflowingly in two points, which are faith and love. Through them a human being is placed between God and one's neighbor as an instrument that receives [gifts] from above and then passes [them] on below, thus becoming a vessel or channel through which the spring of divine goods flows into other people without interruption.[89]

For Luther, then, faith and love serve to describe the way the believer is situated between God and neighbor, such that the believer serves as a "channel" for the communication of God's loving provision and goodness. God communicates his love to the world through the faith of Christians.

In spite of his insistence on the organic unity of faith and love, it must be admitted that there is something right in Milbank's assertion, at least when

---

87. On the simultaneous relation of believers to God and their fellows, see Bernd Wannenwetsch, "Luther's Moral Theology," in *The Cambridge Companion to Martin Luther*, ed. Donald K. McKim (Cambridge: Cambridge University Press, 2003), 134–45. Cf. Mannermaa, *Two Kinds of Love*, 64–6.

88. LW 31:371. The important point, again, is that this is not a cause–effect sequence, but rather there is an organic unity of faith and love. Luther can go as far as to write, "Faith and confidence brings along with it hope and love. In fact, when we see it properly, love comes first, or at any rate it comes at the same time as faith." "Treatise on Good Works, 1520," LW 44:30.

89. WA 10 I/1:100, 7–13. Translated by Krisi I. Stjerna as cited in Mannerma, *Two Kinds of Love*, 66.

granted in reference to justification, that Luther "tends to displace the centrality of love in favour of themes of trust and hope."[90] The question is why does Luther effect this displacement? First, it must be noted that in his explicit discussion of this question in the "Lectures on Galatians 1535," Luther is speaking specifically within the language game of justification.[91] Berndt Hamm's work on the state of the discussion at the time of the Reformation is particularly illuminating on this point. He gives the following description of what Luther viewed as the prevalent concept of justification he opposed:

> The nature of justification, its *forma*, is the new quality of grace shown in love, a quality that is acquired by man, and here indeed the giving and working of God has become so much his own that they are the well-spring of his own free movement and self-realization resulting from his actions, with the aim of achieving eternal life. The working of God as the autonomous first cause opens up to man the possibility of cooperation (*cooperatio*) in his own salvation through the outpouring of grace and perhaps in addition through the actual aid of God's grace.
>
> Here we come to the understanding of the nature of existence characteristic of the medieval doctrine of salvation, an ontology of righteousness determining man's righteous conduct and relation to salvation from the viewpoint of moral quality, and ideologically relating that morality in action to man's final acceptance into sanctification. A crucial point is the dominant idea here of causality or contingency: that justification of the sinner, his pardon and acceptance as a child of God, are expressed where he is made righteous and his soul transformed through the quality of grace . . . this means that the process whereby the sinner is made righteous, a process expressed in moral virtues and good works, is the reason, the necessary prerequisite and condition for the final absolution of man at the Last Judgment.[92]

The key aspects to be noted in Hamm's explication are the nature of justification as an acquired quality of grace in humans, which shows itself in love, the cooperation

---

90. Milbank, "Alternative Protestantism," 33. However, one might point out against Milbank once again the inseparability of faith and love for Luther. In "The Magnificat (1521)," Luther says that faith "comes to experience the works of God and thus attains to the love of God." LW 21:307.

91. This neglect of Luther's "language game" of justification would be my primary critique of Voegelin's account of Luther. Voegelin's repeated acknowledgment that Luther does not seem to be much of a "theorist" betrays his failure to understand this basic aspect of Luther's way of doing theology. For an account of Luther's theology as having its coherence at the level of grammar—which is to say that he engages in different language games that form an overall harmony—rather than at the level of formal system, see Wannenwetsch, "Luther's Moral Theology," 120.

92. Berndt Hamm, "What Was the Reformation Doctrine of Justification?" in *Reformation of Faith*, 187–8.

of humans in their own salvation, and a "characteristic" ontology that centralizes moral quality as a necessary prerequisite for salvation. Behind all of this is the centrality of "causality or contingency." Works of love are understood to be the "necessary prerequisite or at least the *causa sine qua non* for making man's sanctification possible."[93] So then, love understood as a moral quality or capacity in humans is central to justification understood as a causal and conditional process. Works of love, and hence human agency, are essential to a contingent salvation. Luther will move against this centrality of human agency and contingency, while nonetheless maintaining the organic unity of faith and works of love.

Hamm traces the concept of love, which predominated in Luther's historical situation, back to the work of Bernard of Clairvaux (1090–1153) and Peter Abelard (1070–1142). Both grounded their thought in what Hamm calls "a new kind of internalization and individualization" that had come to ascendancy in their time. Central to their concern was finding a true penance that took the form of a change in the inner will. Such change came about by the experience of God's freely given love, which stirs the human heart to reciprocal love that makes possible true repentance. Love, therefore, understood as a "motivating impulse" in the inner man, became the key to redemption.[94] William of Ockham transformed the understanding of love articulated here into a natural moral freedom or capacity that humans have to love God above all else, and therefore to be truly contrite as necessary for the forgiveness of sins. The furthest position from Ockhamism in terms of late-medieval theology was that represented by the theologians of the Augustinian order (Luther's own order). They held that the merciful love of God must first enter the soul and God's justifying grace be received before one is capable of a love of God based in more than simply calculated fear of punishment ("gallows remorse"). However, in both accounts, it was the moral quality of love that inhered in the Christian (whether infused or natural) that was decisive in justification and sanctification.[95]

---

93. Ibid., 188.

94. Hamm, "From the Medieval 'Love of God' to the 'Faith of Luther'—A Contribution to the History of Penitence," in *Reformation of Faith*, 133.

95. See H. A. Oberman, "*Iustitia Christi* and *Iustitia Dei*: Luther and the Scholastic Doctrines of Justification," in *The Dawn of the Reformation*, who argues that Luther thought "all the 'doctors in Papatu' are to be regarded as pelagians, though Occam and his disciples, as worse specimens, are 'peiores'" (116). Therefore, Oberman argues, despite these distinctions, Luther nonetheless still opposed the scholastic tradition as a whole on the question of justification. In the medieval tradition as consummated at Trent, the righteousness of Christ (*iustitia Christi*) was granted as grace or love to the sinner in justification. However, this is not granted together with the righteousness of God (*iustitia Dei*), but rather the righteousness of God is the *telos* of the Christian on pilgrimage. As such, the "*iustitia Dei* is the standard according to which the degree of appropriation and the effects of the *iustitia Christi* are measured and will be measured in the Last Judgment" (120). For Luther, on the other hand, the righteousness of God and Christ are coincident

We gain a more precise understanding of the concept of justification Luther is opposing in the "Lectures on Galatians 1535" by his description of his opponents there. He does not name specific individuals, but rather terms his opponents the "scholastics."[96] The basic error at the beginning of the scholastic concept of justification is the *facere quod in se est* (to do what is within oneself), the idea that a person through use of her natural powers can achieve the preconditions of salvation. That is, God has so ordained that those who do all that they can according to their natural powers will be granted His grace.[97] This grace, which is received as a result of preceding works, is termed a "merit of congruity." The grace that comes as a result of this merit "is a quality that inheres in the will, granted by God over and above the love we have by our natural powers." This quality makes a person "formally righteous and a true Christian." Following upon this, the person is then able to perform good works deserving of eternal life, what "the scholastics" term "merit by condignity."[98] The role of the concepts of faith and love (and grace) in this process of meriting salvation are particularly important in understanding Luther's opposing concept of justification and the way he himself uses the terms "faith" and "love."

Hamm shows that in the medieval conception, faith was understood as important to the Christian life, but "completely insufficient" for salvation. It was understood as an essentially cognitive or intellectual recognition or acceptance of the truth as revealed by Scripture and the church. As such, faith was understood as being fundamentally oriented to the word. "It is meant to hear and obey the authoritative word of the divine truth."[99] The cognitive element in faith was

and granted by faith, so that *fides Christo formata* has replaced the medieval *fides cartiate formata*. Or, "in other words, 'faith living in Christ' has come in the stead of 'faith active in love' as it has been formulated and defined in a unanimous medieval tradition and as it can be found with Thomas Aquinas, Duns Scotus, Gabriel Biel, et al., including the Council of Trent" (120–1).

96. In the following paragraphs, I imitate Luther in using "the scholastics" to refer to his opponents in the debate concerning justification. Kenneth Hagen writes, "Luther was interested in the theological position being promoted or attacked; following Paul, he did not single out individuals for evaluation." Hagen, *Luther's Approach to Scripture as seen in his 'Commentaries' on Galatians, 1519–1538* (Tübingen: J.C.B. Mohr, 1993), 142.

97. For an early statement of Luther's opposition to the *facere quod in se est*, see the "Disputation against Scholastic Theology, 1517," esp. theses 26, 27, 29, 30, 33, and 40. In opposition to the *facere quod is se est*, Luther argues, "The best and infallible preparation for grace and the sole means of obtaining grace is the eternal election and predestination of God," thesis 29 and, "On the part of man, however, nothing precedes grace except ill will and even rebellion against grace," thesis 30, LW 31:11. For a full discussion of the *facere quod in se est*, see H. A. Oberman, "*Facientibus Quod in Se Est Deus Non Denegat Gratiam*: Robert Holcot O.P. and the Beginnings of Luther's Theology," in *The Dawn of the Reformation*, 84–103.

98. "Lectures on Galatians 1535, Chapters 1–4," LW 26:130.

99. Hamm, "Why Did 'Faith' Become for Luther the Central Concept of the Christian Life?," in *Reformation of Faith*, 155.

stressed such that faith remained always at the level of the *intellectus* and never went to the level of the heart (*affectus*). Given this rational element, faith was "the least qualitatively descriptive" of the medieval concepts used to describe the Christian life. Its formlessness was such that it was even held possible that faith could coexist with mortal sin and even lack of love. In fact, Hamm writes, "faith is not constituted by the existential relationship to God's loving-kindness but by the cognitive relationship to divine truth, not becoming good but becoming free of error."[100] Given this rather weak concept of faith, the tendency was to focus instead on love. Faith had to progress through stages from acquired to infused, and from unformed to formed, all determined not by faith itself, but by grace and love, in order to bring faith up to the level of a spiritual quality capable of morality. In this account, Hamm argues, "what is most important in the life of a Christian is not *fides* but *caritas* and the meritorious and satisfactory good works it motivates in the justified person."[101] Unlike faith, love was held to be active and hence essential to salvifically required works.

Two points in this otherwise wanting conception of faith were the key to its usefulness for Luther, namely, its emphasis on receptivity and its linkage to the Word of God. The "scholastics" to whom Luther opposed himself understood faith to be entirely receptive, in opposition to the always active and working love. The receptivity of faith will be maintained by Luther as essential to the way he uses the term to describe justification. As Hamm puts it, "Seen from the perspective of late medieval theology and piety, there was no other concept which could appear to [Luther] so suited to express what was crucial in the relationship between God and humankind than this ready-minted understanding of faith."[102] As opposed to "the scholastic" understanding of love, which posited it as an affective capacity within man, the pure receptivity of faith as a gift outside natural human capacity provided Luther with the means to describe justification wholly in terms of grace received without any reliance on meritorious works. However, in maintaining the receptivity of faith, Luther also significantly broadened the concept of faith to include the affects and posited its activity, setting up an entirely different soteriological grammar.

In describing the receptive nature of a faith that is nonetheless highly active, Luther makes the distinction between faith understood abstractly and faith incarnate. Faith can be understood either apart from or with the work of love. Sometimes Scripture speaks "about an abstract or an absolute faith and sometimes about a concrete, composite, or incarnate faith." Here Luther uses a Christological analogy:

> Scripture sometimes speaks of Christ as God, and sometimes it speaks of Him as composite and incarnate. Faith is absolute or abstract when Scripture speaks

---

100. Ibid., 157.
101. Ibid.
102. Ibid., 165.

absolutely about justification or about those who are justified . . . But when Scripture speaks about rewards and works, then it is speaking about faith as something compound, concrete, or incarnate.[103]

Luther then cites several examples of "incarnate" faith in Scripture, including Galatians 5:6: "faith working through love." Why, Luther asks, would it not make sense for Scripture to speak of faith in these ways, when this is how it speaks of Christ as God and man? "In this sense I can truly say: 'The Infant lying in the lap of His mother created heaven and earth' . . . it is said correctly that 'the man created,' because the divinity, which alone creates, is incarnate with the humanity, and therefore the humanity participates in the attributes of both predicates."[104]

In the same way that Scripture can attribute divine activity (creation) to the humanity that participates in the divinity (i.e., "the man created"), so it can attribute faith to "doing" (i.e., "faithful doing").[105] Speaking this way allows Luther to maintain that faith alone justifies, but the faith that justifies is never alone; works accompany it always. It also makes clear that everything attributed to works belongs to faith. Further, he argues that this prevents "theological" and "faithful" works from being looked at in a moral sense, meaning as proceeding from a good humanity alone. Works understood in this latter sense is a kind of "'doing' according to the moral grammar, which does not apply in theology."[106] Again, what seems at stake here for Luther is preventing works or morality from having autonomy from faith, which is to say, the works of a Christian which are really good works must always be seen as flowing from the union with Christ and not from any inherent qualities or virtues in the Christian considered in herself. The failure to distinguish the two is a failure to distinguish between theological and moral–philosophic grammar, and therefore a failure properly to attribute to Christ every good work performed by the Christian.

Incarnate faith—faith that works—works because faith always means, as stated earlier, a creation of new hearts or a transformation of the affections.[107] What the strands in the late-medieval tradition that Luther came to oppose called an "unformed" faith, a faith in need of formation by love, Luther called no faith at all. A faith at the level of the *intellectus* alone may hear and grasp "God, Christ, and all the mysteries of the incarnation and redemption," and might even speak with beauty about such things, but even in such a case remains a false faith (as opposed to a merely "unformed" faith) if it does not renew and change the heart and "produce a new man."[108] Luther calls this changed heart "a new creation, by

---

103. "Lectures on Galatians 1535, Chapters 1–4," LW 26:264–5.
104. Ibid., 265.
105. Ibid., 266.
106. Ibid., 268.
107. See Mark Louis Metzger, "Luther and the Finnish School," *WTJ* 65 (2003), 201–13, who likewise stresses the importance of transformation of the affections in Luther's understanding of faith and justification.
108. "Lectures on Galatians 1535, Chapters 1–4," LW 26:269.

which the image of God is renewed." He is very clear that this transformation goes all the way down and is a renewal of the mind, will, flesh, and even the senses.[109] This transformation, the creation of a new heart and a renewed mind (an entirely "new man"), can hardly be termed a merely extrinsic imputation. Rather, faith transforms the entire human person.[110] However, this transformation does not mean that the new mind and senses become an inherent disposition possessed by the believer, but rather are grounded in the believer's union with Christ. The believer takes on the affections of Christ.

In terms of Luther's grammar, what is being displaced is not so much an abstract "love," in favor of an abstract "faith," but rather he is opposing a meritorious account of justification with a description of the Christian life that prioritizes the action of God, specifically his act of address to humankind which is received by his Word. It is Luther's emphasis on the priority of God's concrete address to humankind in His Word, rather than on the priority of man's movement toward God, that distinguishes his theology, and therefore his account of politics, from that put forward by Milbank with his focus on ontological participation. It is to Luther's theology of the Word that I turn in the next chapter, which will include treatment of Milbank's criticism of "Luther's *sola scriptura*" presented in the current chapter while further setting out the grammar of Luther's theology. This will be followed by a chapter that lays out the specific understanding of politics that accompanies this theology of the Word, where Milbank's more specific criticisms of the political consequences of Luther's thought as set forth in this chapter will be given a response. More constructively, I will show that a political theology consistent with Luther's thought both stands alongside Milbank in his critical stance toward much of the modern liberal political paradigm, and yet departs from him in allowing for greater positive encounter between the *ecclesia* and *politia*.

---

109. "Lectures on Galatians 1535, Chapters 5–6," LW 27:140.
110. Cf. "The Magnificat, 1521," LW 21:306: "Such a faith has life and being; it pervades and changes the whole man."

Chapter 2

THE WORD OF GOD IN LUTHER'S POLITICAL THEOLOGY

Luther's theology is frequently (and accurately) described as "a theology of the Word."[1] Perhaps unexpectedly, in his understanding of the Word, Luther's thought shows its greatest resonance with the critical elements in John Milbank's political theology, especially as directed against what Milbank terms "Protestantism" and the politics that results from a focus on the individual abstracted from language and culture and on a direct unmediated experience of God. However, it is also Luther's recurring emphasis on the Word as the concrete address of God to humankind (as it encounters humankind in the present), rather than Milbank's primarily metaphysical emphasis on an ontology of peace (referring back to a protological harmony), that accounts for the sharp differences between the two political theologies. This chapter elaborates a response to Milbank's charges relative to Luther's nominalism and univocal ontology in the previous chapter, while also responding to his criticisms of Luther's ecclesiology and understanding of Scripture. In his understanding of the church and of Scripture, Luther is primarily interested in what it means for Christ to be present in faith. In discussing this theme, I intentionally use the terminology "Word" rather than "Christology" to describe this aspect of Luther's thought, as I think it lends itself to a more concrete account of Jesus Christ and his presence to the church rather than to a more ontological "Christological" account, such as one finds in Milbank.[2] Luther's focus

---

1. Regin Prenter, "Luther on Word and Sacrament," in *More about Luther: Martin Luther Lectures*, Vol. 2 (Decorah, IA: Luther College Press, 1958), 65.
2. Marc Leinhard argues that Luther's Christology "is directed toward the Word and faith, toward the union between Christ and believer." Leinhard, *Witness to Jesus Christ*, 388. Stanley Hauerwas expresses a concern that "Christian ethics has tended to make 'Christology' rather than Jesus its starting point." Hauerwas characterizes the difference as follows: "Christologies which emphasize the cosmic and ontological Christ tend to make Jesus' life almost incidental to what is to be assumed as a more profound theological point. In particular the eschatological aspects of Jesus' message are downplayed." Hauerwas, *The Peaceable Kingdom: A Primer in Christian Ethics*, 2nd ed. (Notre Dame; SCM Press, 2003), 73. In spite of his rightly demonstrated caution regarding "Christologies," I have a concern that Hauerwas goes too far in the opposite direction. For example, he writes that

is more on the presence of Christ himself to his church, whereas Milbank's focus tends to be on an ecclesial poetic renarration of Christ, which is to say that Jesus Christ becomes a form of life.[3]

Further, Luther's theology of the Word allows that the *polis*, as part of creation, a creature spoken into existence together with humankind, has a positive good that allows for far greater *en*counter between the church and *polis* beyond a reactionary[4] model of the *ecclesia* as a countersociety, which Milbank seems to promote by relegating the *polis* to the realm of necessity—an ultimately unreal realm, because it is a realm of privative evil.[5] Luther sees politics as a creature of

---

Jesus "proclaims that the kingdom is *present* insofar as his life reveals the effective power of God to create a transformed people capable of living peaceably in a violent world" (83). However, might it not be better said that the kingdom is present *not* "insofar as his life reveals, etc.," but rather that the kingdom of God is present insofar as Christ is present. This does not deny, of course, that Christ's presence is also a transformed people, but that the kingdom is not merely something revealed by the life of Christ, but rather is in an important sense the person of Christ himself, his presence. Where Luther puts Christ himself, I worry that Hauerwas, at least in this instance, puts Christ's "embodiment of a way of life." Does this not lead to a separation between the person and work of Christ, which Hauerwas rightly seeks to keep together—albeit in the opposite direction in which they are separated by "the cosmic and ontological Christ?" See Hauerwas, "Remembering How and What I Think: A Response to the *JRE* Articles on Hauerwas," *JRE* 40.2 (June 2012), 296–306. Of course, we must recognize that Christ's presence does necessarily involve "a way of life," but the way of life is at one with Christ present, and not an embodiment of something supposedly more primal behind the way of life. The Christian life is characterized above all by the worshipping community gathering around the present Christ who has given of himself in Word and sacrament. This act of giving-receiving is the empowering center of the community's way of life, which points to nothing beyond or behind itself.

3. Milbank argues that the gospels do not tell the story of Jesus, but "the story of the (re) foundation of a new city, a new kind of human community." In fact, Milbank goes so far as to say that Jesus "cannot be given any particular content," but can only be identified with the "general norms" of a practice. *WMS*, 150, 152. For criticism of Milbank's Christology on these points, see Fredrick Christian Bauerschmidt, "The Word Made Speculative? John Milbank's Christological Poetics," *Modern Theology* 15.4 (October 1999), 417–32; cf. D. Stephen Long, *Divine Economy: Theology and the Market* (London: Routledge, 2000), 250–4.

4. On the "reactionary" nature of Milbank's project, see Richard H. Roberts, "Transcendental Sociology? A Critique of John Milbank's *Theology and Social Theory beyond Secular Reason*," *SJT* 46.4 (November 1993), 527–35.

5. For Milbank's use of the terminology "counter-polity," see *Being Reconciled*, 105. Cf. Bernd Wannenwetsch, "The Political Worship of the Church: A Critical and Empowering Practice," *Modern Theology* 12:3 (July 1996), 273. In a quite different vein from Milbank, Hans Ulrich writes: "The Church does not replace the *politia* . . . because God's kingdom is present in many different ways, including those deeds that belong to the *politia*." Ulrich, "Stations on the Way to Freedom: The Presence of God—the Freedom of Disciples," in *Who*

the living and active Word of God. The externality and materiality of the Word allows for Luther's emphasis on institutionality, which is central to Luther's constructive contribution to political theology.[6] While we hold off a full treatment of Luther on the institutions to Chapter 5, the present chapter lays the groundwork in demonstrating how Luther views the Word as the key formative agent in human life, whether encountered positively in the form of faith or negatively in the form of unbelief. Chapter 3, to follow, will spell out specifically how the difference of faith or unbelief in response to the Word is politically formative in contrast to Milbank's Augustinian account of human loves as the most basic political reality. However, the task of the current chapter is to continue laying out the grammar of Luther's theology, a task begun in the previous chapter with respect to justification and the relation of faith and love, while bringing to the surface the political meaning of the sacraments for Luther, a theme largely neglected in accounts of his political thought.

This chapter is divided into three sections. In the first section, Luther's theology of the Word is considered generally. Especially important here is God's presence to God's creation, which is shown to be understood by Luther not in nominalist or univocalist terms, but rather to the extent to which Luther can be said to have a metaphysics, it would have to be seen as more a Hebrew metaphysics. As such, Luther could be said to have a highly embodied and political metaphysics, standing in contrast at key moments to the neo-Platonic ontology of Milbank, which, I will argue, allows too much to the hermeneutics of suspicion and its undermining of the political. However, despite important differences from Milbank, Luther's theology of the Word of God displays a great deal of agreement with Milbank's project in terms of its critical capacity relative to many of the assumptions of modern liberal/neoliberal secularism. As such, I hope to show that Luther can prove a valuable ally in much of Milbank's critical project, but also serve as a correction to much in his more constructive project.

In the second section, I articulate Luther's understanding of Scripture in response to Milbank's criticism of Luther's *sola scriptura*. As will be shown here, Luther's theology is quite inimical to the *sola scriptura* principle described by Milbank as replacing "a traditional accumulation of meanings" with "methodological guarantees" that the interpreter can "reproduce 'the original' and untrammeled word of God."[7] Luther's theology of the Word, especially his focus on the sacraments and the attendant ecclesiology, works strongly against this stream of thought in the

---

Am I? Bonhoeffer's Theology through His Poetry, ed. Bernd Wannenwetsch (London: T&T Clark, 2009), 164.

6. Oswald Bayer notes the Luther understands the whole of creation as a word of institution and promise. Therefore, a "comparison of the words of institution of baptism and the Lord's Supper with those of station or estates . . . is something we encounter frequently in Luther." Bayer, "Luther's View of Marriage," in *Freedom in Response: Lutheran Ethics: Sources and Controversies* (Oxford: Oxford University Press, 2007), 179.

7. *TST*, 79.

tradition that Milbank identifies with "the Protestant view" of the church, which "understands it as an association of individual believers who possess outside the social context, their own direct relationship to God."[8] Contra Milbank's attribution of a depoliticization of the church to the "Lutheran *sola scriptura*,"[9] Luther's understanding of Scripture within his larger theology of the Word actually serves to reinforce a political grasp of the church against individualist or voluntarist understandings. The theme of marital union cannot be set up on an individualist basis, as though the union under consideration is essentially one of the individual believer to Christ. Rather, the union is between Christ and the church (Eph. 5:32). Therefore, our being brought to Christ for salvation is likewise our being brought into the church. As David Yeago argues:

> Justification by faith is not, for Luther, the establishment of a private, individual relationship to God, which may subsequently find expression in adherence to the church. Justification is incorporation into the communal priesthood of the church, into the unity of the Body of Christ with its head . . . sharing in the hidden mystery of the church's union with Christ takes place in, with, and through participation in the church's common life and its holy practices.[10]

However, while Luther, like Milbank, places emphasis on material embodiment in the sacraments and the church's nature as a public body, Luther's ecclesiology also stands in sharp contrast to Milbank's. Specifically, Luther applies the *simul* logic not only to individual believers, but to the church as a whole. In this way, the Word of God reigns supreme over the church, which is a *creatura verbi*. In this insistence, Luther's theology provides an important chastening to Milbank's tendency to draw everything into the *ecclesia*. Thus, I close out the second section of this chapter by spelling out the political significance of this difference.

As has already been clearly indicated, Luther's treatment of the sacraments is essential in positioning Luther's thought relative to Milbank's project. In the third section of this chapter, I turn specifically to the Eucharist to show how Luther's understanding of ecclesiology and the sacraments allows worship to shape politics in the way propounded by Milbank and those who have followed after him, but unlike the latter trajectory, Luther is better able to preserve the utter gratuity of justification without undermining the public and political nature of the church. I will make this case especially with reference to the work of William Cavanaugh, who has done a great deal of political theology along the lines set out by Milbank and who has engaged Luther specifically on this question.[11] However, before turning to the questions of Scripture and the sacraments, it is necessary first to

---

8. *TST*, 403.
9. *TST*, 19–21.
10. David Yeago, '"A Christian Holy People": Martin Luther on Salvation and the Church," *Modern Theology* 13.1 (January 1997), 116.
11. See William Cavanaugh, *Theopolitical Imagination* and *Migrations of the Holy*.

discuss Luther's theology of the Word, which is the larger framework within which the two are set.

Luther's Theology of the Word of God

God's Word as Address and God's Self-Giving

The centrality of faith is one with the centrality of the Word of God for Luther. The Word is not merely static propositional statements compiled into "Scripture" and abstractly referring to a reality other than the Word itself. Rather, for Luther the Word is a living Word, a creative Word, it is reality. It is a Word of power, an effective Word, which accomplishes what it expresses.[12] It is precisely this understanding of the Word of God that Oswald Bayer calls Luther's "Reformation discovery." Against a reduction of language simply to a sign system referring to a reality outside of itself, Luther discovered that in God's promissory speech "the verbal sign (*signum*) is itself the reality (*res*),"[13] that it "represents not an absent but a present reality."[14] For Luther, then, the basic way of speaking of God and the world is not in terms of a conceptual ontological unfolding of being (even a Trinitarian unfolding), but rather in terms of forms of communicative action—not being and participation, but speech and deed (as inseparable) are central. As Bayer puts it, God's Word does not disclose being, but rather it creates it in the first place.[15] Encounter with God comes in the form

---

12. "Confession Concerning Christ's Supper, 1528," LW 37:181; The Large Catechism I, 100–101, in *BoC*:400. This stands in contrast to Milbank's assertion that in reducing Christ to a sacrifice, the Reformers thought Christ could be fully "represented" by "a neat set of propositions" absent the narrative of his life. *BSO*, 79. However, in stating Luther's understanding of the Word in this way, we are not denying that Scripture has stable propositional content, we are simply denying the referent "Word" can be so narrowly circumscribed. On the question of revelation and propositions, see Colin Gunton, *A Brief Theology of Revelation: The 1993 Warfield Lectures* (London: T&T Clark, 1995), 7–17, 79–81, 100–101.

13. Oswald Bayer, *Theology the Lutheran Way*, eds. and trans. Jeffrey G. Silcock and Mark C. Mattes (Grand Rapids, MI: Eerdmans, 2007), 129. Cf. Robert Jenson: "The body and blood are at once both *signum et res*." Jenson, *Systematic Theology* Vol. 2, 250.

14. Bayer, "Luther as Interpreter of Holy Scripture," in *Cambridge Companion to Martin Luther*, 75. For Luther's discussion of the Hebrew דבר as both the uttered word and a thing, see his "Lectures on Genesis, Chapters 1–5 (1535–36)," LW 1:16. For a fuller discussion of this point, see Jaroslav Pelikan, *Luther's Works: Companion Volume: Luther the Expositor: Introduction to the Reformer's Exegetical Writings* (St. Louis, MI: Concordia Publishing House, 1959), 54 ff.

15. Bayer, "Poetical Theology: New Horizons for Systematic Theology," *International Journal of Systematic Theology* 1.2 (July 1999), 159.

of an address. The task of theology is to discern what this address is saying *to us*.[16] Theology in the strict sense is not speculation on the nature of being, but rather an analysis of language, specifically the language of the divine address and of the human response in the form of worship, a form that has itself always already been given by the Word.[17] This is not merely an epistemological point, in which access to being is denied to the finite creature without being's prior self-disclosure (although this is true), but rather is itself an ontological point—namely, that language speaks to the very constitution of reality itself. To put the point sharply, God is God's Word.[18]

To say that God is God's Word is to say that in addressing us God gives Godself to us. The address character of "the Word" is essential if it is not to become yet another "signifier" in an idealistic schema, such as in prevalent "cause-effect" orientations. Understanding creation as divine address keeps the communicative character of reality in view.[19] The human is a "communicative being,"[20] finding herself always as the addressee of God's Word. Luther replaces Aristotle's insistence that we are what we apperceive by seeing, with the insistence that we are what we hear.[21] Robert Jenson writes:

> This contrast [between seeing and hearing] may be reduced to a point so simple and fundamental as to seem at first unserious: I have flaps on my eyes but none on my ears and can aim my eyes but not my ears. Sight, stretching across space, is a controlled and controlling relation to external reality; hearing, stretching

---

16. Bayer, *TLW*, 125–38. Hans Schaeffer, commenting on Bayer's interpretation of Luther, writes, 'Theology is not an analysis of existence, but of the language of the Church's proclamation of the gospel." In this way, theology does not seek "(re- or de)construction of reality or existence. Theology is about human perception of reality which is brought forth by God's promising word." Schaeffer, *Createdness and Ethics: The Doctrine of Creation and Theological Ethics in the Theology of Colin E. Gunton and Oswald Bayer* (Berlin: Walter de Gruyter, 2006), 122.

17. Schaeffer again: "Because being a theologian starts with the recognition and experience of God's address to me along with all the creatures, theology is primarily a 'linguistic discipline,' concerned with the 'forms of life' and the forms of worship such as prayer, the blessing, and classical liturgical texts." Schaeffer, *Createdness and Ethics*, 128.

18. Robert W. Jenson, *Visible Words: The Interpretation and Practice of Christian Sacraments* (Philadelphia: Fortress Press, 1978), 31, and idem, "Luther's Contemporary Theological Significance," in *Cambridge Companion to Martin Luther*, 284. Jenson argues that in so understanding the Word, Luther does not say that God *has* being, but that He *is* being. Here it is quite clear that Luther does not succumb to the univocity of being or onto-theology.

19. Bayer argues that Luther understands creation as "speech-act." *MLT*, 101–105.

20. The term is found in Schaeffer, *Createdness and Ethics*, 109.

21. Jenson, in "Luther's Contemporary Theological Significance," writes, "The soul—we may say—is a great ear, rather than a great eye" (282–3).

across time, is uncontrollable. I see what I choose to look at; I must hear what is contingently addressed to me.[22]

We are what God says to us in God's creative Word. Luther's stress on the priority of hearing over seeing indicates the passive receptivity of humankind before the divine address.

God's first word to humankind is a command that promises: "And the LORD God commanded the man, 'You may eat freely of every tree of the garden'" (Gen. 2:16).[23] That the Word takes the form of a promise is vital to Luther's understanding. "We can have no intercourse with God," he writes, "save by the word of him promising and by the faith of man receiving the promise."[24] The relation between God and the world is a communicative relation, even a conversation.[25] Again, the emphasis for Luther is always on the prior action of God. Humans never begin the process or "lay the first stone," but rather "God alone—without any entreaty or desire of man—must come first and give him a promise."[26] The discovery of God's Word of promise is "the source of Luther's new understanding of language and the world."[27] In the speech-act that promise is God gives humanity existence and establishes the community within which it is empowered to be a free existence. As those whose existence is free gift, humanity names those who respond to this gift and its Giver.

The proper response to the gift is obedient praise or worship, which for Luther is presented to us most clearly in the Psalms. For Luther, the speech of the saints in the Psalms is revelatory of anthropology. He writes, "There is no mightier or nobler work of man than speech. For it is by speech, more than by his shape or by any other work, that man is most distinguished from other animals."[28] In the Psalms, the speech of the saints lays bare their hearts toward God and fellow humans.

---

22. Jenson notes, "Metaphysically, it is the difference between a doctrine of being as being mentioned and one of being as appearing." Jenson, *Systematic Theology* Vol. 2, 286. Elsewhere, Jenson writes, "Sight is thus the chief medium of *objectifying* consciousness: consciousness that intends realities as located in that world out there which I am not, and seeks to control my relation to them, to handle them as indeed the 'objects' of my subjectivity. The God of Israel willed to be spoken for, but refused to be visibly depicted." *Visible Words*, 13; emphasis in the original.

23. "Lectures on Genesis, Chapters 1–5 (1535–36)," LW 1:103. A fuller treatment of this passage is given in Chapter 5.

24. Quoted from a December 1519 letter to George Spalatin (LW 35:5) and repeated in "The Babylonian Captivity of the Church, 1520," LW 36:7.

25. Jenson argues that "Christianity is an abnormal religion" in that its God refuses to fall silent. Rather, "this God's word is eternally spoken." Jenson, *Visible Words*, 30–1. As such, he argues that "the being of God is conversation." Jenson, *Systematic Theology*, Vol. 2, 270.

26. "A Treatise on the New Testament, 1520," LW 35:82.

27. Bayer, "Luther as interpreter," in *Cambridge Companion to Martin Luther*, 75.

28. "Prefaces to the Old Testament," LW 35:254.

What it is to be human, to be one addressed by God and empowered for response, is presented in the praise and prayers of the Psalms. Words reveal the heart.[29] They show life[30] and death.[31] This is true to such an extent that Luther can write:

> And that [the saints] speak these words to God and with God, this, I repeat, is the best thing of all . . . When these words please a man and fit his case, he becomes sure that he is in the communion of saints, and that it has gone with all the saints as it goes with him, since they all sing with him one little song. It is especially so if he can speak these words to God, as they have done; this can only be done in faith, for the words [of the saints] have no flavor to a godless man.[32]

Again, it must be stressed that for Luther, none of this is understood in merely individualist terms. Rather, in the Psalter, we see "the holy Christian Church painted in living color and shape, comprehended in one little picture . . . Indeed you will find in it also yourself and the true *gnothi seauton*, as well as God himself and all creatures."[33] Remarkably, what Luther suggests here is that our access to reality comes through our participation with the communion of the saints in worship where we most unambiguously encounter God's Word. Not adequate grasp of ontologies, not adequate hermeneutical procedures (i.e., Milbank's rightful rejection of certain renderings of *sola scriptura*), but attentiveness to God's Word as God gives Godself in and to the community to which God has promised Godself makes possible perception of reality. The key insight in this approach is that a point of view outside of history, which is to say outside of creaturely finitude, is not required to have access to reality—in fact, it is eschewed as an impossible idolatry that cannot help but obscure reality and deform it in one's own image. Postmodern genealogy is ultimately undermined here. Instead, there is reception and giving forth of the world as it is given to us in our being placed between God and neighbor. As those always already embedded in this communicative givenness, the only tale of history that we can tell is the one whereby we chime in to the tale always already told by the Word. In taking up the divine words of praise given to us in the Psalms, we are conformed to reality, which (who) is Christ.[34] This is because

---

29. "For the first things that burst forth and emerge from the heart are words." The Large Catechism I, 50, in *BoC*:392.

30. "There you look into the hearts of all the saints, as into fair and pleasant gardens, yes, as into heaven itself." "Prefaces to the Old Testament," LW 35:255.

31. "There again you look into the hearts of all the saints, as into death, yes, as into hell itself." Ibid., 256.

32. Ibid. On entering into Scripture as belonging to the communion of saints diachronically in such a way that historical distance is overcome, especially as this relates to questions of historical-criticism in biblical studies, see Jenson, *Systematic Theology*, Vol. 2, 279–82.

33. "Prefaces to the Old Testament," LW 35:257.

34. On this point, see Brian Brock, who writes, "Language is the place God has given so that he can use it to claim us. In prayer and praise we take up God's words to expose our

this Word is constitutive of history, and we have no access to a realm outside or beyond/behind this Word (for such a realm does not exist). Further, that this Word is a free, living, and creative Word means we must always recognize this Word as the sovereign of history, which is to say that all cause–effect schemas of history must be eschewed. History is not opened up to us in that manner, because history is not constituted independently of this free, living Word. Again, this is not merely an epistemological point—that somehow the (near) infinite number of causes that go to make up history always exceed our grasp. Rather, it is, again, an ontological point—a denial of any independent status to history relative to the Word. God *makes (speaks?)* history in God's free self-communication, which is a denial of independent historical causality.

That God gives Godself in history is but a way of saying that God always gives Godself by the Word, or that we receive God's Spirit always by the material and external.[35] We "must insist that God does not want to deal with us human beings, except by means of his external Word and sacrament."[36] Luther argues, "God has determined to give the inward to no one except through the outward." The obvious implication of Luther's view of mediation is that it safeguards against Gnostic temptations to downplay or even despise the material and concrete in favor of the "spiritual" and abstract.[37] The priority of the external to the internal proves to be a strong point in Luther's theology against the idealism and transcendentalism characteristic of much modern and contemporary understanding of the political and the church. It is also constitutive of Luther's refusal of antinomian or "spiritualistic" downgrading of creation and the institutions through which God preserves it. Creaturely means are themselves the way in which God preserves his good creation.

> Our parents and all authorities—as well as everyone who is a neighbor—have received the command to do us all kinds of good. So we receive our blessings not from them, but from God through them. Creatures are only the hands, channels, and means through which God bestows all blessings.[38]

More important, for our present purposes, than the affirmation of the material is what this *kind of* affirmation means for our trust in appearances and "others" in opposition to the hermeneutics of suspicion that funds genealogical deconstruction. That God is God's Word means that Christian worship is a form

language and lives to divine remaking. Thus prayer is the dialogical relationship with God in which the regeneration of human life originates and is sustained." Brock, *Singing the Ethos of God: On the Place of Christian Ethics in Scripture* (Grand Rapids, MI: Eerdmans, 2007), 177.

35. "The Holy Spirit must always work in us through the Word." The Large Catechism II, 58, in *BoC*:438.
36. The Smalcald Articles III, 8, 10, in *BoC*:323.
37. "Against the Heavenly Prophets, 1525," LW 40:146.
38. The Large Catechism I, 26, in *BoC*:389.

of life that knows something of taking things as they appear.[39] There could hardly be a stronger antidote to the implicit idealism that makes the hermeneutics of suspicion possible with its insistence on the distinction between "saying" and "meaning." As Bernd Wannenwetsch argues, the assumption that thinking is prior to speaking "is sustained by a very un-Hebrew metaphysics, according to which there is a 'meaning' supposed to be in the head or one's inner self, which is masked by the body and must be decoded by hermeneutical operations."[40] For Luther, on the other hand, there is not something more real behind the embodied encounter with the Word in worship. Rather, the embodied is a trustworthy mediator of reality—that is, reality, the Word, is necessarily an embodied Word in its encounter with humans. Against a Cartesian-like dualism underlying the hermeneutics of suspicion, a "hermeneutics" following Luther would have to affirm that what is spoken, heard, tasted, and touched in the worship of the church is itself the "meaning," the reality with which we have to deal, and not mere signs of a more fundamental reality behind them. Luther's trust in the senses, at least in the senses as engaged in the worship life of the church, suggests that reality is most truly perceived in a *political* way. Rather than deconstructing all politics as mere power play, an embrace of the politics that is the church at worship means that it is only in a political form of life that we are set free *from* determination by the politics of domination and narrow grasping after self-interest and *for* a genuine politics of exploration of the common good. On the other hand, the hermeneutics of suspicion is decidedly apolitical, if not antipolitical. It must always be suspicious of any form of political "expression," any form of shared life, for such forms are mere covers for a more fundamental power play.[41] However, following Luther, one can see the worshipping church as engagement in a shared form of life in which the trustworthy Word of God is encountered audibly and visibly—that is, in a highly sensual fashion. The communal sharing in this form of life, and the trust that it generates, enables the worshippers to engage freely, and not out of necessity, in common action, to carry out works of love toward neighbors. The church at worship is a political community engendering the trust that makes possible a politics of exploring the common good in contrast to a politics as will-to-power, which is fundamentally antipolitical, and hence ultimately self-destructive.

The Word and God's Presence

As we have demonstrated, what Luther understands by God's communication in the Word is that God communicates Godself. To put this more concretely in

---

39. Bayer shows how Luther's hermeneutic excludes the distinction between "appearance" and "essence." See his *TLW*, 137.

40. Wannenwetsch, "The Political Worship of the Church," 288. For this entire paragraph, see this essay and also idem, *Political Worship*, 104–16, 286–94.

41. In the next chapter, I will take up the question of whether Milbank makes an adequate distinction between "power" and "domination" or "violence."

Luther's terms, Christ is really present in the Word and sacraments. Luther holds that "the Spirit cannot be with us except in material and physical things such as the Word, water, and Christ's body and in his saints on earth."[42] Further, for Luther, there is no "realm" of creation or reality absent God's grace. In speaking of the reality of divine grace as present everywhere, Luther forecloses the possibility of God being one being alongside other beings, such that there could be some kind of autonomous realm. In his teaching on the sacraments, Luther shows himself to stand strongly against both nominalism and the tradition of univocal ontology to which Milbank ties him. Rather, God is present to all of reality. God is in every single being, "more deeply, more inwardly, more present than the creature is to itself."[43] Milbank's assertion to the contrary, for Luther there is no finite space into which God could *enter in*, because there is nowhere that is not already a place of God's presence.[44] Luther argues that "the Divine Majesty is so small as to be present in essence in a kernel, on a kernel, above a kernel, throughout a kernel, inside and outside—and, even though it is one single Majesty, can nevertheless be completely and entirely present in every individual thing." However, although there is no world where God is not, because God is simple in God's unity,[45] it

42. "That These Words... 'This is my Body', 1527," LW 37: 95.

43. Ibid., 60. In the discussion of God's presence to all creatures, I deliberately speak in terms of "the Word" and avoid passages where Luther is making a case for the ubiquity of the human body of Christ. I do this because I am not certain that Luther's understanding of the relation of God to creation necessarily results in the speculation concerning the ubiquity of Christ's body which Luther carries out in opposition to the Zwinglian wing of the Reformation. Dietrich Bonhoeffer argues that Luther moves into foreign territory in an attempt to answer the "Reformed question" of *how* Christ is present in the sacrament rather than his usual insistence on the question of *who* Christ is. Dietrich Bonhoeffer, *Christ the Center*, trans. Edwin H. Robertson (San Francisco, CA: Harper, 1960), 55–8. At this point, I differ from Jorgenson, "Ubiquity and a Theology of the Public," who makes Luther's teaching on ubiquity decisive for his interpretation of the significance of Luther's understanding of the sacraments for politics. However, Jorgenson notes, Luther "posits the possibility of explicating real presence in other modes, and thereby proposes the doctrine of ubiquity as something other than foundational" (362). In this chapter, I show the political significance of the sacraments for Luther without necessitating a strong position on the *mode* of Christ's presence in the sacraments.

44. As we saw in the previous chapter, Milbank argues regarding the two natures in Christ that Luther cannot "think this reality other than on the model of a single finite thing 'within which' God has somehow entered." Milbank, *Being Reconciled*, 111. Jenson expresses what I take to be consistent with Luther's understanding when he writes, "Therefore the difference between God's being in heaven and his being on earth can only be a difference between styles of his presence; for him to 'come' from one to the other does not require him to leave where he was or arrive where he was not." Jenson, *Systematic Theology* Vol. 2, 254.

45. "We know, however, that God's power, arm, hand, nature, face, Spirit, wisdom, etc. are all one thing: for apart from the creation there is nothing but the one simple Deity

would be inaccurate to subsume God under creation such that creation would not be external to God or that the difference between the Creator and creature is anything but infinite. "On the other hand, the same Majesty is so great that neither this world nor even a thousand worlds could embrace it and say, 'See, there it is.'"[46]

Another way of putting the point about there being no space outside of God, such that God could be alongside creation, is to say that creation is that space that is brought about and sustained by God's creative Word. Creation is not the "effect" of the "cause" the Word. Rather, the Word is always present, as personal presence, in the creation that the Word itself creates and sustains. In his "Lectures on Genesis" Luther conveys this understanding of the Word by asking about the reason for procreation in a hen:

> The hen lays an egg; this she keeps warm while a living body comes into being in the egg, which the mother later on hatches. The philosophers advance the reason that these events take place through the working of the sun and her belly. I grant this. But the theologians say, far more reliably, that these events take place through the working of the Word, because it is said here: "He blessed them and said: 'Increase and multiply.'" This Word is present in the very body of the hen and in all living creatures; the heat with which the hen keeps her eggs warm is the result of the divine Word.[47]

The same logic is seen here as in the previous chapter's discussion of justification. The Word speaks, but in such a way that the speaking never detaches itself from the speaker. The Word does not act out into a realm as a "cause" where its action then takes on a life of its own as "effect" independent of the Word. Rather,

---

himself." "That These Words . . . 'This is my Body', 1527," LW 37: 61. Here we see that Luther's view of God is very different from that ascribed to him by Milbank as being consistent with a nominalist metaphysic whereby "God and creation are thought to 'exist' (qua pure existence taken by itself) in the same bare fashion, rendering them external to each other within a single ontic field," rather than a participatory metaphysics whereby "we cannot really be a part of being as such, which is God, who is utterly simple." Milbank, "Alternative Protestantism," 28. On the contrary, Luther's understanding of the divine simplicity would rather imply that if an ontology where to be ascribed to him, it would be closer to Milbank's "participatory" alternative than to nominalist univocity.

46. "That These Words . . . 'This is my Body', 1527," LW 37:59. Niels Henrik Gregersen: "There are not two 'gods,' one transcendent, another immanent, nor are there two 'aspects' of God, an immanent plus a transcendent God. Rather, *the transcendent power of God must be wholly and fully present at all places.*" Gregersen, "Grace in Nature and History: Luther's Doctrine of Creation Revisited," *Dialog* 44.1 (Spring 2005), 23 (emphasis in the original).

47. "Lectures on Genesis, Chapters 1–5 (1535–36)," LW 1:53. A few pages prior, Luther writes that birds and fish, for example, "are nothing but nouns in the divine rule of language" (49).

the Word always creates and sustains the realm wherein its actions occur. The Word creates the conditions and possibility of its reception.[48]

In holding that there is no "realm" of creation or reality absent God's grace, this does not mean that God's grace can simply be read off creation. Rather, we must seek God in the places where God has promised to give Godself to us. Luther writes:

> Although he is present in all creatures, and I might find him in stone, in fire, in water, or even in a rope, for he certainly is there, yet he does not wish that I seek him there apart from the Word . . . He is present everywhere, but he does not wish that you grope for him everywhere. Grope rather where the Word is, and there you will lay hold of him in the right way. Otherwise you are tempting God and committing idolatry. For this reason he has set down for us a definite way to show us how and where to find him, namely the Word.[49]

At this point it is necessary to be more concrete regarding what Luther means by the "Word" that promises. What happens in our encounter with God's promise in Word and sacrament? The promise of God is good news, gospel.[50] It is good news because it is, specifically, the gift of Christ's presence. As Bayer puts it, the promises of God, such as those of the performative Word in the sacraments, "are the concrete way and manner in which Christ is present."[51] In general terms, for Luther Christ is present everywhere. More importantly, however, in the Word and sacrament Christ is present *pro nobis*. Luther writes, "Because it is one thing if God is present, and another if he is present for you. He is there for you when he adds his Word and binds himself, saying, 'Here you are to find me.'"[52] That Christ is present in this manner means that he is to be sought in the worship of the church. The emphasis on Christ's presence in the sermon leads to a quite different understanding of Scripture than that assumed in the "Lutheran *sola scriptura*"

---

48. Gregersen argues the point as follows: "In all cases, *Luther is interested in nature as localized interactive events*, not as one continuous line of existing 'things' . . . A mirror is normally conceived as a dead thing (and it surely is!) but in the event of mirroring it becomes active. In the same way with sounds and voices: they may be conceived as material waves (and they surely are!) and ears may be labelled as a mechanical systems (as sense organs certainly also are!) but in the event of the listening, sounds and voices are transformed into messengers of meaning and sensual-spiritual presence." Gergersen, "Grace in Nature and History," 24 (emphasis in the original).

49. "The Sacrament of the Body and Blood of Christ against the Fanatics, 1526," LW 36:342.

50. "The gospel, strictly speaking, is a promise without any demand, a pure promise (*promissio*), a gift." Bayer, *TLW*, 125.

51. Bayer, *MLT*, 53.

52. "That These Words . . . 'This is my Body', 1527," LW 37: 68. In differentiating between Christ's presence and Christ's presence for us, Gregersen remarks that "a distinction must

principle as presented by Milbank. Further, the deep connection between the sacraments and Christology puts a particular emphasis on ecclesiology in Luther's theology, in stark contrast to what Milbank terms the "Protestant" understanding of the church conceived individualistically.[53] Here we consider more concretely what it means for Luther that Christ is present according to his promise in the church's preaching and administration of the sacraments and what this means for Christianity as a politically embodied form of life. This will prove important in Chapter 5 when we speak of the relation of the sacraments and the estates. The estates follow a quite similar logic to the words of institution in the sacrament. However, as we will see at that point, there are also significant differences between the sacraments and the estates, but their common tie is the Word that institutes.

The Word of God in Scripture and in the Church

As is evident from the earlier discussion, for Luther the Word of God is not simply the Scriptures. Jaroslav Pelikan explains, "Most of the time Luther, like the Scriptures themselves, did not mean the Scriptures when he spoke of the 'Word of God.'"[54] However, at times, he does. Luther attributes several forms to the *one* "Word of God" and his rich understanding is necessary to discern what he means when he calls Scripture the Word of God.[55] The Word of God includes God's speech to Godself in eternity apart from the creation, but this speech of God, what Pelikan terms the "cosmic" sense of the term, is also God's Word spoken in the creation.[56] Further, this "cosmic" Word of God is also the Second Person of the Trinity, the eternal Logos, before either creation or redemption. However, the Word of God in redemption is the historical Jesus Christ of Nazareth. As such, Pelikan suggests, "The Word of God in creation could not be simply identified with the Word of God in redemption ... But they could not be separated either, as though creation were beneath the dignity of the God who redeemed men through the Word that was in Christ; for the cosmic Word of God had become flesh in Jesus of Nazareth."[57] Thus, for Luther, Christ is central in both creation and redemption, and in this way Luther holds creation and redemption inseparably together, but without collapsing them into one another. This point will prove important in Chapter 5 when we fully exposit Luther's teaching on the institutions, which frequently (and, as we will argue, incorrectly) are referred to as "orders of creation."

---

be made between the question of the proper *way of approaching God*, and the *reality of divine grace*." Gregersen, "Grace in Nature and History," 19; emphasis in the original.

53. *TST*, 403.
54. Jaroslav Pelikan, *Luther the Expositor*, 67.
55. Lohse, *Luther's Theology*, 192.
56. Pelikan, *Luther the Expositor*, 50–1.
57. Ibid., 53.

Despite the inseparability (though not strict identity) between what Pelikan calls the "cosmic" and the "historical" Word, he notes that the primary emphasis in Luther's theology is on the "historical" Word, that is, on the sense of the "Word of God" as a deed of God.[58] All concrete things in the world are a word of God for Luther, but in the special "historical" sense, only those things and deeds which God has chosen to attach Godself to in a special way for the purposes of redemption and revelation are "God's Word." "A Word of God was a deed through which God chose to act redemptively... a deed was the Word of God if through it God conferred the forgiveness of sins."[59] In Christ, God spoke God's Word "through both words and deeds," and it is the Word of God spoken in the church that makes redemption in Christ contemporary.[60] In the church this Word takes audible/oral (preaching) and visible/tasteable (sacraments) form.[61]

The Word Written and Preached

It has already been suggested earlier that for Luther Scripture is not merely a depository of propositional truths,[62] but rather is a means of God's self-communication, it is God's Word. For Luther, then, the Scripture is the one Word of God in written form. As such, Scripture's authority is not formal, but material. Its authority lies in its ability to create faith, its power to give life.[63] This highlights the intersubjective nature of Scripture. As the Word of God, it is not an object

---

58. On the "deed" or "event" nature of "word," Gerhard Ebeling comments, "Word is therefore rightly understood only when it is viewed as an event which—like love—involves at least two. The basic structure of word is therefore not statement—that is an abstract variety of the word-event—but appraisal, certainly not in the colourless sense of information, but in the pregnant sense of participation and communication." Ebeling, *Word and Faith* (London: SCM Press, 1963), 326.

59. Pelikan, *Luther the Expositor*, 55–6.

60. Ibid., 60, 63.

61. One can easily see here the importance of Luther not identifying the Word of God simply with the Scriptures. Pelikan writes, "It is not a coincidence that those theologies which have equated the Word of God exclusively with the Bible have ended up by depressing the importance of the Sacraments into forms of instruction and reminders about what the Bible taught." Ibid., 221.

62. James Samuel Preus argues that for Luther the Bible is not a book of doctrine, but rather "a book which places man himself *coram deo*, and exposes and subjects him to God's concrete judgment and mercy (*iudicium* and *misericordia*)." Preus, *From Shadow to Promise: Old Testament Interpretation from Augustine to the Young Luther* (Cambridge: Harvard University Press, 1969), 190.

63. Bayer, *MLT*, 69, 75. Gerhard Ebeling, in his criticism of the usual distinction between *sola scriptura* as the "formal" principle of Protestantism and the doctrine of justification as the "material" principle, notes that such distinction reveals a "mode of thought characteristic of the modern world... in which a distinction is made between the bare empty 'form,' and the essential 'content.'" "'Sola Scriptura' and Tradition," in *The Word*

that can be appropriated under formal, prior hermeneutical procedures in such manner as to provide, in Milbank's rendering, "methodological guarantees" that will produce the "original untrammeled word of God."[64] Rather, it is God's address to its readers/hearers, an address that is always killing and making alive (cf. Deut. 32:39). Exposure to Scripture is suffering the encounter with the free and living Word in and with the community of the faithful.

Crucial to Luther's understanding of Scripture is its relation to the Word preached, to the proclamation of the gospel. He emphasizes the oral form of the Word, arguing, "And the gospel should really not be something written, but a spoken word which brought forth the Scriptures as Christ and the apostles have done. This is why Christ himself did not write anything but only spoke. He called his teaching not Scripture, but gospel, meaning good news or a proclamation that is spread not by pen but by word of mouth."[65] Elsewhere Luther writes:

> Christ has two witnesses to his birth and his realm. The one is Scripture, the word comprehended in the letters of the alphabet. The other is the voice or the words proclaimed by mouth. St. Paul and St. Peter call this same word a light and a lamp [2 Cor. 4:4, 2 Pet. 1:19]. We cannot understand Scripture unless the light shines. For by the gospel the prophets are illuminated, so that the star must rise first and be seen. In the New Testament, *preaching must be done orally and publicly, with the living voice*, to produce in speech and hearing what prior to this lay hidden in the letter and in secret vision.[66]

The stress on the preached Word is essential to Luther, for to speak of God's living Word is to say not only that it makes alive, but also that the "Bible has to be addressed to God's people here and now in His name. Thus it appears as His personal word through the 'living voice', the *viva vox* of His servants."[67] Here again we see God's use of creaturely means to address God's creatures. More importantly, however, we see how God uses these means to give Christ to us. The Word of God preached is Christ present to us. Luther notes, "When you open the book containing the gospels and read or hear how Christ comes here or there, or how someone is brought to him, you should therein perceive the sermon or the gospel through which he is coming to you, or you are being brought to him. For the preaching of the gospel is nothing else than Christ coming to us, or we

---

of God and Tradition: Historical Studies Interpreting the Divisions of Christianity, trans. S. H. Hooke (Philadelphia: Fortress Press, 1968), 118.

64. Milbank's description of *sola scriptura* in TST, 79.

65. "A Brief Instruction, 1521" LW 35:123. Ebeling notes that in the Christian tradition generally the primary referent for the Word of God is "to something that happens, viz. to the movement which leads from the text of holy scripture to the sermon ('sermon' of course taken in the pregnant sense of proclamation in general)." Ebeling, *Word and Faith*, 311.

66. "The Gospel for the Festival of Epiphany," LW 52:206–7 (emphasis mine).

67. Prenter, *Luther on Word and Sacrament*, 72.

being brought to him."[68] In preaching (i.e., the Word audible) Christ is present according to his promise. Christ's presence means that Christ, the Word Himself, is mediated to us in preaching and Scripture.[69] Significantly, this means that the Word is mediated, not by our own interpretations or hermeneutical methodology, but rather by the Word Himself.[70]

The Church as Creatura Verbi

Luther's understanding of Scripture is inseparable from the church. As Bayer puts it, "In his interaction with the Bible Luther knew he was positioned deep within the tradition of the one, holy, catholic, and apostolic church."[71] While the Scripture does effect—interprets—the individual believer, it does so only from within the communion of saints at worship. The primary locus of transformation is at the level of the *communio sanctorum*,[72] which translates into the creation of a new humanity. Scripture guides the community in its transformative encounter with Christ as it learns to participate in God's transformation of the world. However, the centrality of the role of the church in interpreting Scripture must not eclipse Luther's insistence that the church is a creature of the Word. Luther's ecclesiology is never ontologized in a static fashion, but rather Luther understands the church as the *event* of Christ's presence to the community gathered in worship, and therefore understands the church as a creature of the Word, a creature that is both fallible and hidden.[73] Here Luther stands strongly against both ecclesiological

---

68. "A Brief Instruction, 1521" LW 35:121.

69. For all the stress on the Word preached, Luther does not set the spoken gospel above or over and against the written gospel. As Bayer writes, "Scripture aims to make the verbal happen; but the verbal does not set itself up as a rival or as an alternative to what is written." *MLT*, 79. Rather, preaching is, in Luther's words, "setting forth Scripture and building on it."

70. Bernd Wannenwetsch, in a discussion of Bonhoeffer, argues, "The Christ that 'gets in between' is precisely Christ, the Word—the Word that actively addresses us and withstands our attempts at domestication through interpretation." Wannenwetsch, "The Whole Christ and the Whole Human Being: Dietrich Bonhoeffer's Inspiration for the 'Christology and Ethics' Discourse," in *Christology and Ethics*, ed. F. LeRon Shults and Brent Waters (Grand Rapids, MI: Eerdmans, 2010), 95. For the parallel between Luther and Bonhoeffer in their understanding that we must rely on the Word of God and not our own interpretations of Scripture, see Brian Brock, "Bonhoeffer and the Bible in Christian Ethics: Psalm 119, the Mandates, and Ethics as a 'Way,'" *Studies in Christian Ethics* 18.3 (2005), 9–10.

71. Bayer, *MLT*, 72.

72. The Holy Spirit "first leads us into his holy community, placing us in the church's lap, where he preaches to us and brings us to Christ." The Large Catechism II, 37, in *BoC*:435–6.

73. In his treatise "Concerning Rebaptism, 1528," Luther states that there is much that is Christian and good under the papacy, "indeed everything that is Christian and good is to be found there and has come to us from this source." In the papal church there are true holy Scriptures, true baptism, the true sacrament of the altar, the true keys, the true office

idealism and positivism. "The church is indeed holy, but it is a sinner at the same time."[74] The church continually stands in need of the judgment of its savior as it continually listens to (and falls under the critical power of) the Word that it also proclaims. In the ministry of the church, therefore, an already present grace is communicated among her members. Life in the institution of the church is responsive to and structured by the always-prior divine activity. We will see in the next chapter that as in the *ecclesia*, so in the logic of the institution of *politia*, human rule and government is always first a response to the gracious divine rule and the already granted common good and is thus not grounded in human activity (whether human will, love, consent, etc.).[75]

In his "On the Councils and the Church (1539)," Luther lists as the first of the *notae ecclesia* the possession of the Holy Word. He writes, "Wherever you hear or see this word preached, do not doubt that the true *ecclesia sancta catholica* must be here, for God's Word 'shall not return empty'" (Isa. 55:11). That the church stands continually under the operation of the Word is reflected in Luther's statement that this "chief holy possession purges, sustains, nourishes, strengthens, and protects the church."[76] Elsewhere, Luther writes, "The church was born by the word of promise through faith, and by this same word is nourished and preserved. That is to say, it is the promises of God that make the church, and not the church that makes the promises of God." The status of the church as a creature of the Word allows Luther to say that "the Word of God is incomparably superior to the church."[77] To put this point in terms of Scripture specifically, the authority of Scripture is not granted to it (e.g., by the church in the canonization process), but rather recognized as already existing. The church does not confer authority on Scripture, but rather recognizes in it the living voice of her creator Lord.[78] In recognizing a voice that

---

of the ministry, and the catechism. Of course, this does not negate Luther's judgment that the papacy of his time was the anti-Christ who takes his seat in the temple of God (II Thes. 2:4). LW 40:231.

74. "Lectures on Galatians 1535, Chapters 1–4," LW 26:109.

75. For this point, see Bernd Wannenwetsch, "'Members of One Another': *Charis*, Ministry and Representation: A Politico-Ecclesial Reading of Romans 12," in *A Royal Priesthood? The Use of the Bible Ethically and Politically: A Dialogue with Oliver O'Donovan*, ed. Craig Bartholomew, Jonathan Chaplin, Robert Song, and Al Wolters (Grand Rapids, MI: Zondervan, 2002), 196–219.

76. "On the Councils and the Church, 1539," LW 41:150–1.

77. "The Babylonian Captivity of the Church, 1520," LW 36:107.

78. In a discussion of canonization, John Webster, although without reference to Luther, argues in a similar manner that the church does not constitute the canon in an ontological sense, but rather that the church receives the canon as a means of grace. Interestingly, he argues, "Such a depiction as this does not command much attention in modern theology, partly because the instinctive nominalism of modern culture . . . and partly because [of] a proclivity to voluntarism." Webster, *Word and Church: Essays in Christian Dogmatics* (Edinburgh: T&T Clark, 2001), 42–3. Yet again, we see how Luther's ecclesiology stands contrary to voluntarist and nominalist trends.

is not her own, the church is able to escape the vicious circle of the hermeneutics of suspicion by attending to an external and alien voice that is promised to *this* community in *these* events (preaching and sacraments).

In subjecting the church to the Word (as *creatura verbi*) and in his insistence on the hiddenness (not invisibility) of the church, a significant difference arises between the political theology of Luther and that of Milbank. Milbank's ecclesiology is largely tragic given that "for the most part, the Church failed to bring about salvation, but instead ushered in the modern secular" by failing to embody its peaceful ontology.[79] Whereas Milbank's ecclesiology assumes the enactment of "the vision of paradisal community," that is, it perhaps comes dangerously close to seeking to live out an ideal form, Luther's stress on the hiddenness of the church requires a focus on particular signs, which do not point beyond themselves, and which do not leave the church at its own disposal in such a way that it could "embody" or "enact" its own true being. Further, the signs, as places of assurance, prevent a ceaseless searching for the "true" church or an insistence that the church as a whole (or even its individual members) is responsible in any kind of ultimate sense for itself. One gets an occasional sense of an ecclesial self-importance of this type in Milbank, particularly in passages like that which begins *The Word Made Strange*:

> Today, theology is tragically too important. For all the current talk of a theology that would reflect on practice, the truth is that we remain uncertain as to where today to locate true Christian practice. This would be, as it has always been, a repetition differently, but authentically, of what has always been done. In his or her uncertainty as to where to find this, the theologian feels almost that the entire ecclesial task falls on his own head: in the meagre mode of reflective words he must seek to imagine what a true practical repetition would be like. Or at least he must hope that his merely theoretical continuation of the tradition will open up a space for wider transformation.[80]

For Luther, the Church dependent on the promise of the risen Christ's presence in Word and sacrament can never find itself in the predicament that Milbank here describes. Rather, the true Church always has its "practices," it could not be otherwise, for then it simply would not be the church. The church is always a concrete, real presence, and not the outworking of an ideal or vision. The promise of its practices and the promise of its continuation (i.e., Christ's promise that "I am with you always, to the end of the age," Matt. 28:20) are one and the same promise.[81]

---

79. *TST*, 383.
80. *WMS*, 1.
81. In an interesting critique of this same passage, Steven Shakespeare argues that Milbank shows himself quite inconsistent at this point given his insistence on the importance of practice for thought: "If the Church is no longer sustaining true Christian practice, then

However, that the church is subject to the Word does not mean for Luther that private interpretation of Scripture can ever be other than subject to the church. Pelikan complains that Luther's views on preaching and interpreting the Bible have frequently been divorced from his doctrine of the church. The emphasis on the Sacrament in Luther's teaching works against individualistic and private notions of interpretation, which could lead to rampant sectarianism, as frequently happened in those communities that neglected the Sacrament. Therefore, in addition to stressing preaching (the oral Word), which locates the use of the Bible centrally in the church, his stress on the sacraments (the visible Word) also ties Luther's understanding of the Word to the church, and the sacrament of the Lord's Supper, especially, reveals the very political understanding of the church and the Christian life that Luther holds. In fact, the Eucharist is at the core of Luther's political theology. As such, it is to the Eucharist that we now turn.

The Word of God and the Eucharist

In Luther's view, unlike in the view of much subsequent "Protestantism," the sacraments are not secondary to the preached Word, but rather as another form of the same Word, the sacraments are central to the life of the church.[82] Scripture and preaching are sacramental and the sacraments are proclamation.[83] In particular, the centrality of the Eucharist means that the worship of the church is political.[84] As we will see in this section, Luther's theological grammar allows for human activity even in the Eucharist, but in such a way that the assurance of salvation is not threated, which can only be the case if salvation is the work of God alone. By

---

the theologian's task ought to be impossible. Theory cut off from practice is lifeless. It can only be a misrepresentation of Christianity, not its continuation." Shakespeare, *Radical Orthodoxy: A Critical Introduction* (London: SPCK, 2007), 93.

82. Jenson, in his Lutheran exposition of the Word and sacrament, writes, "As we move between proclamation and sacrament we simply move inside the borders of *one* event: God's real self-communication to us, which is always at once audible and visible in order to be the communication of the particular God who in fact is." Jenson, *Visible Words*, 208. See also Hermann Sasse, *This Is My Body: Luther's Contention for the Real Presence in the Sacrament of the Altar* (Adelaide: Lutheran Publishing House, 1977), 303.

83. In instituting the Supper, Luther argues, it was as if the Lord were saying, "As often as you use this sacrament and testament you shall be preaching of me." "A Treatise on the New Testament, 1520," LW 35:105.

84. Kyle Pasewark writes, Luther's "sacramental theology is an expansive social theory. Much of his protest against radical thought is directed at the essential privacy of their alternative." Pasewark, "The Body in Ecstasy: Love, Difference, and the Social Organism in Luther's Theory of the Lord's Supper," *The Journal of Religion* 77.4 (October 1997), 537. The sacramental elements in Luther's theology, so often overlooked in his political theology, will prove especially important in Chapter 5 in connection to the *politia*, *oeconomia*, and *ecclesia*, which, like the sacraments, are filled by the Word.

relieving our work of soteriological significance (i.e., in relieving us of the burden of being self-creators), but maintaining space for human response and the bonds formed within such response, Luther's view frees us to relate to God and humans without justificatory pressure. We can let them be what they are since Christ stands between and mediates.

Some contemporary theologians have taken Luther to task for his treatment of the Eucharist, arguing that it leads to harmful political consequences. Although Milbank himself tends to be vague in his treatment of Luther's Eucharistic understanding, others associated with "Radical Orthodoxy," particularly William Cavanaugh, have been more explicit. Interestingly, however, on this question, Luther's thought shows itself to be closer to Milbank's writing on "gift" than is Cavanaugh in his criticism of Luther. Without rehearsing in too detailed fashion the familiar question of whether, or in what sense, the Eucharist is a sacrifice, or the nature of the atonement, it will be helpful nonetheless to consider Luther's understanding of the Sacrament's gift nature in the context of contemporary discussions of "gift" as it further elucidates the way in which Luther's sacramental theology is crucial to his political theology.

Milbank and the Gift

Milbank treats the question of gift exchange in conversation with the work of Jacques Derrida and Pierre Bourdieu.[85] Following what Milbank discerns as a Kantian logic of gift that posits the goodness of a gift in the purity of the will or motivation of the donor, Derrida argues that a gift cannot be given because any notion of gift is self-refuting. Gratitude, or even acknowledgment by the recipient, translates into a reward for the giver, thus negating the gift. And even in the absence of acknowledgment, the giver's enjoyment in giving means a return that cancels the gift. As such, for Derrida, a true gift would be of nothing to no one from no one. However, Milbank argues, in the case of the divine gift, this logic does not apply. The divine gift does not pass through a "neutral" territory to a recipient on the other end, but rather divine gift giving is a gift to no one as it establishes creatures themselves as gifts and receives a return from them simply by the fact of their being. Further, Milbank puts forth the possibility of purified (but not "pure")

---

85. John Milbank, "Can a Gift be Given? Prolegomena to a Future Trinitarian Metaphysic," *Modern Theology* 11:1 (January 1995), 119–61. For a recent discussion of Milbank on the gift, see J. Alexander Sider, *To See History Doxologically: History and Holiness in John Howard Yoder's Ecclesiology* (Grand Rapids, MI: Eerdmans, 2011), 183–94. For the broader conversation, see Sarah Coakley, "Why Gift? Gift, Gender and Trinitarian Relations in Milbank and Tanner," *SJT* 61.2 (May 2008), 224–35. For treatment of "gift" from a Lutheran perspective, see Risto Saarinen, "Forgiveness, the Gift, and Ecclesiology," *Dialog* 45.1 (Spring 2006), 55–63. J. Todd Billings has considered Milbank on "gift" from a Reformed perspective, "John Milbank's Theology of the 'Gift' and Calvin's Theology of Grace: A Critical Comparison," *Modern Theology* 21.1 (January 2005), 87–105.

gift-exchange characterized by delay and nonidentical repetition, a gift-exchange that "is what Christian agape claims to be."[86] Such an account stands opposed to Derrida's purist logic, which Milbank argues can be illuminated with reference to a theological strand, characterized by Anders Nygren, that interprets *agape* in an "over-rigourous" and "self-defeating" fashion. Although delay and nonidentical repetition save gift by refusing a disinterested "suicidally sacrificial will against oneself,"[87] Milbank still has to contend with Bourdieu, who argues that the form of gift-exchange as delay and nonidentical repetition serves to "conceal from view a brute contractual reality, that 'giving' is a deceitful appearance disguising demands arising from quasi-legal agreements, which themselves are grounded in various exercises of coercive power."[88] At bottom, then, gift exchange is "a nakedly contractual and usurious reality."[89]

In reply, Milbank argues that this logic is not self-evident and necessary except for on the model of self-interested behavior as produced by capitalism. However, with the agonistic elements eliminated and coupled to a refusal of intentional "purity," delay and nonidentical repetition allows for a conception of giving as "a kind of *ecstasis*, or continuation of oneself out of oneself," which is simply to recognize that human being has an exchangist social nature and that there is an ineradicable connection with others.[90] Gifts are inalienable from the giver, and in receiving the gift one receives the giver. Refusal to enter into gift-exchange is refusal of relationship with others.[91] On the other hand, the church in its practice of the Eucharist participates in the purified Christian agapetic gift-exchange.[92]

86. Milbank, "Can a Gift be Given?" 131.
87. Ibid., 132.
88. Ibid., 125–6.
89. Ibid., 129.
90. Ibid., 132. We will bring up the question of purity of intention in Luther in Chapter 4, given that this issue is crucial to Jennifer Herdt's criticism of Luther.
91. Milbank's treatment of sin at this point shows a highly "Luther-like" logic according to which sin is a refusal of receptivity, which closes itself to receiving either "from God or from other creatures." In this closing off, "the sinful self is left merely with the empty gesture of freedom, and absolute control over its own illusory and contentless stability, and robbed of the freedom to do this or that, which is inseparable from a freedom *for* this or that, involving receptivity." Ibid., 135; emphasis in the original. One thinks here of Luther's definition of the sinner as *homo incurvatus in se ipsum*, "Lectures on Romans (1515–16)," LW 25:391; WA 56.304, 25–9.
92. Milbank, "Can a Gift be Given?" 152. Bayer argues, "The logic of life is giving and receiving, receiving and giving." He explicates the logic in terms of tradition: "The giving forth of that which has been received and taken is 'a passing along, a handing on, a bestowal'; the Greek and Latin equivalents of this concept of 'tradition' contain the verb 'to give,' namely, *paradido, nai* and *tradere* (=*trans-dare*)." The sense of gift in the logic of tradition, Bayer argues, can be "transferred and broadened to include the history of the whole of

The Eucharist and Society

William Cavanaugh: The Medieval Social Imaginary With this discussion of "gift" in the background, William Cavanaugh argues that Luther's Eucharistic theology evidences a modern contractual rather than a medieval organic conception of society, which succumbs to the difficulties of modern gift-exchange logic as set forth by Derrida and Bourdieu.[93] Particularly troublesome for Cavanaugh is what he perceives as Luther's excision of sacrificial language from his treatment of the Eucharist in favor of the language of gratitude.[94] Sacrifice refers to something that we give, while promise refers to something that we receive. The two cannot go together for Luther, as is shown, Cavanaugh argues, by his statement in the "Babylonian Captivity (1520)," that "the same thing cannot be received and offered at the same time, nor can it be both given and accepted by the same person."[95] Cavanaugh argues that this "zero-sum logic" is necessary if Luther is to hold onto justification by faith understood as absolute dependence on God. However, this is not to deny the human response of praise and thanksgiving. But if we can only *respond*, and not positively *give* a sacrifice, since the sacrifice of Christ on the cross was a sufficient and once-and-for-all (unrepeatable) sacrifice, then we cannot offer

---

human and non-human life—even to the nature of the genetic code and the changes that it undergoes." Bayer, "The Ethics of Gift," *LQ* 24.4 (Winter 2010), 449.

93. William Cavanaugh, "Eucharistic Sacrifice and the Social Imagination in Early Modern Europe," *Journal of Medieval and Early Modern Studies* 31.3 (Fall 2001), 586. For the larger connections Cavanaugh draws between the Eucharist and politics, see his *Torture and Eucharist: Theology, Politics, and the Body of Christ* (Oxford: Blackwell Publishers, 1998). Milbank likewise considers one of the distinguishing marks of modern political ontology to be the view that "the formal and material aspects of human social existence are seen as concurrently coinciding, rather than as organically blended." *BSO*, 4.

94. Cavanaugh argues that for Luther, "our faith is not a work but a sheer response of gratitude for the gift of mercy received." Cavanaugh, "Eucharistic Sacrifice," 587. Cavanaugh's argument echoes Voegelin's concern in the previous chapter that Luther displaces love of God with gratitude as motivating good works. However, as Wannenwetsch shows, this is to turn the directly active thanksgiving in the Eucharist into a disposition of gratitude. For Luther, a dispositional or motivational account of response to the Eucharist would be far too idealized. Rather, Luther's logic is consistent with Wannenwetsch's statement, "The *specific* grace which is mediated to believers in worship is not some good thing or other, for which they are to give thanks; it is the life with God, and of this all individual things (forgiveness, consolation, and so forth) are merely different facets." Further, Wannenwetsch shows that the thanksgiving in worship is that appropriate to those who know that as children of God they have free access to the divine presence, whereas gratitude is consistent with a slavish mind set according to which the celebrants are not worthy of God's presence. *Political Worship*, 49. Pelikan likewise argues against ascribing a morality based on gratitude to Luther, *Luther the Expositor*, 247–8.

95. Quoted in Cavanaugh, "Eucharistic Sacrifice," 587.

the Mass for others, whether living or dead. The effect is to sever the connection between the *ecclesia militans* and the *ecclesia triumphans* and *penitens*.[96] It also means that it is not the sacrifice of Christ that is made present in the Lord's Supper, but rather the fruits of the sacrifice are distributed with a focus on individual receipt.[97]

Luther's Eucharistic theology, Cavanaugh argues, idealizes sacrifice as gift and so contributes to the conception of a contractual society that characterizes modernity. Whereas the medieval social imagination was construed according to organic body imagery (1 Cor. 12:12–26) in which the Eucharistic played a central role in the construction of the social imagination in the sense that all were incorporated into the body, in the modern social imagination a hypothetical "state of nature" dominates, according to which each member begins as a radically differentiated individual who enters into relations of exchange for mutual benefit. Rather than exchange based on mutual obligation, contract forms the basis. According to this logic, gift does not serve the function of bringing individuals together, but rather sets one off from the rest in the mode of self-negation. While Cavanaugh acknowledges that Luther's Eucharistic theology shows traces of the medieval organic social body, such as has been demonstrated by Kyle Pasewark, Cavanaugh argues that this is only the case because Pasewark ignores Luther's treatment of sacrifice.[98] If one places emphasis on Luther's explication of sacrifice as gift, Cavanaugh argues, Luther can be seen to "most closely anticipate the modern social imagination" with its sharp contrast of gift and exchange according to which

---

96. Cavanaugh argues that in making this move, Luther "tends to de-eschatologize not just the communion of saints, but Christ's priesthood as well." Ibid., 589. For an argument to the contrary, see Wolfgang Simon, "Worship and the Eucharist in Luther Studies," *Dialog* 47.2 (Summer 2008): 144.

97. "Precisely because he wishes to avoid the appearance of the repetition of Christ's once-and-for-all sacrifice on Calvary, Luther speaks of the Lord's Supper as that ritual in which the living Word distributes the fruits won in that long ago sacrifice." Cavanaugh, "Eucharistic Sacrifice," 595.

98. Pasewark argues that Luther's conception of the Eucharist and its social effects is "organic-charitable" (in contrast to "organic-functional"), but that "in contrast to his sacramental theology, Luther's political theology of the 'station' or 'estate' (*Stand*) . . . is a veritable paradigm of static social thought." Pasewark, "The Body in Ecstasy," 521, 538. For Cavanaugh's criticism of Pasewark, see "Eucharistic Sacrifice," 593. It will be part of the task of Chapter 5 to show the connection between Luther's sacramental theology and his teaching on the institutions, both of which prove to be anything but "static." For present, I note that Pasewark appears to assume a necessary bifurcation between sacramental thought, which is therefore ecstatic, and political thought which must be nonecstatic if it is to render models for social life. However, beyond Pasewark, I would argue with Piotr Malysz that the Eucharist for Luther does not merely provide a social model or paradigm, but rather "radically restructures those relationships." Malysz, "Exchange and Ecstasy: Luther's Eucharistic Theology in Light of Radical Orthodoxy's Critique of Gift and Sacrifice," *SJT* 60.3 (2007), 308.

altruistic self-sacrifice is the only means of stepping outside of reciprocity in a manner consistent with the logic of gift (which ultimately preserves the self and excludes mutual participation).[99] Maintaining the purity of the gift is important for Luther, Cavanaugh states, because of his zeal to maintain passivity before God in justification. "Faith, as well as our offering of praise and thanksgiving to God, is therefore not something given back to God, but a sheer effect of God's gift of self in the individual believer." The believer, outside of the Sacrament, returns the gift of Christ's sacrifice, not to God, but to others. However, for Luther the benefits of Christ's sacrifice cannot be passed on but only received by the individual believer in faith. What is passed on, then, is not Christ's self, but the believer's own self transformed by Christ.[100] It is Luther's insistence on the once-for-all-nature of Calvary (the *ephapax*) that puts Luther into this position precluding return of the gift, its purity ensured by its "pastness." So while Luther is accurate to insist on "a logical absolute priority of God's grace" to our reception, he fails to see that the gift of grace itself creates the conditions for its receipt. In contrast to Luther, Cavanaugh argues "the same thing *can* be both received and offered at the same time by the same subject. There is no causality or work to our offering, nor is our offering simply a response to God's offering. Our offering simply *is* being drawn into the divine life—deification."[101]

"Members of Christ and the Church": Luther's Eucharistic Teaching In response to Cavanaugh, we refer, first, to our previous chapter where we showed how for Luther justification is union with Christ, rather than a mere contractual exchange as posited in more formal and solely forensic accounts of justification.[102] In rejecting sacrifice in the Mass, then, Luther is not rejecting participation, but rather any notion of self-justificatory merit. What is given is a return of our God-given self in Christ and a giving of ourselves to other believers, also in Christ. I do not merely offer the "benefits" of my justification, but rather Christ whose

99. Cavanaugh, "Eucharistic Sacrifice," 596.

100. "The modern logic of self-possession haunts Luther's account here. Without a stronger rendition of human participation in the sacrifice of Christ, self-sacrifice is in danger of becoming mere altruism . . . My self-offering to another is merely the fruits of my justification; whether or not that other is justified is between God and the other." Ibid., 598.

101. Ibid., 599; emphasis in the original. Cavanaugh's interpretation of Luther proves to be consistent with Milbank on this point, who writes that although Luther recognizes that we exist in receiving, "one can add to Luther a more Catholic stress that one can only receive God who is charity, by sharing *in* the giving of this charity—faith *is* (against Luther) from the outset a *habitus* and from the outset the work of charity, our work only in so far as it is God's." Milbank, *WMS*, 228; emphasis in the original.

102. Although I have not stressed the point, one of the strengths of Luther's Christology relative to the Reformational tradition more generally is his insistence on predicating the work of Jesus Christ in the first instance, not on the natures, but rather on the person. This proves highly fruitful in elaborating the participation of the church in the life of Christ. See Jenson, "Luther's Contemporary Theological Significance," 274–7.

presence is precisely the benefit of justification. Significantly, that justification is mediated means that in Christ the obliteration of either the self or the other as required in "purist" conceptions of the gift are overcome. Cavanaugh argues that in Luther's account what is passed on is not Christ's self, but the believer's own self transformed by Christ. However, this is a failure to understand the ecstatic conception of the self in Luther.[103] The believer's self is constituted (received) in Christ and the neighbor, as one placed in between. Whereas Cavanaugh's stress is on *Christ being mediated* to us, Luther's focus is on the way in which *Christ mediates* the Triune God and our neighbor to us. How this plays out in terms of Eucharistic practice will be discussed later in relation to Luther's treatment of the "collect." First, however, we consider the centrality of the words of institution in Luther's Eucharistic theology and how he allows for a return of the gift outside of the sacramental context (without precluding it from that context).

While retaining the real presence, Cavanaugh argues that Luther puts the stress on the words of institution and not the Sacrament itself. Thus, Cavanaugh states, "If only the word were present, and not the body and blood, the forgiveness of sins would still be present in the sacrament."[104] In this, Cavanaugh continues, Luther "ironically maintained and highlighted one of the most problematic aspects of late medieval worship—an almost exclusive focus on the words of institution as a singular moment when the body of Christ became present on the altar."[105] However, as Wolfgang Simon shows, in emphasizing the words of institution, Luther was not concentrating on a singular moment of consecration, but rather stressing the distinction between God's word and human words. In so doing, Luther ensured not just the gratuity, but also the certainty, that obtains in receipt of the Supper.[106]

Further, I would argue that Cavanaugh fails to acknowledge that for Luther Christ and his gifts are inseparable, that is, in terms of Milbank's explication, the gift and the giver are in an important sense inseparable. Cavanaugh abstracts the words of institution from Christ in a manner that Luther does not. For the latter, the words spoken in the institution are the living words of the present Christ himself.[107] Cavanaugh's interpretation of Luther applies to the separation of Word and sacrament found in much subsequent "Protestantism," but this separation is inimical to Luther himself. Likewise, for Luther the believer/s give herself/

---

103. On this point, and for this paragraph generally, see Malysz, "Exchange and Ecstasy," 294–308. Suggestively, Malysz wonders whether Luther's understanding of mediation might not be "one way of conceptualizing the mutual participation of the finite in the infinite, the mode of which, by Milbank's own admission, remains mysterious and incomprehensible" (301). Simon likewise argues that Cavanaugh's claim that Luther holds to an absolute dependence on God that reads sacrifice being of ourselves to God and one another is "unfounded." Simon, "Worship and the Eucharist," 155, n. 42.

104. Cavanaugh, "Eucharistic Sacrifice," 590.

105. Ibid., 591.

106. Simon, "Worship and the Eucharist," 145.

107. "A Treatise on the New Testament, 1520," LW 35:88–9.

themselves back to God in that they return to God their entire God-given selves. Again, the gift remains inseparable from the giver, but more importantly, Luther is correct when he argues that some "thing" is not exchanged in the Eucharist. Rather, there is a communication of persons (in Luther's terms a "fortunate exchange"). As such, "*we offer ourselves as a sacrifice* along with Christ . . . and do not otherwise appear before God with our prayer, praise, and sacrifice except through Christ and his mediation."[108]

All of these themes, which refute a link to Luther and an individualist modern-gift exchange logic, are spelled out with especial clarity in Luther's treatise on the Lord's Supper, "The Blessed Sacrament of the Holy and True Body of Christ, and the Brotherhoods (1519)."[109] There he argues that the Sacrament "signifies the complete union and the undivided fellowship of the saints."[110] Luther describes this fellowship in explicitly political terms:

> Hence it is that Christ and all saints are one spiritual body, just as the inhabitants of a city are one community and body, each citizen being a member of the other and of the entire city. All the saints, therefore, are members of Christ and of the church, which is a spiritual and eternal city of God. And whoever is taken into this city is said to be received into the community of saints and to be incorporated into Christ's spiritual body and made a member of him. To receive this sacrament in bread and wine, then, is nothing else than to receive a sure sign of this fellowship and incorporation with Christ and all saints. It is as if a citizen were given a sign, a document, or some other token to assure him that he is a citizen of the city, a member of that particular community.[111]

To be a member of this city, to be in union with Christ and his saints, means to share this community's spiritual possessions, which "become the common property of him who receives this sacrament."[112] This includes sharing one another's sufferings and sins as common property. Harm to one citizen is harm to all citizens; benefit to one citizen is benefit to all citizens.[113] Employing ancient imagery, Luther

---

108. Ibid., 99 (emphasis mine). In addition to the objections to Cavanaugh that I have laid out here, Malysz makes the interesting point that Luther's insistence that the Christian can make an offering of sacrifice in contexts outside of the Eucharist means that on this point Luther's teaching actually corresponds more closely to the requirement of delay and nonidentical return and is less transactionalist than Cavanaugh, who criticizes Luther for not restricting a direct return to the Eucharistic context. "Exchange and Ecstasy," 303.

109. "The Blessed Sacrament of the Holy and True Body, and the Brotherhoods, 1519," LW 35:45–73.

110. Ibid., 50.

111. Ibid., 51.

112. Ibid.

113. Here Luther cites 1 Corinthians 12:26: "If one member suffers, all suffer together with it; if one member is honored, all rejoice together with it."

discusses how the actual materials of the Eucharist show its meaning. Just as the many grains are mixed together and form one loaf of bread, and as the many drops of wine become the common wine in the cup, "so it is and should be with us." Here again Luther uses the logic of the *communicatio idiomatum*, which characterized his description of justification as we presented it in the previous chapter. He again refers to the marital imagery from Ephesians, but in expositing the Eucharist, it is made even more explicit that the *communicatio* is not only between Christ and the believer, but also between the believers themselves, between the community of saints. "In this sacrament," Luther writes, "the believer is thus united with Christ and his saints and has all things in common . . . Christ's sufferings and life are his own, together with the lives and sufferings of all the saints."[114]

As Cavanaugh acknowledges, Luther's opposition to the private mass, so prevalent in his time, was based on its neglect of the fellowship intrinsic to the Eucharist. In other words, the private mass lacks the political character proper to the worship of the church. Luther complains,

> We at present see to our sorrow that many masses are held and yet the Christian fellowship which should be preached, *practiced*, and kept before us by Christ's example has virtually perished. So much so that we hardly know any more what purpose this sacrament serves or how it should be used. Indeed with our masses we frequently destroy this fellowship and pervert everything.[115]

In contrast to the private masses, Luther sets forth the practice of the early church, when "this sacrament was so properly used."[116] The proper use was evidenced particularly in the "collect"—the gathering of food and material goods in the church to be distributed to those in need as part of the celebration of the Eucharist. One finds little here in the way of a private relationship between the believer and God outside of the "social context." On the contrary, for Luther, the church is the social context without which the Christian faith makes absolutely no sense. The privatization of faith could not be more inimical to Luther's teaching and it could be argued that such understanding was precisely what he was fighting against. In fact, rather than private "self-seeking love," Luther found in the Eucharist the practice that makes possible a very political seeking of "the common good of all."[117]

However, that the Eucharist is so politically significant for Luther does not mean that Cavanaugh has not noted some important shortcomings. For example, he points to Luther's dismissal of the kiss of peace in the "Formula Missae," which had served previously to make clear the connection between the communal body

---

114. "The Blessed Sacrament of the Holy and True Body, and the Brotherhoods, 1519," LW 35:52.
115. Ibid., 56 (emphasis mine).
116. Ibid., 57.
117. Ibid., 67.

and the body on the altar. Further, Cavanaugh's suggestions regarding the patristic Eucharistic understanding could be developed in interesting ways with respect to Luther's broader Eucharistic theology. This is particularly the case with the ancient church's practice of the offertory rite, whereby there was a sense in which the members of the church sacrificed themselves *into* the Eucharist by their offering of the very materials that constituted the elements of the Supper, with whatever remained afterward being distributed to the poor. The gifts in the offering were not raw material, but rather were bread and wine, such that human labor and effort, with all its ambiguity and impurity, are included.[118] In this way, we could go a step beyond Luther's recognition of the early church's practice of the collect to a liturgical practice that more clearly highlights the communal nature of the offering as inseparable from the Eucharist, and actually helping, quite literally, to constitute it, at least in terms of the elements. Nonetheless, contra Cavanaugh, it is necessary to maintain the prominence Luther gives to the words of institution. Such prominence ensures that the sacrificial offering is not falsely conflated with Christ's sacrifice on behalf of the congregation and that the place of Christ alone as mediator is maintained. As sole mediator, the words of Christ must be distinguished from human words, and foregrounded such that emphasis is on the Christ who stands between in mediating the Triune God to the participants and to one another. Here, again, we do not have a purist gift, but a mediated and asymmetrical gift. This nuancing of the logic of the Eucharist retains its political significance as explicated by Cavanaugh, while simultaneously foregrounding the prior divine self-giving and preserving the gratuity and certainty of salvation.

Conclusion

Having begun a response to Milbank's criticisms of Luther relative to justification in the previous chapter, in the current chapter I have continued my response to Milbank by examination of Luther's theology of the Word of God. I have demonstrated that Luther understands the Word as underlying all of reality in such fashion that nominalist or univocalistic construals of Luther's theology prove inaccurate. More importantly, I have argued that the trustworthiness of this Word means that Luther's theology provides a strong corrective to the hermeneutics of

---

118. See Bernd Wannenwetsch, '"Hier Liegt Ihr Auf Dem Altar". Darbringung Der Gaben Und Die Konsekration Der Gemeinde," in *Gottesdienst Der Kirche: Handbuch der Liturgiewissenschaft*, ed. Martin Klöckener, Angelus A. Häußling, and Reinhard Messner (Regensburg: Verlag Friedrich Pustet, 2008), 393–4; cf. Wannenwetsch, *Political Worship*, 161–3. Bayer notes regarding Luther's associating the words of institution with the word that institutes the estates, "[Luther] is saying that just as bread and wine are the fruit of the earth and of human toil, and are embraced and taken up in the Word of God, so nature and culture are also embraced and permeated by this Word that confers, imparts and bestows fellowship with no strings attached." Bayer, "Luther's View of Marriage," in *FR*, 179.

suspicion that runs strongly throughout Milbank's political theology.[119] I have also responded to Milbank's charges relative to the negative political consequence of Luther's "*sola scriptura*" by highlighting the ecclesial location of Scripture and its interpretation for Luther contra voluntarist and individualist readings. However, in stressing the supremacy of the Word to the church, Luther's theology further provides a corrective to Milbank's political theology in chastening the latter's tendency toward an ecclesiological colonialism.[120] Finally, I argued that Luther's Eucharistic theology retains all of the political significance of the Eucharist as explicated in Radical Orthodox theology, but does not do so at the expense of the certainty of salvation that can be had only if the Word of God in Christ is clearly distinguished from human words and activity. Again, here the key is the supremacy of the Word for Luther. In the next chapter, I move from a responsive posture to a more constructive one as I demonstrate how Luther's political theology retains the critical elements found so powerfully in Milbank's version of Augustinianism, but does so in such a manner that theology can move beyond deconstruction to the positive task of pointing to those places where the rule of God can be encountered with certainty beyond the bounds of the *ecclesia*.

---

119. In spite of Milbank's assertion that he avoids a foundationalist principle of suspicion by deriving his criticism from within the "rationally unfounded Christian cultural code." *TST*, 391.

120. For evidence of this disposition, note Milbank's assertion that a "viable and adequate" global order "would have to involve the emergence of a symbolic and representative centre of world government . . . which was at least not opposed to Christian aims, and ideally made explicit acknowledgement of them, and more ideally still recognized the spiritual primacy of the Pope." In response to skepticism on this front, Milbank argues that all that would be required for such a global order would be for Christians to "recover their inspiration and reignite their will." *BSO*, 257.

Chapter 3

"THE TWO" IN MILBANK AND LUTHER:
CIVITATES OR *ECCLESIAE*?

In his magisterial *The Desire of the Nations*, in a subsection entitled "Christendom: The Doctrine of the Two," Oliver O'Donovan masterfully spells out the history of what he calls the doctrines of a "Two-Kingdoms-Christendom" and a "Two-Governments-Christendom." The former conception, which dominated until the end of the patristic period according to O'Donovan, saw the church and the secular as two distinct societies that belonged to two different eras of salvation-history. The latter conception, which coincided with the rise of the Germanic kingdoms, viewed society as one single homogeneous entity, with two centers of authority signified by kings and bishops.[1] In this chapter, I argue that Luther holds together the best insights of both traditions by retaining the critical force of the former Augustinian conception as interpreted by Milbank, but can allow more to the divine origin of political rule as a positive good than does Milbank given Luther's insistence that political societies are not generated in the first instance by human love, but rather by the Word to which humans attend either in faith or in unbelief. Luther is able to achieve this combination by his teaching on the two "ecclesiae" and the two "regiments," the former that retains the critical elements of Milbank's two *civitates* reinterpretation, and the latter that maintains the positive good of politics and foregrounds the divine activity in constituting human society.[2] Given that Luther's teaching on both these doctrines can be explicated only within his

---

1. Oliver O'Donovan, *The Desire of the Nations: Rediscovering the Roots of Political Theology* (Cambridge: Cambridge University Press, 1996), 196.

2. Vítor Westhelle likewise suggests that Luther combines the Augustinian tradition with the medieval tradition of the "two swords." See his "The Word and the Mask: Revisiting the Two-Kingdoms Doctrine," in *The Gift of Grace: The Future of Lutheran Theology*, ed. Niels Henrik Gregersen (Minneapolis: Fortress, 2005), 167–78. Risto Saarinen also sees a close similarity between the "two kingdoms" and the "two swords." "Ethics in Luther's Theology: The Three Orders," in *Moral Philosophy on the Threshold of Modernity*, eds. Jill Kraye and Risto Saarinen (Dordrecht: Springer, 2005), 195. Further, for this argument, see John R. Stephenson, "The Two Kingdoms and the Two Governments in Luther's Theology," *SJT* 34.4 (August 1981), 330.

larger theology of the Word of God, this chapter carries forward the importance of the Word as explicated in the previous chapter and begins to show how that Word is generative for politics. In Chapter 5, we will make the connection between the Word of God and politics even more explicit when we consider Luther's largely neglected teaching on the three "estates" or "institutions." But first, we turn to the task of this chapter, comparing Milbank and Luther in their understanding of "the Two."

The Doctrine of "the Two" in Milbank

I have noted Milbank's explicit mention of the "two kingdoms theology" in Luther earlier. However, to attain a fuller picture of the constructive differences between the political theologies of Milbank and Luther, it is helpful to contrast Luther's framework with Milbank's generally positive appraisal of Augustine's political thought. In an "attempt to retrieve and elaborate"[3] Augustine's account of the opposing histories of the two *civitates*, Milbank seeks to show how the historical narrative of the city of God alone grounds an ontology of peace, while the contrasting historical narrative of the earthly city grounds an ontology of violence (thus the language of "ontologies" replaces Augustine's language of "loves").[4] He claims to follow Augustine, whose criticism of antique political society is funded by this ontological distinction and for whom the ontological priority of peace over conflict is "arguably the key theme of his entire thought."[5] The peace of the earthly city is only a semblance of peace, for underlying it is really the management of a preceding chaos and anarchy by means of the arbitrary.[6] Pagan virtue is thus reactive and parasitic on an always already existing vice that must be defeated.

---

3. *TST*, 391.
4. Augustine famously states: "Two cities, then, have been created by two loves: that is, the earthly by love of self extending even to contempt of God, and the heavenly by love of God extending to contempt of self." Augustine, *The City of God*, XIV.28, 632. For Augustine, all human communities ("peoples") are generated and held together by desire: "a 'people' is an assembled multitude of rational creatures bound together by a common agreement as to the objects of their love" (XIX.24, 960). See also XIV.13, 609–10, where Augustine divides the cities between love of God and love of self, where the latter has its origin in the pride of humans trying to make themselves their own ground rather than remaining obedient to the true ground of their being. One notes the stress on desire and ontology, whereas in Luther we will find a stress on faith and word. In his "Lectures on Galatians 1535, Chapters 1–4," Luther writes, "Civil and domestic ordinances are divine, because God Himself has established and approved them," but "my loving is not a divine ordinance." LW 26:296–7.
5. *TST*, 392.
6. *TST*, 393.

While Augustine argues that pagan virtue fails to be truly justice because it does not worship the true God, Milbank interprets this to mean that for Augustine the pagans were unjust in refusing true social harmony given their failure to place peace and forgiveness at the ontological forefront.[7] In contrast, the heavenly city worships the God from whom all things originally come in the form of peaceful gift.[8] In this city, a virtue of "self-forgetting conviviality" takes the place occupied in the earthly city by a virtue of reactive domination. It envisions a peace before the sinful pride of the earthly city and its employment of domination. Salvation from this sin, Milbank argues:

> must mean "liberation" from cosmic, political, economic and psychic *dominium*, and therefore from all structures belonging to the *saeculum* . . . This salvation takes the form of a different inauguration of a different kind of community.[9]

This community, the city of God, is the church. In fact, Milbank expresses disagreement with those who underplay the identity between the heavenly city and the church visible in Augustine's thought.[10] He argues, the church is "the

---

7. *TST*, 414–15.
8. *TST*, 394.
9. *TST*, 394. In an essay predating *TST*, Milbank argues, "For Augustine, it is quite precisely the political order (the order of the *polis*) that we are to be saved from. Even if Augustine considers that the Church is in future 'to make use' of the restricted peace of the earthly city, it is nevertheless clear that he wishes human social relationships to be more and more brought within the true *asylum* that is the Church." Milbank, "An Essay against Secular Order," *The JRE* 15.2 (Fall 1987), 209. I will argue that rather than "liberation" from the structures of the *saeculum*, Luther's framework allows us to look toward a transformation and redemption of such structures. The latter is possible because in Luther's account these structures are not reducible to *dominium* nor do they originate in the force and coercion that tragically all-too-often characterizes them in the *saeculum*.
10. *TST*, 406. Here, Milbank is consistent with Oliver O'Donovan's reading of Augustine. The latter: "For the definite identification of the two cities with Rome and the church, often denied, cf. *Ep*. 95.5 and *City of God* 16.2.3 respectively." O'Donovan, *Desire of the Nations*, 203. William Cavanaugh argues that, for Augustine, it is "true in one respect" that the church is the city of God and "inaccurate in another . . . As Christ's body, the church is ontologically related to the city of God, but it is the church not as visible institution but as a set of practices. The city of God is not so much a space as a performance. Likewise, the earthly city is a particular tragic performance of the *libido dominandi*. It is true that the city of God and the earthly city are ideal moral communities whose actual performance in time is, for Augustine, the history of Israel and the church, on the one hand, and the history of the Babylonian and Roman Empires, on the other. But what we are not given is anything like a theory of church and state, or civil society and state." Cavanaugh, *Migrations of the Holy*, 59.

realized heavenly city . . . the *telos* of the salvific process."[11] This city enjoys a peace "coterminous with all Being whatsoever," in contrast to the earthly peace, in which the dominant merely provide the dominated protection from external enemies.[12]

On Milbank's interpretation, Augustine's *civitas terrena* "is the vestigial remains of an entire pagan mode of practice, stretching back to Babylon." As such, the earthly city has no meaning of itself, but rather serves a "use" (*usus*) function by the heavenly city.[13] The earthly city, necessarily reliant on coercive force, is "natural" only in the sense that coercive political rule is in accordance with God's will to curb sin after the Fall. In fact, Milbank argues, a case may even be made that, for Augustine, the institution of slavery after the Fall is "virtually one and the same event" as the institution of political power.[14] (Otherwise, the only other "natural" political rule for Augustine is that those who are intellectually and morally superior should guide their inferiors.) "(I)nsofar as *imperium* lies outside *ecclesia*, it is an essentially *tragic* reality, involved in a disciplining of sin, which constantly threatens to (even, in fact, *always is*) itself nearer to the essence of sin as the self-exclusion of pride from the love of God."[15] Again, Milbank argues, "this is a curbing of sin by sin, and, in a way by more serious sin, because more self-deluded in its pride and claims to self-sufficiency." Nonetheless, the church is to make *usus* of this peace, which includes slavery, coercion, and compromise, for the ends of heavenly peace. However, the church "must never derive these things from its own rule and order." Because the earthly city serves this use by the church, and because of this "ambiguous" service alone, the earthly city continues to be distinguished from the church.[16] In its proper, prelapsarian mode, the political sphere could in

11. *TST*, 407.
12. *TST*, 394.
13. *TST*, 410.
14. *TST*, 411. Cf. Oliver O'Donovan, "Augustine reminds us of the patristic tradition that government and slavery were a provision of providence for a fallen world and no part of an order of creation." O'Donovan, "The Political Thought of *City of God* 19," in *Bonds of Imperfection*, 67–8. See also Katherine Chambers, "Slavery and Domination as Political Ideals in Augustine's *City of God*," *HeyJ* LIV (2013), 12–28. She argues that "domination was the very nature of political rulership" for Augustine, although the meaning of dominion had to be distinguished in the case of politics and slavery respectively (19, 25).
15. *TST*, 419.
16. *TST*, 411. Milbank notes that the "natural" necessity for coercive political rule after the Fall is where "Augustine's social thought is most problematic." For an account of the relation between Christians and civil government, similar to Milbank's interpretation, see John Howard Yoder's exposition of Romans 13:4, which, he argues, shows that divine providence can make use of Rome, "without declaring that the destructive action by pagan powers which God thus 'uses' is morally good or that participation in it is

no way be distinguished institutionally from the church. In a sense, then, there is no political before the Fall—only an unpolitical social. This is reflected in Milbank's prescription that the boundary between the church and the state be kept "extremely hazy" in order to foster a complexly interwoven social existence in which sovereignty is not assigned to the state nor "static hierarchy" to the church.[17] Instead, the expectation is that political governance will be gradually drawn into ecclesial rule.[18]

Given this account of the two cities, it comes as little surprise when Milbank collapses all "political theory" into ecclesiology.[19] He argues that Christian social theory "is first and foremost an *ecclesiology*, and only an account of other human societies to the extent that the Church defines itself, in its practice, as in continuity or discontinuity with these societies."[20] The postlapsarian "political" (which is the *only* political) is of necessity imperfectly social because of its dependence on compulsion and compromise. Augustine, Milbank argues, points to a true sociality beyond the political.[21] "True society implies consensus, agreement in desire and harmony amongst its members, and this is . . . exactly what the Church begins to provide."[22] However, despite its sinfulness, Milbank notes that Augustine still resigns himself to the necessity of worldly government in the *saeculum*:

> As long as time persists, there will be some sin, and therefore a need for its regulation through worldly *dominium* and the worldly peace, which takes the form of a bare "compromise" between competing wills. There can be no doubt that Augustine here contributes to the invention of liberalism, though in a negative manner, by insisting that in the economy of things there remains a place for a kind of political rule which is not really justice, indeed whose presumption is the essence of sin.[23]

incumbent upon the covenant people." Yoder, *The Politics of Jesus*, 2nd ed. (Grand Rapids, MI: Eerdmans, 1994), 198. While I agree that providence may include the sense of "using" Rome here, the question still remains whether there is ever the possibility for a *politia* that is not merely made "use" of, but which can actually be seen as God's own work in such a way that it is "morally good" and that "participation" in it is in fact "incumbent" on God's covenant people.

17. *TST*, 413.
18. *TST*, 403.
19. *TST*, 410.
20. *TST*, 380.
21. *TST*, 422. For an analysis and defence of the "political" over and against an all-encompassing "social," see Hannah Arendt, *The Human Condition*, 2nd ed. (Chicago: The University of Chicago Press, 1958), esp. section II.6, "The Rise of the Social," 38–49.
22. *TST*, 406.
23. *TST*, 402.

For Milbank's Augustine, the political is "intrinsically sinful."[24] Therefore, it cannot be subject to Christian norms. Instead, the earthly peace (what I am here referring to as "the political") can only *be made use of* by Christianity.[25]

The question that arises is whether there can be a conception of the political and the ecclesial that does not simply divide them along the lines of coercion and noncoercion. That is, can there be a noncoercive political that is part of the original good of creation, that is distorted by fallenness, yet not outside God's ordinance and providence in the *saeculum*, and that is therefore part of the original creation ultimately reconciled and being redeemed in Christ? Milbank, and his reading of Augustine, suggests that the answer is finally "no." The political belongs only to the *saeculum*, and therefore, ironically, "the good ruler must reduce the scope of the political precisely insofar as he is a good ruler."[26] For Augustine, on this reading, "salvation *means* the recession of *dominium* (of the political, of 'order')." However, Milbank argues that Augustine's concessions to punishment goes too far against this basic insight, and therefore, one should hold, beyond Augustine,

---

24. On this point, Milbank sees an irreconcilable difference between Augustine and Catholic thought following Aquinas's Aristotelian account of politics, *TST*, 414. He writes, "By beginning to see social, economic and administrative life as essentially natural, and part of a political sphere separate from the Church, Aquinas opens the way to regarding the Church as an organization specializing in what goes on inside men's souls." In so doing, Aquinas "has moved too far" in the direction of allowing "a sphere of secular autonomy." If the political comes to be viewed as a "permanent natural sphere," with its own ends, "then, inevitably, firm lines of division arise between what is 'secular' and what is 'spiritual'. Tending gardens, building bridges, sowing crops, caring for children, cannot be seen as 'ecclesial' activities, precisely because these activities are now enclosed within a sphere dubbed 'political.'" These newly designated "political" activities are then put under the rule of a centralized sovereignty to the detriment of mediating institutions. *TST*, 412. However, in his more recent *BSO*, Milbank gives a more positive spin to Aquinas's political thought, arguing that the latter points a way forward for integrating the natural with the political (social/artificial), and both with supernatural charity. In this integration, Milbank sees Aquinas returning to "Augustine and Gelasius, yet via the prompting of Aristotle" (244–5). In this latest trajectory in Milbank's thought, he is closer to the view of Luther that I set forward in this chapter than was the case in the earlier *TST*.

25. *TST*, 407.

26. *TST*, 425. I would argue that this is true in some instances, but in others, the reverse may actually be the case. Following Oliver O'Donovan, one could say that the question of "reducing/increasing" the scope of the political is always relative to the particular missionary situation in which the church finds itself in any given time and place. For O'Donovan, this has been, historically, the instrumental use of the doctrine of "the Two," which serves to prevent the church from either accommodating itself to or falsely assuming control over the state, and hence serves the church's "opportunities for preaching the Gospel, baptizing believers, curbing the violence and cruelty of empire and, perhaps most of all, forgiving their former persecutors." See his *Desire of the Nations*, 192–226, quotation taken from 212.

"that all punishment, like the political itself, is a tragic risk, and that Christianity should seek to reduce the sphere of its operation."[27] This does not mean the end of punishment, just as it does not mean the end of the political, but rather a deeper recognition of the tragic nature of both.

Violence and Politics: Hannah Arendt

Milbank's account of politics is perhaps most problematic in its strict association of the *polis* with *dominium* and hence violence and force, which seem to be coequal with power.[28] In an early critique of Milbank's *Theology and Social Theory*, Nicholas Lash argues that Milbank "too easily adopts Nietzsche's habit of confining the sense of 'power' (*Macht*) to domination and the violence which it entails."[29] However, Lash notes that not all power is violence. Therefore, he calls *not* for a giving up of the language of "power," "virtue," and "politics," but rather, in a quite Luther-like manner, argues that the "theological task is better seen as taking good words up and purifying them of misuse by setting them in the context of a Christian understanding of God's outpoured love."[30] In this section, I pursue this task, first

---

27. *TST*, 427.
28. *TST*, 334. Here is a point of agreement between the ancient and modern Hobbesian conception of politics grounded in a foundational antagonism. However, the truth in Milbank's argument, that the ancient city, by violent means (marked by its walls), created a space for violence-free activity, must not be allowed to overwhelm the meaning of politics. That is, the church witnesses to the politics of the eschatological *polis*, a politics that speaks to the true and original dignity of the *polis* as a founding of the divine Creator and whose true *praxis* is a form of worship of the Creator. See Reinhard Hütter, "The Church as Public: Dogma, Practice, and the Holy Spirit," *Pro Ecclesia* 3:3 (Summer 1994); and Hütter, *Suffering Divine Things: Theology as Church Practice*, trans. Doug Stott (Grand Rapids, MI: Eerdmans, 2000), 160–9. Put somewhat differently, rather than an antipolitical theology, what is called for is a genuine theological politics, the reconciliation and redemption of the *polis*. As we will see, this is what is provided for in Luther's account of politics against both ancient and modern liberal agonistic conceptions of politics.
29. Nicholas Lash, "Not Exactly Politics or Power?" in *Modern Theology* 8:4 (October 1992), 358. For a more recent and developed critique of Milbank's strict association of power with violence and oppression, see Christopher Insole, "Against Radical Orthodoxy: The Dangers of Overcoming Political Liberalism," *Modern Theology* 20:2 (April 2004), 213–41. In a response to criticisms of his use of "power" in *TST*, Milbank seems to recognize the possibility for a distinction between power and violence. In response to the question whether persuasion has a violent character, he writes, "Certainly, to be persuaded is to be forced, is to succumb to what is taken to be superior power. This power is 'violent' (arbitrary, domineering) unless what is persuasive has the force of 'truth' and one is 'truly' persuaded." Milbank, "Enclaves, or Where is the Church?" in *The Future of Love*, 140.
30. Lash, "Not Exactly Politics or Power?" 362. See also Debra Dean Murphy, "Power, Politics and Difference: A Feminist Response to John Milbank," *Modern Theology* 10.2

by treating Hannah Arendt's discussion of power, violence, and politics, and then showing how Luther's own understanding of politics is ultimately more consistent with such a stance in contrast to the negative connotation given to power and politics in Milbank's retrieval and elaboration of Augustine.[31]

Arendt challenges the view that violence is a manifestation of power, as supposed by Max Weber, according to whose definition the state is "the rule of men over men based on the means of legitimate, that is allegedly legitimate, violence."[32] Equating political power with "the organization of violence" in Weberian fashion presupposes that the state is merely an instrument of domination by those who rule.[33] Arendt opposes this presupposition with the tradition of thought identified with the Athenian city-state, the Roman *civitas*, and eighteenth-century republicanism, according to which politics is in essence power in contradistinction to violence. She defines power as the human ability to act in concert, which always belongs to a group and not an individual.[34] This ability for action is what makes humans political beings.[35] Furthermore, action, by which Arendt means the sharing of words and deeds, makes human living together worthwhile. The purpose of the *polis* in the Greek self-interpretation was to multiply opportunities for the "immortal fame" coming from speech and deed and to ensure an enduring remembrance of such actions without reliance on the poets.[36] Accordingly, the political realm arises directly out of acting together, the "sharing of words and deeds. Thus action not only has the most intimate relationship to the public part of the world common to us all, but is the one activity which constitutes it." The *polis*

(April 1994), 131–42. She argues that collapsing the meaning of "violence" and "power" is inherently sexist (135).

31. For a criticism of the dichotomies set up in Arendt, see Jürgen Habermas, "Hannah Arendt's Communications Concept of Power," *Social Research* 44.1 (Summer 1977), 3–24.

32. Hannah Arendt, *On Violence* (London: The Penguin Press, 1970), 35. Arendt here quotes from Weber, *The Vocation Lectures: "Science as Vocation," "Politics as Vocation,"* ed. David Owen and Tracy B. Strong, trans. Rodney Livingstone (Indianapolis: Hackett Publishing, 2004).

33. Arendt, *On Violence*, 36.

34. Ibid., 44.

35. She argues, "No other faculty except language, neither reason nor consciousness, distinguishes us so radically from all animal species." Arendt, *On Violence*, 82. Elsewhere Arendt writes, "Speech is what makes man a political being." *The Human Condition*, 3; cf. Aristotle who reasons that humans are more political than any other animals because humans alone have speech, *The Politics*, trans. Carnes Lord (Chicago: University of Chicago Press, 1984), 1253a7–10, 37.

36. Arendt, *The Human Condition*, 196. She cites Pericles's famous Funeral Oration as rendered by Thucydides as evidence of the Greek understanding of the function of the *polis*. See *The Landmark Thucydides: A Comprehensive Guide to the Peloponnesian War*, ed. Robert B. Strassler and trans. Richard Crawley (New York: Touchstone, 1996), 2.35.1–46.2, 111–88.

serves to allow for human acting together, but at the same time is itself constituted by acting together. The *polis*, then, "is the organization of the people as it arises out of acting and speaking together, and its true space lies between people living together for this purpose."[37] Significantly, according to this construal, action and speech are not instrumental, but rather their *telos* lies in the activity itself, which exhausts its meaning in its performance. This corresponds to Aristotle's notion of *energia* (actuality), although, as Arendt notes, for Aristotle the greatest achievement of human being lay not in speech and action but rather in contemplation and thought.[38]

Power, then, which is the ability to act in concert, and which arises wherever humans come together and do so, is an "end in itself." Its legitimacy comes from the initial coming together for action, and not from anything that then follows.[39] As noninstrumental, defying means–end categories, power has a "potential" character, and is "not an unchangeable, measurable, and reliable entity like force or strength." Strength is the natural quality of an individual viewed in isolation, whereas "power springs up between men when they act together and vanishes the moment they disperse."[40] Unlike strength, power cannot be possessed, and unlike force, it cannot be applied. It only exists in its actualization. As potential, and as formed in action, political power is not a means to an objective, as in the Weberian *teleological* understanding of power, but rather its exercise (i.e., the coming together of humans in word and deed) is its own end. Hans Ulrich notes the importance of this conception of power for our understanding of politics when he writes:

> Political power is the power to act together, to enact a common deed, and this means to do something independent, something new, something beyond what can be accounted for by cause and effect. Such acts are political and not administrative or governmental; they are related to real (political) power—i.e. the possibility to truly act rather than to rely upon particular technical abilities or competences. Actions are political in this sense.[41]

Here, the *polis* speaks of a shared form of life whose activity both originates it and preserves it as it is its *telos*. As such, the *polis* or "the political" is not a description of the tools or implements used by individuals or groups of individuals ("interests") to achieve their objectives in competition with other individuals or groups. Rather, politics is constitutive of what it means to be human, needing no justification beyond itself.[42]

37. Arendt, *The Human Condition*, 198.
38. Ibid., 206–7.
39. Arendt, *On Violence*, 51–2.
40. Arendt, *The Human Condition*, 200.
41. Hans Ulrich, "Stations on the Way to Freedom," 159.
42. Of course, Arendt's account of politics will need to be heavily qualified theologically, which I will do in my interpretation of Luther. Theologically, we must be more precise and

Violence, in contrast to power, is instrumental in character and uses implements to multiply natural strength (the inherent property belonging to a person or object which is in essence independent of others).[43] Thus, while nothing "is more common than the combination of violence and power," it does not follow that they are the same thing.[44] On the contrary, power and violence are opposites, "where the one rules absolutely, the other is absent." Violence is able to destroy power, but is "utterly incapable of creating it."[45] A loss of power ultimately means the death of the political community. Viewed from the other side, however, the existence of a political community, "the foundation of cities," is the "most important material prerequisite for power," given that the "only indispensable material factor in the generation of power is the living together of people."[46] Power is the keeping and being of people together such that the potential for action is always at hand. Without power, there is no common action, and it is here that violence can be seen clearly in its stark opposition to power. Power relies on the coming together of people, whereas violence can do without them through the use of implements. In extreme form, power is all against one, whereas the extreme form of violence is one against all made possible by instruments.[47] As Arendt writes, "Those who oppose violence with mere power will soon find that they are confronted not by men but by men's artifacts."[48] The rule of violence comes in when power is on its way out. Following this logic, the least powerful and most violent form of government is tyranny, which attempts to substitute violence for power. Citing Montesquieu, Arendt argues that the outstanding feature of tyranny is its dependence on the isolation of the tyrant from those subjected to him/her and the isolation of the subjected from one another. This isolation fosters impotence and robs the subjects of tyranny of their capacity to speak and act together (i.e., of power).[49] Viewed in this way, then, power is of the essence of politics, but in contrast to Milbank, violence and domination are the opposite of politics and power. As Arendt articulates the ancient Greek understanding, "To be political, to live in a *polis*, meant that everything was decided through words and persuasion and not through force and violence."[50] Rather than an agonistic conception of

---

speak of *political worship* as an end in itself. That is, politics as worship in response to the prior activity of the Creator and Redeemer. Seen as anything less than this service, politics is in danger of becoming antipolitics, a means of justification in Luther's grammar.

43. Arendt, *On Violence*, 44, 46.
44. Ibid., 47.
45. Ibid., 56.
46. Arendt, *The Human Condition*, 201.
47. Arendt, *On Violence*, 41–2.
48. Ibid., 53.
49. Arendt, *The Human Condition*, 202–3. Arendt notes that terror depends for its effectiveness on social atomization, *On Violence*, 55.
50. Arendt, *The Human Condition*, 26.

power as supposed by modern accounts of politics grounded in the hermeneutics of suspicion,[51] an account of politics followed by Milbank, Arendt sees power as "actualized only where word and deed have not parted company, where words are not empty and deeds not brutal, where words are not used to veil intentions but to disclose realities, and deeds are not used to violate and destroy but to establish relations and create new realities."[52] Rather than deconstructing all politics as mere power play, an embrace of the politics that is the church at worship means that it is only in a political form of life that we are set free *from* determination by power politics and narrow grasping after self-interest and *for* a genuine politics of exploration of the common good. On the other hand, the hermeneutics of suspicion is decidedly apolitical, if not antipolitical. It must always be suspicious of forms of shared life as concealing a more basic play of power. However, following Luther, one can see the worshipping church as engagement in a shared form of life in which the trustworthy Word of God is encountered audibly and visibly. The communal sharing in this form of life, and the trust that it generates, enables the worshippers to engage freely, and not out of necessity, in common action, to carry out works of love toward neighbors. The church at worship is a political community engendering the trust that makes possible a politics of exploring the common good in contrast to a politics as will-to-power that is fundamentally antipolitical, and hence ultimately self-destructive. It is this sense of politics, politics as concerned with the real, and as both constitutive of and determinative of human life, that forms the background for my interpretation of Luther's political theology.

Of course, in addition to Arendt's focus on the acting together of humans, the active presence of God in the Spirit will also have to be considered as a decisive difference from classical/republican accounts of politics and Luther's theological account. That God alone occupies such a place makes it possible to speak of a politics that does not assume a still deeper original violence or agonism, traces of which remain unavoidable in the Arendtian–Aristotelian account, with its distinction between necessity (*oikos*) and freedom (*polis*). Nonetheless, the account provided by Arendt goes a long way in illuminating a tradition of political thought that conceives of political life quite differently from the negative construal of Augustine as reappropriated by Milbank, in which politics is merely the result of human sin, a tragic necessity destined to disappear.

---

51. On the relation between modern liberal Western (unpolitical) accounts of politics as the self-interested pursuit of power over against the interests of others and the hermeneutics of suspicion, see Bernd Wannenwetsch, "The Liturgical Origin of the Christian Politeia: Overcoming the 'Weberian' Temptation," in *Church as Politeia: The Political Self-Understanding of Christianity*, ed. Christoph Stumpf and Holger Zaborowski (Berlin: Walter de Gruyter, 2004), 322–40, esp. 338–9, and Wannenwetsch, "The Political Worship of the Church," 269–99, esp. 288–9.

52. Arendt, *The Human Condition*, 200.

The Construal of "the Two" in Luther

Luther's Teaching on the Two Ecclesiae

As suggested, Luther's understanding of politics allows it an inherent dignity and goodness absent in Milbank, and in Augustinian accounts that reduce politics merely to its negative function of preserving peace in the face of disorder. As a way of beginning to explicate the differences between the two, it will be helpful first to consider what is frequently referred to as Luther's "doctrine of the two kingdoms" in light of Milbank's construal of the two cities. Luther is capable of the criticism of pagan ideologies that Milbank carries out in his use of Augustine's *City of God*. However, unlike Milbank, he does not make the primary distinction rest on rival "ontologies" forming two cities (or in Augustine's language, rival "loves"). Rather, when Luther discusses the division of mankind in the biblical primeval history between Cain and Abel—making explicit reference to Augustine's treatment of the passage in the *City of God*—he does not use the language of two "cities" but instead two churches (*ecclesiam*) formed by two faiths.[53]

Luther's exposition of the two *ecclesiae* can be foregrounded by his discussion of the Fall, in which he refuses to name a specific sin as the nature of the temptation in the Garden, such as idolatry or pride, and instead argues that the serpent aimed to disprove God's goodwill toward humankind and draw them away from God's Word.[54] In so doing, he drives them to unbelief, which results in breaking all of the Ten Commandments.[55] Idolatrously, glory is transferred away from God to works. The primeval parents give up the Word and in its place worship their own thoughts. As with pride and idolatry, it is also the case that the beginning of sin does not lie in false desire, but rather in a turn away from the Word of God.[56] Rather than an ontological focus (seeking for a self-grounding outside of God) or an emphasis on desire (false love), for Luther the original sin is a turn from the Word of God to the false word of the serpent. Luther will divide the two churches along the lines of their attentiveness to the Word.[57] As such, the

---

53. "Lectures on Genesis, Chapters 1–5 (1535–36)," LW 1:252; WA 42.187, 13, Augustine, *City of God*. Cf. note 2 earlier. See also John A. Maxfield, *Luther's Lectures on Genesis and the Formation of Evangelical Identity* (Kirksville, MI: Truman State University Press, 2008).

54. Genesis 3:1: "Did God say, 'You shall not eat from any tree in the garden'?"

55. "Lectures on Genesis, Chapters 1–5 (1535–36)," LW 1:146–7. "The source of all sin truly is unbelief and doubt and abandonment of God's Word" (149).

56. Ibid., 158. The serpent "first attacks man's greatest strength, faith in the Word" (162).

57. In his exposition of Psalm 82 (1530), Luther writes, "For God's Word makes a distinction among the children of Adam. Those who have God's Word are not merely men, but holy men, God's children, Christians, etc.; but those who are without God's Word are merely men, that is, in sin, eternally imprisoned in death, under the power of the devil, and are altogether without God." LW 13:71.

origin of both churches lies outside of humankind, yet without forfeiting human responsibility for sin.[58]

Luther locates the "historical" beginning of the division between the two churches in the narrative of Cain and Abel in the Genesis account, calling the two men the "originators" of the two churches.[59] He notes that Adam and Eve were "pious and excellent" teachers, yet their two sons were two different kinds of *hearers*. Cain has the appearance of saintliness and is confident that he is a lord, as are his parents, as evidenced for Luther by their giving him a more favorable name (Cain meaning "to possess" or "to acquire," compared to Abel, which means "vanity") and by assigning him the role king and priest, that is, concerns of government (*politicum*), while leaving the home (*oeconomicum*) to Abel.[60] However, Cain is a representative of the hypocritical church, for his attentiveness to the word is only contrived.[61] On the other hand, Abel, though deprived of the dignity and honor his brother receives from their parents, represents the true church in bringing his sacrifices in faith in the promise that God is good and merciful, that is, he has faith in the promise of the seed, a promise that would have been conveyed to him by his parents' preaching of the Word (Heb. 11:4).[62]

Whereas Milbank follows Augustine in describing the primary division of humankind in explicitly political terms as two cities, Luther writing in terms of the doctrine of the three institutions stresses that he is doing something different in referring to "the two" as churches.

> These things pertain neither to the state (*politicia*) nor to the household (*oeconomica*); they pertain primarily to the church (*ecclesiastica*).[63] Abel is slain, not because of his activity in the state or in the household but because of his worship of God.[64]

Luther's understanding of the narrative as referring primarily to the *ecclesia* is further reflected in his explanation of the fact that Cain "became very angry, and his face fell" (4:5). Cain's anger is a response to being forced out from the church

---

58. Throughout the commentary, Luther refers to the two churches as the blessed seed and as the seed of the serpent.

59. "Lectures on Genesis, Chapters 1–5 (1535–36)," LW 1:246, 252.

60. Ibid., 243, 246; WA 42. 183, 4–5. Luther notes here already the beginning of God's subversion of false human expectations. While Adam and Eve seem to hold the *ecclesia* and *politia* in higher regard than the *oeconomia*, God's chosen faithful is restricted by the world to the latter. Luther notes that this subversion through raising the humble is repeated throughout the Old Testament history, with Jacob and David (both kept at home) serving as paradigms. Here we see already the raising of the status of the *idiotes* of ancient culture to the status of full citizenship, which they likewise enjoy in the *ekklesia* of the New Testament.

61. "Lectures on Genesis, Chapters 1–5 (1535–36)," LW 1:247.

62. Ibid., 251.

63. A full discussion of the institutions comes in Chapter 5.

64. Ibid., 253; WA 42.188, 1–6.

and simultaneously being "deprived of rule and priesthood" (*regno et sacredocio*).[65] It is not enough for Cain that he has been given the privileged position by his parents, he also wants to bear the mantle of "the church." However, Luther asks, in God's rejection of Cain's sacrifice, "Is this anything else than being cast out and excommunicated from the church?"[66] Cain has lost the fellowship of the saints.[67]

Simultaneous with the loss of the community of the church, Cain "went out from the face of the Lord." In explicating this expression, Luther demonstrates further what it means for Cain to be excommunicated from the true church. According to Luther, the Scriptural meaning of "the face of the Lord" is "those things by which God shows that He is with us." In the Old Testament these included the pillar of fire, the cloud, and the mercy seat, while in the New Testament these things were baptism, the Lord's Supper, and the ministry of the Word, all means by which "God shows us, as by a visible sign, that He is with us, takes care of us, and is favorably inclined toward us." Cain's going out to the east is his loss of the assurance of God's presence and God's good and merciful will toward him.[68]

Tied to the importance of these signs of assurance for Luther is his description of the true church as hidden. In the previous chapter, we discussed Luther's ecclesiology in the negative sense that, as a creature of the Word, "The church is indeed holy, but it is a sinner at the same time."[69] Here, it is important to add to this negative sense Luther's positive stress on the hiddenness of the church, a hiddenness that is at the same time a sign of its faithfulness. The true church has the character of Abel, which is to say that it is "without influence, forsaken, and exposed to suffering and the cross."[70] As was Abel, so Christ (who also was neither a priest nor a king in the eyes of the world) was sent to the cross by priests and kings. And given that the church, too, is to be conformed to Christ (Rom. 8:29), it is the case that true church should expect persecution.[71] In fact, elsewhere, Luther can even refer to such suffering as one of the true signs within which the church is hidden.[72] However, that the church is hidden does not mean for Luther that it is invisible. Rather, it is visible to the eyes of faith. Instead of despairing over its suffering, Luther encourages the faithful to look to baptism and the Eucharist and to find comfort in the fact that "the church has never been deprived to such an extent of outward signs that it became impossible to know where God could surely be found."[73] Cain's punishment consists primarily in being deprived of these signs.

---

65. "Lectures on Genesis, Chapters 1–5 (1535–36)," LW 1:260; WA 42.192, 22–3.
66. "Lectures on Genesis, Chapters 1–5 (1535–36)," LW 1:260.
67. Ibid., 283–4.
68. Ibid., 309.
69. "Lectures on Galatians 1535, Chapters 1–4," LW 26:109.
70. "Lectures on Genesis, Chapters 1–5 (1535–36)," LW 1:252.
71. Ibid., 253.
72. "On the Councils and the Church, 1539," LW 41: 164–5.
73. Of course, Luther insists that these "outward signs" (sacraments) be accompanied by the preaching of the Word, LW 1:248. In addition to preventing a crude empirical

If the true church is known by the assurance of Word and sacrament, then the false church, the church of Cain, is characterized by its being "unsettled," its lack of a "Word or command" from God designating a definite promise with definite places and ceremonies for the worship of God. Here, in furthering his description of the nature of Cain's excommunication, Luther shows that although Cain's sin related to matters of *ecclesia* (namely, that he wanted to be ruler of the church), his punishment is "of a political nature" (*politica poena*).[74] Here, in Luther's exposition of the narrative, we find another strain that, instead of stressing the division of the two churches, focuses rather on the way in which the church is necessarily connected to the city and the home, that is, we see again Luther's employment of a grammar of the three institutions. Although the sin concerned the church, the punishment extended to all areas of human life. In discussing Genesis 4:14,[75] Luther notes Cain's acknowledgment "that he was being driven out, in the first place, from home (*Oeconomia*) and community (*Politia*), in the second place, also from the church (*Ecclesia*)."[76] His being driven out "from the face of the ground" refers to an economic punishment, being left "a wanderer and fugitive on the earth" refers to a political punishment, and being "hidden from your face" refers to the ecclesiastical punishment. Yet, even though Cain's punishment refers to the threefold form of human life, he is not cut off from human life in whole. It addition to still enjoying the signs of God's kindness to all creation, "namely, the enjoyment of sun, moon, day, night, water, air, etc.,"[77] Cain is not deprived of the gift of procreation or of ruling (*dominii*).[78] Despite his punishment, it is still significant than he can marry, have children, found a city and engage in economic and social life.[79] In short, Cain remains human, which means he still lives from the promise of God to govern, care and provide for human life, even when the promise is not acknowledged or held to with the certainty of those who have faith in the promise of Christ.

In answer to the question of how Cain can be the first to build a city when he has been cursed to be a wanderer and fugitive on the earth, Luther answers that just as Cain was deprived of the definiteness that the true church knows in its worship

understanding of the church, the stress on the spoken word in worship reveals Luther's fundamentally political understanding of worship. See Wannenwetsch, "Ecclesiology and Ethics," in *The Oxford Handbook of Theological Ethics* (Oxford: Oxford University Press, 2005), 57–73, esp. 66.

74. "Lectures on Genesis, Chapters 1–5 (1535–36)," LW 1:298; WA 42.220, 13.

75. "Behold, you are driving me out today from the face of the ground, and I shall be hidden from your face; and I shall be a wanderer and fugitive on the earth, and it will come to pass that anyone who finds me will kill me" (quoted in ibid., 298).

76. Ibid., 298; WA 42.220, 5.

77. "Lectures on Genesis, Chapters 1–5 (1535–36)," LW 1:309. Here Luther distinguishes between God's signs of kindness and blessing provided to all creatures from God's signs of "His changeless grace."

78. Ibid., 311; WA 42.229, 24.

79. "Lectures on Genesis, Chapters 1–5 (1535–36)," LW 1:305.

of God, Cain is deprived of the assurance of God's presence and goodwill toward him as he engages in economic and political life. Administration of the household (*Oeconomia*) is left to Cain, but without any blessing, and civil government (*Politia*) is also left to him, but without assurance of its endurance. The way back into the church is even left open to Cain, but without the promise. Unlike Adam, who after his expulsion from the garden was still left with a definite work in a certain place, Cain "is simply sent away to any indefinite place and work without the addition of any promise and command, just like a bird which roams uncertainly in the open air."[80] So although the true church is hidden under suffering and persecution, being driven from place to place, it alone has the signs of assurance; the false church has the appearance of stability and permanence, but without a promise or command of God, so that it is actually the unsettled wanderer. As such, Cain "is truly like a beggar in the church, in the household, and in the government."[81] He cannot know of freedom for the neighbor in *oeconomia* and *politia*, which Luther praises so highly, but instead experiences them in uncertainty and in a turned inwardly self-protectiveness.

Nonetheless, Cain is preserved, and his perseverance is not finally grounded in his own activity. Rather, Luther argues, "because of the elect who had to be saved by accidental mercy," Cain is allowed to live and even procreate.[82] That even in exile Cain still finds his life ordered is a result of divine mercy. Cain is preserved for the sake of Christ and his church (the elect), and in this way, we can say that the good of Cain in economic and political activity is at one with the good of the church. To the extent that Cain's economic and political undertakings further human life, then the city of Cain and the true church share a genuine common good; that is to say, they do not merely use the same goods for different ends, but rather there is an actual coincidence of good between them. But this is only possible because they both share the same origins (the creation of the world for the glory Christ) and the same *telos* (the consummation of the world for the glory of Christ). For Luther, the world never slips out in any way from under the reign of Christ.

It is not until after construing the division between Cain and Abel along the lines of two *ecclesiae* that Luther then begins to use language similar to Milbank's construal of two *cities*. Luther argues that Cain, who was the first "historically" to build a city, did so out of spite of the true church and a desire to suppress it. Luther puts the following words into the mouth of Cain: "I shall build a city in which I can gather my own church. Away with my father and his church!"[83] The logic behind this city is the constitution of a new church to oppose the true church. Cain acts neither out of fear nor defense, but rather in "pride and lust for ruling." On the other hand, "the children of God are concerned with the other city, which has solid foundations and has been built by God Himself, as the Epistle to the

80. Ibid., 300.
81. Ibid., 294; WA 42.217, 20–3.
82. "Lectures on Genesis, Chapters 1–5 (1535–36)," LW 1:302.
83. Ibid., 315.

Hebrews says" (11:10).[84] Significantly, that these are Cain's motives in building a city (which happens to be the "historically" first city built by humans) does not mean that his motivations represent the generative logic behind the earthly city, such that questions of power and politics are resolvable to human pride and will to domination. Rather, the *politia*, at least in the sense in which Cain is not entirely deprived of it in his punishment, was constitutive of life in the true *ecclesia* to which his parents and brother belonged.[85] Understood not as generative in Cain's pride and lust, but as part of God's mercy in not depriving Cain of *politia* (nor *oeconomia*), the earthly *politia* can only have reference back to God's original good creation within which human life is inescapably embedded and in which it is formed. The loss of certainty in God's governance and care, which certainly can be destructive of the *politia* and *oeconomia*, is not identical with their loss. Again, Cain still receives governance and care from God, but without certainty he is always in danger of destroying the very institutions by which God provides these things by self-destructively using them to secure himself (whether out of pride or fear) rather than finding security from trust in God's providence, hence freeing him for whole-hearted commitment to the good of his neighbor in the *politia* and *oeconomia*.

This positive assessment of the origin of the "earthly city" relative to Milbank is evident elsewhere in Luther's writings, both early and late. In a 1521 letter to Philip Melanchthon, Luther considers the place of governmental authority in the New Testament. He argues that Paul (I Tim. 2:1–2) commands prayer for the governing authorities in accordance with the example set by Jeremiah (29:7). Interestingly, Luther understands Paul's command to require an interpretation of Jeremiah that goes beyond merely "using" the peace of the earthly city. He writes, "You will not convince me that prayer could have been commanded by the apostles or prophets for things which were only permitted and were to be endured so that they could continue to exist and enjoy peace. If this were the case, we should pray for robbers and unjust tyrants, that they might continue to be unjust!"[86] Clearly, for Luther, the governing authorities are not merely to be endured or permitted,[87] but to be recognized as servants of God when they perform their task of punishing evil and encouraging the good (Rom. 13). They are servants of God because instituted and ordained by God, and "a concession, or something permitted, cannot have the function of a servant of God."[88] Again, it is important to stress that for Luther

---

84. Ibid.

85. In Chapter 5, where I treat the three institutions in greater detail, I will argue that Luther, although not always consistently, views the *politia* as also constitutive of human life in creation as such, before Adam's sin.

86. "85. Philip Melanchthon: Wartburg, July 13, 1521," LW 48:260.

87. The American Edition of Luther's Works defines "permitted things" in Luther as "things neither commanded nor prohibited by God's Word; they are neutral in themselves and have no direct relationship to man's salvation." Ibid., 259, n. 15.

88. Ibid., 260.

governmental authority does not begin in human initiative, but rather, per Christ's words to Pilate, authority is given from above (Jn. 19:11).[89] In Chapter 5 in the treatment of the institutions, I will spell out in more detail the positive purposes of government in Luther's account, as well as the basis for critical assessment of (and even opposition to) any particular government in light of these purposes. However, at this point I want to concentrate specifically on Luther's treatment of the divine *origin* of political rule, which stands in clear contrast to modern liberal contractarian accounts of politics, as well as Augustinian accounts like Milbank's which ground the beginning of earthly cities (and for Milbank, ground politics as such) in pride and human desire.

Luther spells out this understanding that God alone founds cities in his "Exposition of Psalm 127 (1524)." He seeks to comfort his addressees by urging them to trust God in the management of the household. For when humans seek to build a household on the basis of their own labor, "there covetousness and anxiety quickly arise, and they hope by much labor to acquire much."[90] However, if they were to heed the first verse of the Psalm, they would realize that "unless the Lord builds the house, those who build it labor in vain." As such, Luther argues, "the managing of a household must be done in faith—then there will be enough—so that men come to acknowledge that everything depends not on our doing, but on God's blessing and support."[91] He then extends this logic to the city, given that "a whole community is nothing other than many households combined."[92] Commenting on the second half of verse 1, "Unless the Lord keeps the city, the watchman guards in vain," Luther argues that although communities tend to

---

89. Ibid., 262. Wannenwetsch notes that in the biblical account the New Jerusalem is also pictured as coming down from heaven (Rev. 21:2), not as being generated from human desiring or activity. He writes, "When it comes to the earthly city, Augustine's framework makes it next to impossible to see God's loving providence at work in the gestation of this polity. We must not conflate this theological mistake with a philosophical one, though. Augustine is, of course, absolutely right to point to the socially formative power of human desiring. 'Common objects of love' in fact give shape to human societies, whose organizational patterns can be said to be revolving around such common objects of desire. *But his sociological insight cannot be transposed onto the stage of cosmo-genesis. The categorical difference between the New Jerusalem and the Old is not one that is constituted by different forms of socially formative loves.* Rather, it is God's own creative love that brings into being either of them, only in different ways and for different purposes." Wannenwetsch, "'For in its welfare you will find your welfare': Political Realism and the Limits of the Augustinian Framework," in *Political Theology* 12.3 (June 2011), 462 (emphasis mine).

90. "Exposition of Psalm 127, 1524," LW 45:325.

91. Ibid., 324.

92. Luther states that by the term "community" (*gemeine*), he means "all manner of principalities (*fürstenthum*), dominions (*herrschaften*), and kingdoms (*königreich*), or any other grouping of peoples (*ein gemein hausse*; i.e., community of houses)." Ibid., 328; WA 15.370, 709.

think that it is due to their "own cleverness, reason and strength" that they rise up and endure, it is only because God's allows them that they come to power, and it is only by his work that they remain. Although they may gain prominence "through human wit and arrogance," so much more quickly do they fall. Their failure is never a lack of "manpower, money, goods, and all manner of resources," but because God (the "true watchman") has withdrawn his "watchful care and protection."[93] We find this same understanding of the divine provision behind all communities in Luther's treatment of Psalm 82. Luther argues that the Psalmist calls "all communities or organized assemblies 'the congregation of God,' because they are God's own, and He accepts them as His own work, just as (Jonah 3:3) He calls Nineveh 'a city of God.' "[94] God makes and preserves all communities and they having nothing "that does not come unceasingly from Him."[95] The generation and perseverance of a city can never be finally attributable to human activity, but must always account for the ongoing presence and activity of God in the world.

For Luther, then, whether it is the promised heavenly Jerusalem for which the faithful (those belonging to the true church) wait, or the earthly cities that organize human life in the *saeculum*, in either case, it must be recognized that God is the one ruling. This construal of the narrative of Cain and Abel and of God's founding activity in the case of all *politia* deprives the church of a totalistic "counter-society" or contrast status, in which the church is set up in stark opposition to a *civitas terrena*, which is merely destined to pass away (as it is grounded in unreality), but instead means the church finds itself *in* the midst of a world which is itself being redeemed. Luther, like Milbank's Augustine, can only recognize one true worship and calls all other worships false. This is the real gain to be had from following Luther's use of the concept of two *ecclesiae* (the kingdom of God and the kingdom of Satan) in that he can hold the critical edge that is found in Milbank's understanding of the two *civitates*. However, the *politia* does not have to be resisted and opposed outright in the way that the false *ecclesia* does, but rather, Christians can go beyond merely using the peace of the earthly city and instead more fully

---

93. "Exposition of Psalm 127, 1524," LW 45:329.

94. "Psalm 82 (1530)," LW 13:46. Luther continues, "For mad reason, in its shrewdness, and all the worldly-wise do not know at all that a community is God's creature and His ordinance. They have no other thought about it than that it has come into being by accident, through people holding together and living side by side in the same way murderers and robbers and other wicked bands gather to disturb the peace and the ordinance of God; these are the devil's congregations" (46). For the Augustinian parallel, see the passage where Augustine compares Alexander's kingdom to a band of robbers, *City of God*, IV.4, 147–8.

95. "Psalm 82 (1530)," LW 13:46. "Such communities are God's work, which He daily creates, supports, and increases . . . this word is . . . a great and pleasant comfort to all those who find themselves situated in such a community. It assures them that God accepts them as His work and His creation, cares for them and protects and supports them, as we can, in fact, see with our own eyes. For who could have or keep a cow or a heller if God did not give it and help and guard it?" (47).

participate in exploration of the common good that all humans (Christian or not) share together, exploration which the *politia* as creature together with humankind (and not merely an outcome of human generational love) serves.

Recognition of the common good, however, does not preclude radical criticism of elements in earthly cities that are not truly political, but are rather forms of false worship. The *politia* is not absorbed by the *ecclesia* such that all action in the *polis* stems in total from its (false) worship. Yet, in Luther's teaching on the two regiments, which we treat next, there is far more room for constructive engagement and encounter between the church and the world than in Milbank's framework. Further, it can be argued that this concept is also more effective in preventing the kind of false church–world dualisms that Milbank is so keen on preventing.[96] To put it in Luther's terms, although the kingdom of Satan is real and really evil, to be opposed and ultimately destroyed, even the devil cannot escape the rule of Christ. Of course, seeing the truth that Luther acknowledges a singular rule of God over all human life means that he stands in sharp contrast to many of the later "Lutheran" doctrines of the two kingdoms that claimed to follow his own teaching. For that reason, it is to Luther's teaching on "the two" that we now turn.

Luther's Teaching on the Two Regiments

Given Luther's emphasis on the role of God in establishing political authority, and his rather positive account of "politics" relative to more negative accounts like that of Milbank, he has often been accused of promoting a political quietism and justification of the existing political status quo. This critique is especially focused on what is commonly referred to as Luther's "doctrine of the two kingdoms,"[97] according to which political authority occupies an external "worldly" realm ruled by its own law that stands in autonomous independence of the inward and

---

96. For a criticism of the dualisms in Milbank's project, see Gavin Hyman, *The Predicament of Postmodern Theology: Radical Orthodoxy or Nihilist Textualism?* (London: Westminster John Knox Press, 2001), 70–73.

97. As is often pointed out by Luther scholars, Luther himself never refers to a "doctrine of the two kingdoms." Rather, the term appears to have originated in 1922 with Karl Barth. See Bernhard Lohse, *Martin Luther's Theology*, 154; Braaten, "The Doctrine of the Two Kingdoms Re-examined," *CurTM* 15.6 (1988), 498; James Arne Nestingen, "The Two Kingdoms Distinction: An Analysis with Suggestion," *WW* 19.3 (Summer 1999), 268–9. For a brief account of the development in late-nineteenth- and early-twentieth-century Lutheranism of the two kingdoms doctrine as a concept of two autonomous spheres of life, see Ulrich Duchrow, "Introduction," in *Lutheran Churches—Salt or Mirror of Society?: Case Studies on the Theory and Practice of the Two Kingdoms Doctrine*, ed. Duchrow (Geneva: Lutheran World Federation, 1977), 12–17. For a more recent and detailed account of the same period, see William J. Wright, *Martin Luther's Understanding of God's Two Kingdoms: A Response to the Challenge of Scepticism* (Grand Rapids, MI: Baker, 2010), 17–43.

"spiritual" realm occupied by the church and its rule by the Gospel. In light of such a view, Milbank writes, "[We, the contemporary Church,] must have done forever with Luther's two kingdoms, and the notion that a State that does not implicitly concern itself with the soul's salvation can be in any way legitimate."[98] However, it can be argued that rather than the two *civitates* framework suggested by Milbank, in which the *civitas Dei* eventually absorbs the *civitas terrena*, Luther's conception of "the two" under the "one" reign of Christ allows the doctrine to serve a polemical function in which neither a false politics nor a false church absorbs the other. It is concerned with their proper relation against either an unhealthy accommodation or domination of the church to or by the *politia*. The church not only has a critical role vis-à-vis the world, but the reverse relationship also holds. The church has much to learn from suffering the criticism of the world directed at it. In either case, Luther is not setting one authority off against another, but rather is denying false claims to possess the singular authority of God. Rather than the state being unconcerned with the affairs of the church, Luther claims that in the case of godly rulers, the secular authority acts directly as a servant of the church. He writes, "For with respect to God and in the service of His authority everything should be identical and mixed together, whether it be called spiritual or secular."[99] Here we see clearly that Luther does not propose an inviolable separation of secular and spiritual in the case that godly officers occupy both. However, what Luther always does oppose is the encroachment of either the secular or ecclesial authority on the other when such is not done "with respect to God and in the service of His authority."[100] The crucial point is that in both secular and spiritual matters, it is the one rule and reign of God (i.e., an inseparable authority) that is being expressed. A reading of Luther along these lines requires disentangling Luther's teaching on God's unitary but "two-fold" governance of the world from all-too-common misunderstandings of his "doctrine of the two kingdoms."

In "Temporal Authority (1523)" Luther speaks variously of "the kingdom of God" (*reich Gottis*), "the kingdom of the world" (*reich der welt*),[101] and of God's "two governments" (*regiments*), one "spiritual" (*geistliche*), the other "temporal" (*weltliche*).[102] Luther uses the first distinction (between "two kingdoms") in a seeming echo of Augustine's "two *civitates*." Luther argues that humankind is

---

98. *Being Reconciled*, 209. Here, Luther's commentary on Psalms 101 shows a stark contrast to what Milbank ascribes to him.
99. "Psalm 101 (1534–35)," LW 13:195.
100. See Estes, *Peace, Order and the Glory of God*, 203.
101. "Temporal Authority, 1523," LW 45:88, WA 11.249, 25.
102. "Temporal Authority, 1523," LW 45: 91; WA 11.251, 15–17. The editors of the American Edition of Luther's work note that the word "regiment" occurs ninety-five times in his treatment of Psalm 101. They translate the term variously as "government, charge, administration, kingdom, authority, regime, reign, domination, rulers, realm, exercise of government, governmental affairs, responsibility of government, governmental circles." "Psalm 101 (1534–35)," LW 13:147n. 4.

divided into two classes, "the first belonging to the kingdom of God, the second to the kingdom of the world." The first kingdom consists of "all the true believers who are in Christ and under Christ."[103] The second kingdom consists of all "who are not Christians."[104] So in a very simple sense, the two kingdoms as set up here simply describe the fact that there are believers and nonbelievers in the world. Significantly, Luther does not associate one group with the visible institutional church and the other with the political kingdoms of the world. In this way, the division maps on very neatly to the division Luther makes in the "Lectures on Genesis" between the true and false *ecclesia*. Given this distinction, any association between Luther's "two kingdoms" and "Church and State" simply prove misguided. At this point Luther simply declares that there are those who are faithful to Christ's rule in the world and those who are opposed to it; we might say "a kingdom of Christ" and "a kingdom of the devil."

Where we can begin to derive a political understanding of Luther's teaching understood in the specific and not unproblematic sense of mapping it onto questions of "Church and State" and divisions (institutional) in the world is when he uses the terminology of God's two "regiments." At the outset, it is important to stress that the two regiments do not correspond straightforwardly to the two kingdoms as the latter are formulated in Luther's "Temporal Authority (1523)."[105] Paul Althaus argues that in his writing subsequent to the period in which he wrote "Temporal Authority," Luther dropped the distinction between the terms "kingdom" and "regiment" and instead used the concept of each in the sense of the latter, that is, as referring to God's government of the world rather than a dualism between the kingdom of God and the kingdom of Satan.[106] F. Edward Cranz already finds in Luther's "Temporal Authority" a clear division between the two regiments, arguing that at this point Luther has clearly separated this distinction "from its earlier confusion with the contrast between God's kingdom and Satan."[107] Cranz traces the development in Luther's thought from his very early focus on two kingdoms, understood in the Augustinian sense of the two *civitates*, to his later teaching on the two *regiments* as we have set it out here.[108] Further, both

103. "Temporal Authority, 1523," LW 45:88.

104. Ibid., 90.

105. See James M. Estes, "Luther on the Role of Secular Authority in the Reformation," *LQ* 17.2 (Summer 2003), 207–209.

106. Paul Althaus, *The Ethics of Martin Luther*, trans. Robert C. Shultz (Philadelphia: Fortress Press, 1972), 49–52.

107. F. Edward Cranz, *An Essay on the Development of Luther's Thought on Justice, Law, and Society* (Cambridge: Harvard University Press, 1959), 165–6.

108. Estes argues that in his commentary on Psalms 101, one notes a move in Luther away from a "Two Kingdoms" account of secular government toward the *cura religionis* as promoted by Melanchthon. See his *Peace, Order and the Glory of God*, 205. Basing his argument on Luther's "Lectures on Genesis," David M. Whitford argues that Luther's later writings reveal that he never wavered on his two kingdoms teaching, and that Estes's

Althaus and Cranz argue that although Luther focuses exclusively on the coercive aspect of God's worldly *regiment* in restraining sin in his earlier writings, by the time of "Whether Soldiers Too Can Be Saved (1526)," the positive sense of this regiment begins to be emphasized. While taking this approach, I would argue that it is nonetheless essential to include Luther's two *ecclesiae* as indicated earlier, otherwise there is a danger of losing the critical function that a framework like the two *civitates* provides.[109] According to this reading, while the two kingdoms (or two *ecclesiae* as I have described earlier) depict an eschatological dualism between good and evil in the world, the twofold regiments are entirely misunderstood if they are likewise understood dualistically.[110] Rather, the two regiments refer to the one rule of God over His kingdom in a twofold manner over and against the kingdom of the devil. While the worldly government postlapsum is ruled in part by the temporal sword and law, and is instituted "so that those who do not want to be good and righteous to eternal life may be forced to be good and righteous in the eyes of the world," this providential use does not exhaust the meaning of politics for Luther.[111] The worldly government understood in this context has a merely negative function. The temporal sword ensures that the wicked, "even though they would like to . . . are unable to practice their wickedness, and if they do practice it they cannot do so without fear or with success and impunity."[112] The worldly (or temporal) government serves to maintain peace by punishing the wicked and protecting the upright. However, even in this negative, postlapsum context, the temporal government remains an ordinance of God, established and preserved by God's ongoing activity (here Luther cites Rom. 13 and I Pet. 2). As such, Christians "should esteem the sword or governmental authority as highly as the estate of

---

attribution to Luther of support for the principle of *cura religionis* is misguided. "*Cura Religionis* or Two Kingdoms: The Late Luther on Religion and the State in the *Lectures on Genesis*," *CH* 73.1 (March 2004), 41–62.

109. Ebeling argues that if the dualistic sense of "kingdoms" is not held together with the unity of "regiments," "we evade the problem of the relation between eschatology and creation which is so disturbingly acute in the two kingdoms doctrine . . . Creation and eschatology require to be thought together in theology and not merely held apart like the prelude and finale of a drama." Ebeling, "The Necessity of the Doctrine of the Two Kingdoms," in *Word and Faith* (London: SCM Press, 1963), 397. My argument is, rather than a two kingdoms doctrine, what is required is something like the two *ecclesiae* and a teaching on the two *regiments*, which together interweave creation and eschaton without overlooking the Fall.

110. Duchrow argues that it is a mistake in certain kinds of "two kingdoms" thinking when, "instead of locating dualism in the proper place (namely in the struggle against the power of evil in every sphere of life), a dualism is now introduced on the level of God's twofold governance, whereas Luther's thinking is unmistakably multi-dimensional and complementary." Duchrow, "Introduction," in *Lutheran Churches*, 12.

111. "Whether Soldiers, Too, Can be Saved, 1526," LW 46:99.

112. "Temporal Authority, 1523," LW 45:90.

marriage, or husbandry, or any other calling which God has instituted."[113] Given this understanding of worldly government, Luther is able to write, "Not since the time of the apostles have the temporal sword and temporal government been so clearly described or so highly praised as by me."[114] So with the doctrine of the two regiments, Luther does not split the world into two autonomous spheres. Rather, on the one hand, he highlights the negative aspect that politics has taken on in light of the Fall. Nonetheless, as we saw earlier, this does not entail the full meaning of politics for Luther or set politics in total outside of the church. Rather, it highlights the eschatological tension that follows from living in an age when Christ has triumphed, but his triumph is not fully consummated. To obtain the full picture of Luther's teaching on politics, we will require in addition to the two "ecclesiae" and the two "regiments," Luther's teaching on the three "institutions," where he more stresses the positive sense of politics and its connection to the Word of God. The important point here is that Luther sees temporal government (in both its negative and positive aspects) as still falling under the one rule of God and not as generated in human desire or activity. In this way, temporal government can be viewed as part of God's good creation and a testimony to God's one rule without being viewed as an institute conceived in sin, even if providentially useful in light of such sin.

Conclusion: On the Need for a Doctrine of the Two Ecclesiae and the Two Regiments

As we have demonstrated, when Luther narrates the history of something like Augustine's two cities, he speaks in a doxological rather than a political–ontological register. Two loves do not form two cities, but rather two worships form two *ecclesiae*. The formation of cities remains always the work of God. Milbank's account assumes an original violence at the heart of all political societies/institutions. On this point, ironically, Milbank's approach has an affinity with modern contractarian theories of politics following in the wake of Hobbes. However, Luther's account of politics provides a more theologically grounded alternative to contractarian secular politics than Milbank and Milbank's Augustine. As such, Luther's teaching on the two "kingdoms," when taken in the sense of Augustine's two cities, is not primarily political in the modern sense, such that the temporal kingdom is associated with the state or *politia* whereas the spiritual kingdom is associated with the *ecclesia*,

---

113. Ibid., 100. The stress on divine institution, however, is not Luther's sole reason for insisting on giving high esteem to temporal authority. Rather, as Piotr Malysz argues, "Christians' participation in the socio-vocational structure of society is motivated not only by temporal authority's divine sanction but, first and foremost, by the law of Christian love." Malysz, "*Nemo iudex in causa sua* as the Basis of Law, Justice, and Justification in Luther's Thought," *HTR* 100.3 (2007), 370.

114. "Whether Soldiers, Too, Can be Saved, 1526," LW 46:95.

as in the case of many mistaken interpretations of Luther on the "two kingdoms," which view the "doctrine" as referring to Church and State. Rather, for Luther, the two kingdoms in the Augustinian sense of the kingdom of God and the kingdom of the devil must be differentiated from his teaching on the two regiments of God's singular rule. In other words, we must distinguish Luther's teaching on the two *ecclesiae* from his teaching on the two regiments, while affirming the truth and utility of both. Milbank is partially in agreement with Luther, political thought in the antique sense must be qualified in light of the *ecclesia*, the eschatological gathering of the heavenly *politia*. But this does not mean a withering away of the political or its absorption by the church, except in the negative sense as a restraint on sin. The *politia*, like the church, is a place in which divine action in human life can be expected and encountered.

A fuller spelling out of the *politia* as a place of encounter with God and of concrete obedience to God's commands awaits the treatment of Luther's teaching on the three institutions in Chapter 5. Before doing so, however, it will be necessary to show how Luther distinguishes God's work in the church from God's work in the *polis*, such that the particularity of Jesus Christ and His church remains, and yet His Lordship over all of creation is upheld. To put it perhaps too simply, a distinction needs to be made between God's Word in creation and providence and His Word of redemption. This task will be carried out in conversation with Jennifer Herdt, who challenges the traditional nature and grace distinction and seeks to find common ground between contemporary Christian ethicists and non-Christian moral philosophers in an ethics of virtue.

Chapter 4

VIRTUE AND AGENCY: JENNIFER HERDT'S CRITIQUE OF LUTHER

While it is consistent with Luther to "baptize," as it were, the language of power and politics, Luther's reservations regarding virtue prove to be rather consistent with Milbank's criticism of classical virtue. In this chapter, which examines the work of Jennifer Herdt, I will take up the question of virtue in Luther in greater detail. For all the apparent Aristotelianism in Luther when considering his treatment of politics in comparison with Milbank's Augustine, Luther's political ethics nonetheless prove to be different in crucial respects from the "virtue ethics" of the neo-Aristotelianism that has enjoyed resurgence in the past generation. For Luther, an important area of difference from classical political thought relates to the latter's ideal of self-sufficient magnanimity and the assumption of irresolvable conflict between freedom and necessity (i.e., a persisting agonism as foundational for virtue, which in classical political thought typically takes the form of a *polis* and *oikos* opposition).[1] Luther's teaching on a formed life, lived in obedience to the commandments of God in the *Stände*, stands in opposition to both the underlying individuality in elements of Aristotelianism and the *polis–oikos* antinomy, both of which Milbank masterfully deconstructs in *Theology and Social Theory*.[2] In this sense, I think Luther would be in agreement with Milbank that the interruptive character of Christianity should be emphasized against both modernity and antiquity.

As argued in the previous chapter, Luther leaves ample space for an understanding of all earthly cities as works of God, of His loving provision for His creatures. However, this is not to say that Luther simply sanctions the "political" virtues that, on the human level, enable such cities. Rather, with Augustine, Luther expresses anxiety over pagan virtue and stresses the distinctiveness of both Christ and Christ's particular work, which means that a distinction must be made between God's work in the *politia* and God's work in the *ecclesia*, such that they are not simply set alongside each other in a continuum, but rather remain distinct, although inseparable. To put this in terms of traditional dogmatic

---

1. See Wannenwetsch, *Political Worship*, 133–41, 175–206.
2. *TST*, 402–403. For a more developed version of the argument, see "Can Morality be Christian?" in *WMS*, 219–32.

language, Luther preserves a proper distinction (without separation) between creation and redemption. To carry out the task of articulating the importance of these distinctions in Luther's political thought, we will begin with Jennifer Herdt's account of virtue in the Christian tradition, which aims to preserve the activity of God in the political world and seeks to overcome contrastive models of the relationship between the church and the world, but which, I will argue, does not avoid the problematic arrangement of placing the practices of Christians in the church on a continuum with the virtuous activity of non-Christians in the world. In contrast to Milbank, who seems to leave little space for God's loving providence in politics, I will argue that Herdt leaves too little room for Christian particularity, too quickly identifying any instance of virtue with the specific work of Christ. However, the particularity I seek is not that of a people so transformed that they stand out starkly from the world, but rather the particularity of a people who confess that their identity is hidden in Christ. In this chapter and in the one to follow, I will show that the political elements of Luther's account of sanctification, especially his focus on the three institutions, allows for the kind of engagement and encounter with non-Christians (i.e., the "world") that Herdt seeks, but also retains the critical edge that is so crucial in Milbank's treatment of politics and its readiness to call the principalities and powers "anti-Christ" when the need for such faithful discernment arises.

This chapter is divided into three parts. First, I set out Jennifer Herdt's narrative of virtue in the Christian tradition, highlighting the place she gives to Luther in this genealogy. A significant element of her argument is that the late-medieval and early-modern tradition, following nominalism, began to set divine and human agency in competition, with Luther playing a crucial role. While her work takes much inspiration from the modernity critics, Herdt seeks to temper their approach to allow greater harmony between political theologians/theological ethicists and contemporary moral philosophers/ethicists who seek to promote the values of modern liberal democracy, finding common ground in virtue ethics. She does so by proposing what I would term a "chastened" Augustinianism. Much recent work in political theology has been carried out according to similar frameworks.[3] I focus on Herdt, however, because of her comparatively extensive engagement with Luther and the centrality of his place in her narrative. Second, in this chapter I respond to Herdt by examining the question of pagan virtue in Luther, a key theme for political theology in a pluralistic world. Further, I consider Luther's account of agency and the way he relates creation and redemption, arguing that Luther is more faithful to the biblical witness than is Herdt's account, while avoiding construal of divine and human agency in competitive terms. Finally, in the concluding section of the chapter, I treat the importance of Luther's account of

---

3. I have already noted the work of Luke Bretherton, Charles Mathewes, and Eric Gregory in the introduction, all of whom Herdt indicates as being compatible with her project.

new creation for his understanding of sanctification and politics, a theme that sets up the final chapter to follow on the three institutions.

In the previous chapters we were concerned particularly with Luther's understanding of the *ecclesia* and its implications for politics. In this chapter and the one to follow, we will begin to turn our attention more explicitly to the institution of *politia*. As such, the threads running through all of these chapters is the place of institutionality in Luther's thought as it relates to questions of politics, although we wait to make this theme explicit until the final chapter, where we pull the various threads together. Whereas our treatment of the *ecclesia* dealt primarily with questions of faith and justification, the treatment of *politia* is doctrinally located under the *loci* of sanctification and good works, and thus to the themes highlighted in Herdt's work.

Herdt's Narrative of Virtue Acquisition

In her *Putting on Virtue: The Legacy of the Splendid Vices*, Jennifer Herdt seeks to find greater common ground between contemporary Christian ethicists and non-Christian moral philosophers. As with Milbank's *Theology and Social Theory*, Herdt's project takes the form of a grand narrative, in this case a story of the place of mimetic acquisition of virtue in the Western philosophical and theological tradition. By her account, this history is characterized from Augustine on by anxiety over the semblances of virtue, particularly as related to his accusation that pagan virtue is really prideful self-love. In narrating this history, Herdt hopes to set forth a Christian ethic of acquired virtue that is Augustinian, yet freed from these anxieties over questions of non-Christian virtue.[4] Luther plays an important role in this story, as according to Herdt, he is central in propelling this tradition along a "hyper-Augustinian" trajectory that questions the possibility of habituation into true virtue, requiring instead a complete abandonment of human agency, as well as discarding the eudaimonistic assumptions underlying Augustine's account of virtue.

---

4. *PV*, ix. In a later essay, Herdt argues that she is not attempting a retrieval of "a now lost treasure," but rather that the task of providing an adequate Christian account of virtue still lies in the future. "Back to Virtue," *SJT* 65.2 (2012), 224. A note on the use of the term "virtue" is fitting at the outset. Herdt predominately uses the singular term "virtue" given that her concern is the "general structure" of virtue acquisition rather than particular virtues. Nonetheless, she argues that the singular rather than plural use of the term is an early-modern development that comes from, among other things, a separation of justification and virtue acquisition in "Protestant thought" and therefore a proclivity to see virtue (like salvation) in either/or terms. *PV*, 10–11. I would argue that Herdt is half-correct in this statement, at least with regards to Luther. Soteriologically this either/or is the case. However, in interpreting Luther we need a more nuanced grammar, given that the soteriological language game is not the only language game of theology. Without this distinction, we cannot account for Luther's statement that pagans have much about them that is holy.

Pagan Virtue

Herdt begins her story with Aristotle's account of habituation into moral virtue, according to which we become virtuous by doing virtuous actions. The account raises the problem of the "habituation gap": how do we begin to do virtuous actions if we are not already virtuous? Put another way, the question is, how do we distinguish true virtue from mere semblances of virtue? While Herdt never seems to answer the question of how the gap is bridged, she does trust that the process of habituation is adequate for moving one from the mere semblance of virtue to the true thing.[5] And in answer to the latter formulation of the question, the difference between false and true virtue is, as Aristotle explained, that the truly virtuous do not simply do the right actions, but do them for the right reasons. A truly virtuous person chooses virtuous actions as inherently good, not as means to other ends. Further, she does so reflectively (i.e., the moral agent knows why she is choosing to undertake virtuous actions) and from a place of stable character. Virtue is false (a mere semblance) when it is pursued not for its own sake but for the sake of an external good, and is less than perfect when done out of acknowledgment of the beauty of virtue but without a reflective understanding of the place of virtue in the truly good life. In both cases, there is a failure to appreciate the nature of *eudaimonia*, the truth that the virtuous life is its own end and that human happiness is a life lived according to virtue.

Despite Aristotle's positive account of habituation into virtue, Herdt nonetheless discerns troublesome elements in Aristotelian virtue, especially in his account of magnanimity, which he calls the crown of the virtues. The core problem with magnanimity is its focus on the self, such that one is self-deceived. The magnanimous person is not only worthy of great things (especially honor), but considers herself worthy of them.[6] However, it is not the honor of others that the magnanimous person seeks, for she is godlike in her self-sufficiency, but rather her own perception of herself as worthy of honor. The difficulty here, as Herdt notes, is that a focus on self-perception means an instrumentalization of virtuous activity. The magnanimous person begins to act for the sake of her own self-perception rather than for the sake of virtue as such. In addition, her self-perception is false, magnanimous self-sufficiency requires a forgetting of the proper upbringing and virtuous friendship that made one's acquisition of virtue possible in the first place. One forgets the dependency that enables virtue.[7]

---

5. A failure to take the problem of the habituation gap seriously enough is one of Gilbert Meilaender's chief criticisms of Herdt in his review of *PV*, see "Book Review," *Studies in Christian Ethics* 23.1 (February 2010), 98. However, Herdt does seek to improve on Aristotle's account of habituation by insisting that the subject of the transformation into virtue must love and be loved by the moral exemplar, *PV*, 28.

6. *PV*, 38.

7. *PV*, 41–2. Herdt argues that Aristotle is not uniform in his failure to recognize dependency.

The Augustinian Virtue Tradition

The discussion of Aristotle leads into Augustine and "the legacy of the splendid vices."[8] Herdt argues that Augustine finds no room for genuine pagan virtue. Rather, he equates pagan virtue with Aristotle's account of magnanimity and its ultimate self-focus. This equation means that the virtues acquired by pagan habituation only serve to promote the self-love and pride that really drive the process. Pagan virtue is thus characterized by *superbia*, "the fundamental disorder that orders all things to self."[9] Hence, pagan virtue is only a semblance, for it fails to recognize God as the true *telos*. Importantly, however, Herdt says that a denial of genuine pagan virtue does not mean for Augustine abandonment of mimetic virtue acquisition nor of eudaimonism. Instead, true Christian virtue is dependent upon God to reorder our love from self to God. Acknowledgment of this dependency proves to be an important corrective to Aristotle. Dependency does not mean passivity, however, but rather responsiveness to the grace of God. Augustine retains an emphasis on mimesis, but with better models. Christian habituation takes the form of imitation of Christ, but unlike pagan imitation, it does not seek self-sufficient independence. "Rather, mimesis unites copy with exemplar or, better, reunites copy with exemplar, restoring us to the God from whom we came."[10] Again, it is important to stress that through this process the Christian exercises agency in response to the grace of God. God's grace is required because our final end, which is communion with God, is beyond our abilities. That said, the Christian does not reach this end without active participation. But, unlike the proud and presumably self-sufficient activity of the magnanimous person, the Christian's activity is characterized by humility, by an understanding of human activity that "accepts our own activity as itself God's gift."[11] Furthermore, that Christian virtue is directed toward God as its end does not make virtue instrumental. Instead, on Herdt's reading of Augustine, one's final good is union with God that can only be experienced when one's love is virtuously transformed such that one is "capable" of this union. Accordingly, one's "final end is not just external; even though I cannot in this life fully realize that loving union with God, my loving, virtuous activity is even now an expression of the love of God."[12]

Even in Augustine's Christianized version, virtue acquisition, being conformed to Christ, having one's loves properly reordered, is not only a matter of habituation, but must be preceded by the inspiration that comes from falling in love with God. A moment of conversion is required, and to this conversion we contribute

---

8. *PV*, 2.
9. *PV*, 49.
10. *PV*, 47.
11. *PV*, 58. Herdt argues that this sort of active receptivity is at the core of Augustine's account of proper Christian moral agency. Our virtue consists in responding to God in love. As such, "We find happiness in the perfected activity of receiving and returning God's gift" (57).
12. *PV*, 55.

nothing. However, this conversion only marks the beginning of a gradual process of transformation, and even the conversion itself cannot be given an isolated starting point.[13] Augustine's account of conversion, then, leaves plenty of space for habituation in spiritual exercises (e.g., scripture reading, fasting, communion, and prayer). Imitation of exemplars does not take the place of divine grace, but rather is "one of the concrete ways in which human beings receive grace."[14]

Herdt next turns to Aquinas, who like Augustine recognizes that we must acknowledge the dependence of our virtue on God, but allows a place for true pagan virtue, while being less concerned about hypocritical Christians. Aquinas is able to make this move by utilizing the scholastic distinction between natural acquired and supernatural infused virtue. According to this tradition, acquired virtues are viewed in accordance with Aristotle's account of habituation. These virtues are political in nature and aim at the common good. The infused virtues come through the supernatural infusion of grace from God, and are directed toward enjoyment of God. Aquinas allows for pagan virtue and argues that acquired virtue is directed not only toward the common good, but also toward individual good considered in itself.[15]

In addition to allowing for pagan virtue, Herdt finds in Aquinas a corrective to Aristotelian magnanimity in Thomas's emphasis on gratitude. Magnanimity, according to this view, means an acknowledgment of dependence, which as Herdt holds, is more consistent with Aristotle's overall account of virtue than is his own description of magnanimity. There is no self-deception involved. He preserves the space for pagan magnanimity by allowing a more general recognition of dependence rather than the specific Christian recognition of dependence on the true God. In other words, there is an appropriate pagan piety, which is reflective of a true and genuine, even if not perfect, virtue.

Aquinas appears to provide a solution to one of the central concerns of Herdt's book, namely, accounting for true pagan virtue in such manner that mimetic habituation does not merely entrench pride even absent directedness toward God. However, Herdt argues, the solution proves to be unstable given its grounding in the infused/acquired virtue distinction (and its attendant natural/supernatural distinction). Later thinkers would err in positing that salvation comes on the basis of the infused virtues alone, rendering it an external reward that does not require transformation of the person. Further, they would take the distinction between the natural and supernatural so far as to allow for an independent natural human agency. While, Herdt claims, Aquinas himself avoided the dangers in the instability by arguing that infused virtues are at the same time "intrinsic dispositions to act," and that they can increase over time, thus preserving both human dependency

---

13. *PV*, 68.

14. *PV*, 67. Herdt argues, "Augustine is thus able to absorb into the Christian life many of the ascetic spiritual exercises of pagan philosophy, although these are now chastened by the humble recognition of dependency" (70).

15. *PV*, 72.

4. Virtue and Agency

and moral agency, the same was not true for those who came to succeed him, and who came to accept the late medieval voluntarist view of divine–human agency on a contractual and competitive basis.[16]

The "Hyper-Augustinians"

In sixteenth- and seventeenth-century theology, Herdt's story continues, the Augustinian legacy forms into a suspicion of virtue acquisition by means of mimetic habituation because it is seen as dishonest. Not only is there no room for genuine pagan virtue, but there is no room for acquired virtue whatsoever. Herdt, following Charles Taylor, names this early-modern tradition "hyper-Augustinian,"[17] and puts Luther at its forefront. The "hyper" refers to these Augustinians going further than Augustine in extending dependence on God over the acquisition of virtue to such a degree that it results in the complete abandonment of mimesis and one's agency (i.e., complete passivity before God). Habituation into virtue as such, pagan or otherwise, is necessarily an unhelpful magnification of human moral agency. This view contrasts with Augustine, for whom habituation only becomes problematic if we fail to have our proper *telos* in view, that is, if we forget that we are to be formed into Christ by imitating Christ's example and participating in his virtue. However, according to Herdt's Luther, "such an effort to put on virtue will only be a 'put-on,' and putting on Christ is instead properly understood as assuming a mask. The attempt to act virtuously in order to become virtuous is seen as essentially hypocritical."[18] Additionally, the "hyper-Augustinians" depart from Augustine's eudaimonistic legacy for reasons similar to their discarding of habituation—it

---

16. *PV*, 73.

17. Herdt states that she uses the term "hyper-Augustinian" in a manner consistent with Charles Taylor, *Sources of the Self*, 246–7. Besides Luther, she includes in this category "the Puritans and other radical Calvinists, and the Jansenists." However, she argues that some Puritans left place for human agency by providing an account of secondary causality (*PV*, 355, n. 2). Taylor deploys the term in his account of the history of the Christian doctrine of grace and nature. He argues that for the first millennium and a half of Christianity, Christian thinkers followed the concept of the natural good that had been developed by pagan thinkers. Grace was seen as needing to supplement this natural good in two ways: (1) by making possible human participation in God's salvific action, something required given that God calls humans to a good beyond the natural good, and (2) by making it possible to discern the natural good in the first place given the depravity of the human will resulting from the Fall. The tradition has typically held onto both accounts of the necessity for grace, with varying emphasis on one or the other. Where (1) has been emphasized, Taylor argues, a Thomistic affirmation that grace perfects rather than destroys nature is typical (here, Taylor includes Erasmus). Where (2) is radically emphasized, "there is suspicion and hostility to the search for natural perfection, and at the extreme the ancient moralists are denounced (as with Luther)." It is this latter group which Taylor names the "hyper-Augustinians."

18. *PV*, 2.

gives too much place to the "self," being founded not in a love of God for Godself, but rather is a love of God as means of securing the good of one's own self. That is, eudaimonism is ultimately self-love. As is obvious here, in both these cases—the call for abandonment of human agency in favor of pure passivity and the suspicion of eudaimonism—God and the human are set against one another in a competitive relationship. Either God's agency is at work in the moral formation of the human, or the human agent is at work, but the latter is not seen as participation in or enablement by the agency of the former.[19] Likewise, there can be either a love of God or a love of self, but not a love of God that includes a proper love of self. The human is fully passive before God's agency and is entirely self-forgetting in her love of God.

Christian Mimesis

Given the aspects of the story described thus far, it might be tempting to read Herdt's tale simply as a narrative of decline. However, she finds much hope for the constitution of a Christian virtue ethic freed from Augustinian suspicion. In fact, she finds resources for such within the early modern tradition itself, particularly in Erasmus and the Jesuit theatrical tradition. She locates Erasmus within a Christian humanist tradition that views virtue as intrinsic to the Christian life, rather than as simply necessary for the political ends of peace and order.[20] In Erasmus, she holds, one finds the positive characteristics of the Augustinian tradition that sees habituation into virtue as an imitation of Christ, but beyond Augustine Erasmus serves as a "model" of Christian liberality toward non-Christian virtue. He rightly sees that "Christians and pagans alike are in *via*, both grasping only in an obscure and clouded way the full truth of our dependent agency."[21]

Erasmus was able to give an account of mimesis without suspicion over semblances of virtue given his belief that humans can be transformed inwardly by means of external imitation. He held that Christians become conformed to Christ by imitating Christ.[22] As Herdt describes it, "To imitate exemplary virtues— the charity of Christ and the saints—is not to do something merely 'external'; to honor and admire exemplary virtue without imitating it is."[23] Erasmus is not

---

19. *PV*, 332.
20. *PV*, 106.
21. *PV*, 10. However, Herdt does note a danger of Pelagianism in Erasmus, claiming that "the confrontation with Luther's extreme position on sin and freedom of the will made it easy to shift in this direction" (113). To my view, she does not do enough to address the charge against Erasmus. Further, I would not call Luther's view on sin extreme, but rather quite Augustinian. For her account to be truly Augustinian, I would argue that Herdt would have to give much greater place to an account of sin. But then, that would greatly complicate the use of virtue as a bridge to non-Christian contemporary moral philosophy.
22. *PV*, 107.
23. *PV*, 109.

overly concerned about the motives behind mimetic activity as long as the virtues imitated are appropriate. According to Herdt, Erasmus gives a helpful account of human and divine interaction in that he does not parse in detail the agency of either actor, but rather "simply insists on the priority of grace, on free human response, and on the dependency of this response."[24] Consistent with Aquinas, then, Erasmus views human agency as "enabled" by divine grace—imitation of Christ is human participation in divine agency.[25]

Erasmus views all virtue, pagan and Christian, as on a single continuum. In acting the part of virtue, one may eventually actually become virtuous—in fact, there is no other way. Even pride can drive us to engage in virtuous practices, and through such practices, one may eventually become virtuous. Such transformation through theatrics is possible because, even after the Fall, humankind continues to exhibit the image of God. The fallen creation, likewise, retains the marks of the Creator and can draw us to God.[26] "Pagans, too," according to Herdt's Erasmus, "by practicing virtue . . . are in the process of being transformed by Christ's beauty, even if they do not yet know how to name this."[27] The importance of this conception for Herdt is that Erasmus could conceive a participation in Christ through imitation that doesn't require a prior acknowledgment of Christ. Rather, "Erasmus is open to the possibility that persons can, in imitating the exemplars whose moral beauty they *are* able to recognize, already begin to be assimilated to Christ by grace."[28] Erasmus, then, is concerned that our virtue is being formed in the right direction rather than that we have an explicit, propositional grasp of Christ. Herdt thus summarizes the importance of Erasmus to her project:

> We encounter, after all (as Aquinas himself affirms), not a simple dichotomy between nature and grace but manifold forms of grace-enabled human agency. We can affirm the radical dependence of all human agency on divine sustenance while also insisting that the quality of that dependence is transformed when acknowledged and embraced. We can affirm the redemptive activity of the Word at work throughout created-but-fallen nature while also insisting that the quality of that redemptive activity is transformed when the Word is known as Jesus Christ and His Spirit is known in the church. Just such an account is offered . . . by the Christian humanism of Erasmus.[29]

Herdt's Luther

Having traced the contours of Herdt's overall story, we can now discuss the particular place of Luther within it before looking at what she sees as the relevance

24. *PV*, 113.
25. *PV*, 113.
26. *PV*, 125.
27. *PV*, 126.
28. *PV*, 126; emphasis in the original.
29. *PV*, 97.

of her narrative for contemporary theological and philosophical debate. As we have seen, Herdt places Luther's theology within the context of the late-medieval voluntarist and nominalist tradition. In a move similar to Milbank, Herdt traces the difficulties presented by hyper-Augustinian suspicion of virtue back to late-medieval voluntarism, mentioning specifically Duns Scotus and William of Ockham. Voluntaristic thought is marked by an emphasis on contract rather than participation in its description of divine and human agency.[30] Being formed in this context, Luther cannot posit a view of divine–human relations that allows for Erasmus's conception of grace-enabled human agency.[31] In fact, Luther serves in Herdt's book somewhat as a foil to Erasmus.

According to Herdt, Luther's holds, in contrast to Erasmus, that external practices cannot have an internal transforming effect—not even the practice of neighbor love. She quotes Luther's "Freedom of a Christian (1520)": "It is evident that no external thing has any influence in producing Christian righteousness or freedom, or in producing unrighteousness or servitude."[32] While both Erasmus and Luther seek restoration of the image of God, for Luther this has been "utterly destroyed," making it impossible that mimesis of Christ could lead to becoming "participants in the divine activity of assimilating copy to exemplar."[33] Instead of imitation, Herdt argues, for Luther, we must begin first with the recognition of God's agency and entirely deny our own. Honest confession of ourselves as sinners, not copying the actions of the virtuous (which only leads to hypocrisy without the prior acknowledgment of our sinfulness and dependence), is the beginning of the Christian life.[34] Without "a perfect subjective acknowledgment" of this passivity,

---

30. *PV*, 92–3. Elsewhere, Herdt argues that although Luther is able to maintain a noncontrastive account of God's transcendence in elements of his thought, he nevertheless understands freedom in terms of a liberty of indifference, meaning that human and divine freedom are placed in a competitive, univocal relationship, consistent with freedom as conceived by Scotus, Ockham, and Biel, "Affective Perfectionism: Community with God without Common Measure," in *New Essays on the History of Autonomy: A Collection Honoring J.B. Schneewind*, ed. Natalie Brender (Cambridge: Cambridge University Press, 2004), 40–1. See also Herdt, "The Invention of Modern Moral Philosophy: A Review of *The Invention of Autonomy* by J.B. Schneewind," *JRE* 29.1 (Spring 2001), 164, 167–8.

31. Similarly to Herdt, Reinhard Hütter argues that Luther's nominalistic metaphysics force him to deny genuine contingency as such would turn into competition with divine causality, "St. Thomas on Grace and Free Will in the *Initium Fidei*: The Surpassing Augustinian Synthesis," *Nova et Vetera* 5.3 (2007), 521–54.

32. *PV*, 174.

33. *PV*, 174.

34. Thus, "For Luther the honest sinner is closer to righteousness than the aspirant to virtue" (*PV*, 176). Of course, this would only be true in terms of the righteousness that comes from faith alone. It seems that Herdt's statement here needs to be nuanced with the acknowledgment of Barth's reminder to Brunner: "According to Luther, man is not a 'sinner' by nature. He has to *become* one, and it is 'a rare thing and a hard one' to become a

without a posture of pure trust, sanctification cannot begin.[35] As such, there is no place in Luther for God's grace to be at work in non-Christian attempts to mimic the virtuous.[36]

Given the strong contrast that Herdt finds in Luther between external appearances and internal realities, the emphasis on "a conscious experience of faith in Christ (though not of righteousness)" proves crucial.[37] As Luther holds to limited election, his emphasis on prior trust rather than virtuous imitation opens the floodgates to the deep, dark waters of personal assurance of salvation, a problematic that would later give rise to Puritan attempts at extreme self-scrutiny in light of existential anxieties over election. Instead of faith in the promises of the Word, believers are ironically thrown back onto their own faith.[38] An inward directed spiral follows the inability to make distinctions between merely apparent and truly good works.[39]

Another important difference between Erasmus and Luther is related to their starting points. While the former focused mimesis on Christ, with union to Christ

---

sinner (Comm. On Romans 1515/16, Ficker II, lxxi. 1f.). As the righteousness of God lives in us through *faith*, so it is also with sin; that is, we must *believe* that we are sinners (lxix, 10)." Barth argues that Calvin is in agreement with Luther on this point, holding that "true knowledge of self in real humility cannot precede the knowledge of God, it must follow the latter." Karl Barth, "No!" in *Natural Theology*, trans. Peter Fraenkel (London: The Centenary Press, 1946), 118–19.

35. *PV*, 193.
36. *PV*, 194.
37. *PV*, 193.
38. *PV*, 194.
39. In making this argument, Herdt relies on Randall Zachman, *The Assurance of Faith* (Minneapolis: Fortress, 1993). I would argue however, for Luther, the point is precisely that we are not to make such distinctions. Such distinctions belong to the Holy Spirit alone. In looking to Christ, we are freed from such questions. Luther insists that the gaze remain radically fixed on Christ. It seems that Herdt would like to give us a little room for self-assurance to avoid extreme self-scrutiny and election. But Luther's point is that there can be no self-assurance. Our works are always a mixed bag, and yet that is our freedom, because our salvation is not in our works. We are free to prayerfully discern and then move forward, knowing that we walk in forgiveness. If we could make the distinction via self-reference, between moral striving and the fruit of the gift, our gaze would turn back on ourselves, and would then be one of self-righteous approval or self-loathing despair, instead of focusing our gaze entirely on Christ and finding there alone our justification such that we are free for works toward our neighbor (free from self-satisfaction and from despair), precisely because we do not have to be obsessed with intentions. On the contrary, our trust and gaze is focused simply on Christ and his love for the neighbor, freeing us from the spiral of *Anfechtungen*, or worse, spiritual smugness. The Christian doesn't have to worry whether her virtue is in some respect mere performance, because it most likely is. Thus there is need for confession, but also the freedom of forgiveness. The starting point is not "pure trust"; Luther would not find such possible.

being the end of "a long healing process," Luther held that union to Christ through faith, not imitation of Christ, restores the image of God to us. Union with Christ, rather than being the endpoint of the sanctifying process, is the beginning given that "human agency is entirely enslaved to sin and incapable of anything good."[40] In this union God can accept the sinner. "For Luther," Herdt argues, "what is front and center here is our juridical relationship with God." Christ's righteousness is imputed to the sinner, yet the sinner remains in himself "fundamentally unlike God."[41] In placing union with Christ at the outset of the process, Herdt argues along lines similar to Milbank that Luther displays something like a monophysite Christology with its "physicalist" reductionism.[42] Union as precondition rather than culmination radically changes the meaning of justification as well: "participation in the divine life is no longer understood as requiring transformation of the human person."[43] At this point, other than the reduction to physicalist terms, I would argue that this is indeed Luther's understanding, and that it is in fact superior to Erasmus. Transformation is not humanly possible, but requires transformation by divine activity, in which the human person participates in the sense of the *vita passiva*. How could the human come to such a point as to participate in the divine life unless God first comes to the human and offers her participation in the divine life as a free gift? How could we possibly be prepared for participation in the divine life without already, in some sense, participating in it? This question is parallel to the question of the habituation gap, which as we noted earlier, Herdt does not really account for. Luther, on the other hand, does not have this problem. The Christian can begin to participate in the divine life, because, in Christ, the Christian has already been brought into the divine life by the agency of another.

The result of moving union with Christ to the beginning of justification, Herdt argues, is Luther's famous *simul justus et peccator*. But, Herdt asks, does this not just exchange one hypocrisy for another? Rather than pretending to act virtuous when we are not, we instead "put on" Christ and wear his righteousness while "God, audience of this cosmic drama, applauds the disguises."[44] What saves the latter from hypocrisy, Herdt argues, is for Luther simply the recognition that one is justified and righteous merely on the basis of union with Christ, while empirically remaining sinful. However, Herdt acknowledges, at least at this point in her account, that Luther's view of justification is not wholly forensic, as he does not make the strong separation between justification and sanctification that was to characterize the later Lutheran tradition.[45] Here Herdt acknowledges

40. *PV*, 175.
41. *PV*, 178.
42. *PV*, 178–9.
43. *PV*, 179.
44. *PV*, 179.
45. *PV*, 178. Herdt alludes to Alister McGrath's argument that prior to Protestantism, justification was seen as both an act and process, without distinguishing between justification and sanctification (390, n. 14). Unfortunately, Herdt does not maintain this nuanced account of Luther on justification throughout. Elsewhere in the book, when

the Finnish interpretation, particularly the work of Simo Peura, which develops the distinction Luther makes in his "Against Latomus" between grace and gift.[46] According to this distinction, grace refers to our forensic status before God, while the gift of faith works to effect an inner transformation. Grace is God's favor, God's good disposition toward the sinner for whom God was wrathfully disposed previously. The gift is "infused" faith and the indwelling presence of Christ, which works to gradually form the believer into the form of Christ. While grace is total and complete, the gift is partial and gradual. Thus, according to the famous distinction, proper human agency is passive before God (*coram Deo*) but active before humankind (*coram hominibus*).[47]

The *coram Deo*/*coram hominibus* distinction also makes it possible, Herdt argues, for Luther to reject habituation in terms of our relationship to God, while nonetheless preserving room for an Aristotelian habituation into *civic* virtue. That is, mimesis is appropriate when the merely temporal end of the common welfare of the state is in view. But in terms of our final and true end, civic virtue is inadequate. This move is made possible by the distinction between "a sincere heart and good will" in theological and temporal matters. A good heart in pursuit of the common welfare, while temporally good (i.e., good *coram hominibus*), is not good in the sight of God (*coram Deo*). While civic virtue requires the full engagement of human agency, right standing before God only comes via a full displacement of human agency to be replaced by the agency of Christ.[48] Attempts at forming one's own character will necessarily lead to a further entrenching of prideful self-reliance instead of the purity of will and intention that, Herdt claims, Luther is after.[49] But, Herdt asks, if justification is entirely God's unmerited gift, could there not be a place for pagan salvation in Luther? Her answer is no, given Luther's insistence that the Holy Spirit and faith come only by means of the Word and sacrament. However, even for this institutionally mediated faith to be effective it must be preceded by "explicit trust in and acceptance of our absolute dependence on God."[50]

The difficulties arising from a competitive account of the relation of divine and human agency can also be seen, according to Herdt, in Luther's famous distinction between the inner and the outer person in his "Freedom of a Christian (1520)." The outer person who belongs to the temporal and bodily sphere can experience

---

comparing Luther to the Jansenists on justification, she argues that Luther pulls justification and sanctification apart (236, 341).

46. Peura, "Christ as Favor and Gift," in *Union with Christ*, 42–69.

47. *PV*, 184–5.

48. *PV*, 183.

49. She says that while impurity of intention "casts a shadow over all the impure strivings of this life" for Augustine, "Luther goes beyond this, requiring that this purity be already fully present coram Deo and that even in the world of time human agency be exercised as the yielding of agency." *PV*, 189.

50. *PV*, 182–3.

growth and transformation, while the inner spiritual person takes somewhat "the traditional place of reason," guiding the outer person to perfection.[51] Absent the bodily and temporal, perfection would have been immediate upon receipt of the gift. But since the outer person remains, it is necessary that faith grows and increases over time. Herdt charges Luther with "groping for his own substitute for the infused virtues" at this point.[52]

Related to Luther's account of the virtues, Herdt argues, is his antieudaimonism. Luther rejects the eudaimonism that characterizes both Aristotle and Augustine given his suspicion that human agency, even after conversion, remains trapped always in a prideful self-centeredness.[53] Love of God remains always, this side of eternity, a partially disguised self-love.[54] But given such strong antieudaimonism in Luther, with its requirement of passive agency, Herdt wonders how he can allow for "gradual assimilation to Christ."[55] Herdt finds the marriage of passivity and divine agency extremely troubling, particularly as grounded in a competitive construal of divine and human agency resulting in a "paradoxical account" of progress in virtue.[56]

Herdt argues that Luther's paradox leads to disastrous political consequences. She demonstrates this with reference to his writings on education. Despite the impossibility of preparation for faith, Luther nonetheless promotes "external enticements" in preparing children to hear the preaching of the Word and in learning basic Christian doctrine and practice. Here habituation and the semblance of virtue can genuinely become the real thing, such that Herdt writes, "Luther on education can sound remarkably like Erasmus."[57] Nonetheless, for Luther, the promotion of habituation is always accompanied by the suspicion that the process may ultimately only serve to entrench prideful self-love. Pagan virtue is finally a hopeless contradiction in terms. The only sure way to true Christian righteousness and virtue is through the Word and sacrament, the only means by which the Holy Spirit works. In light of the social unrest that would characterize the later decades of Luther's life, this ultimate underlying suspicion of anything like pagan virtue would lead to the assertion of the need for a powerfully coercive government. Among entirely depraved humankind, the best that can be hoped for is imposition of order. Such order can only be achieved by coercing "virtuous" external behavior. Although this creates a false virtue that only further ingrains pride, in light of a disintegrating social order, Luther saw no other option. This goes against Luther's teaching regarding passivity, but without grace among the

51. *PV*, 187.
52. *PV*, 187.
53. *PV*, 188.
54. Herdt relies on Peura's interpretation of Luther for this point. See his "What God Gives Man Receives: Luther on Salvation," in *Union with Christ*, 76–94.
55. *PV*, 188.
56. *PV*, 188.
57. *PV*, 191.

pagans, what other alternative is there? Herdt writes, "In the end, then, Luther accepted the infantilizing practices of authoritarian state religion and the danger of hypocritical goodness because of his fear of disorder."[58]

Contemporary Relevance of Herdt's Genealogy

Herdt argues that contemporary Christian ethicists should move beyond the Augustinian suspicions uncovered in her narrative in order to more fruitfully engage with contemporary moral philosophers and find common ground in virtue ethics. On the whole, Herdt finds that Christian ethics has, indeed, moved in the right direction in the past few decades. There has been a shift in focus to the way communal narratives and practices form character, especially liturgical practices. Christian identity has also come to be seen as formed gradually through participation in such practices rather than "through an instantaneous evangelical rebirth."[59] Refusal of a sharp division between nature and grace has meant more space given to secondary causality in the understanding of divine and human agency, allowing space for the operations of grace within human agency.[60] Further, overemphasis on purity of motives and intentions has been overcome.[61] In light of these developments, Herdt is hopeful that a genuinely Augustinian account of habituation into virtue can be provided, absent Augustine's suspicions about pagan virtue.

Nonetheless, in spite of these developments, Herdt still discerns too much hesitancy with respect to virtue ethics among Christian ethicists, including a concern that it leads to a self-focused cultivation of character rather than a loving concern for one's neighbor.[62] Further, virtue ethics, it is charged, problematically understands the virtues as self-achieved possessions deserving of honor. In order to overcome these challenges, Christian ethicists have tended to draw a sharp distinction between Christian and other virtues, stressing the distinctive particularity of Christian virtue.[63] Coupled with this is a use of the language of virtue to provide hostile critiques of modernity.[64] Following many of the criticisms

---

58. *PV*, 192.

59. *PV*, 350. This will be a key difference between Herdt and Luther. For the former, we are what we do. Participation in practices makes us who we are. For Luther, we are what we hear. We are those who are addressed by God and God's address to us defines our identity. As a result, we begin within the space created by this Word, rather than ending there. "We do not become righteous by doing righteous deeds but, having been made righteous, we do righteous deeds." Luther, "Disputation against Scholastic Theology, 1517," thesis 40, LW 31:12.

60. *PV*, 351.

61. *PV*, 350.

62. She refers to Gilbert Meilaender's *The Theory and Practice of Virtue* (Notre Dame: University of Notre Dame, 1984) as an instance of such concern.

63. *PV*, 169.

64. *PV*, 346.

of Stanley Hauerwas voiced by Jeffrey Stout, Herdt argues that Christian ethicists have made an overly sharp distinction between Christian and non-Christian habituation.[65] The result has been a surrendering of all agency to churchly practice and an idealization of the church at the expense of acknowledging God's work outside its walls. While acknowledging that Stout has missed much of the nuance in Hauerwas's thought, she agrees that "Hauerwas's rhetoric does feed these tendencies at times."[66] Milbank, she argues, moves even further in this direction by simply equating modern and pagan, leaving no room for any sort of virtue ethics. For Milbank, Aristotle's magnanimous man is the epitome of pagan virtue, the heroic victorious warrior who stands in fundamental opposition to the Christian priority of peace.

In response to these lingering hyper-Augustinian anxieties, Herdt calls for a focus on habituation into virtue that less emphasizes Christian distinctiveness and finds possibility for such development outside of church practice. Virtue thus understood would be mimetic "in that it regards virtue as a finite reflection of God's infinite perfection."[67] Grace and nature would be brought more closely together as nature would be understood as "already fallen and in the process of being redeemed."[68] Therefore, humans can transform their character through action, and this does not exclude divine agency, even absent recognition of human

---

65. Jeffrey Stout, *Democracy and Tradition* (Princeton: Princeton University Press, 2004).

66. *PV*, 347. However, elsewhere Herdt points to aspects of Hauerwas's thought that she finds promising for her own project. She notes that his emphasis on "character" allows for an understanding of the moral agent over time, an agent who grows morally, contra Protestant emphasis on justification with its attendant inner/outer distinction and its individualistic and occasionalist understanding of the self. Character goes beyond this focus on the isolated moment of decision-making. Nonetheless, Herdt is still concerned with what she sees as the exclusively particularistic direction of much of Hauerwas's thought, especially as evident in his rhetoric. For a Christian particularism of the sort that appeals to Herdt, which is one that she sees as more open and engaged in the world and less interested in preserving identity, she instances Gregory, Mathewes, and Bretherton as cited earlier. Key to these accounts is recognizing shared common goods among Christians and non-Christians.

67. *PV*, 344. In discussing her understanding of virtue as performative, Herdt argues that her point about the example of Christ being infinite is analogous to Samuel Well's referring to the Christian life not according to script (provided by Scripture) but rather by improvisation based on Scripture. Against Kevin VanHoozer, who would give more place to the external authority of Scripture, Herdt argues that this move toward improvisation puts Christ and his "indefeasible example," rather than Scripture, at the center of focus (165, 168). Seeking a more expansive account of the way in which the character of Christians are developed, she argues that too narrow a focus on ecclesial practices in virtue formation neglects "Christ's lordship over the rest of creation" (170). Given the infinitude of God found in Christ, Herdt affirms with Stout the rejection of any fixed *telos*.

68. *PV*, 351.

action's dependency on God. Since divine grace is front and center, and since recognition of dependency on grace is not required, there is no need to make careful distinctions about identity. Instead, "we must trust wholly in God, even as we embrace the practices of the church and strive to develop our own moral agency."[69]

Response to Herdt

As discussed earlier, Herdt's critique of Luther in broadest terms is his purported enclosure within the late-medieval nominalist and voluntarist tradition, according to which human and divine agency are understood in competitive terms and freedom is understood as liberty of indifference. This framework leads to a stress on utter human passivity before the justifying work of God and relates this passivity problematically to sanctification. In fact, Herdt argues, it finally leads to a dangerous separation of justification and sanctification. Although she acknowledges Luther's emphasis on union with Christ as recovered by the Finnish interpreters of Luther, Herdt argues that placing union at the beginning of the sanctifying process requires that justification continue to be divided into forensic and effective aspects in such manner that God's agency swallows human agency and renders Luther's account of sanctification paradoxical in leaving no room for imitation of Christ, putting confession based on a pure intention in place of mimesis. His problematic distinction between inner and outer reality, Herdt further charges, and the requirement that virtue in the latter must be preceded by conscious acknowledgment of Christ in the former, leaves no place for grace in pagan life, and thus no room for true pagan virtue. The political consequences are an authoritarian state and a negative politics aimed at maintaining order among a corrupt and sinful humanity.

In responding to Herdt, I continue to argue that Luther holds justification and sanctification organically together, while still making the proper distinctions that prevent a tendency toward Pelagianism as found in Erasmus. Without either collapsing the distinction between justification and sanctification or separating them, Luther is still able to break free from the understanding of divine and human agency prominent in the nominalist and voluntarist traditions, allowing for

---

69. *PV*, 352. Herdt nicely summarizes her aims for contemporary Christian ethics in a subsequent essay, noting that Christians should affirm true, even if imperfect, secular virtues, in cases "when virtue is pursued for its own sake rather than for the sake of external goods, when those who seek virtue recognize in some fashion the dependent character of human moral agency, and when they are oriented towards proximate ends capable of being further directed towards our ultimate final end of communion with God. It is a conception which should allow Christian ethicists to move beyond a preoccupation with Christian distinctiveness and identity while furthering recent emphases on the social formation of Christian virtue." Herdt, "Back to Virtue," *SJT* 65.2 (2012), 225–6.

genuine human response to the prior activity of God. Further, I show that tied into Luther's accounts of agency and sanctification is an insistence that God's gracious activity is found also among pagans, a providential care that is seen most fully in Luther's teaching on the three institutions and its positive account of politics. However, a distinction, again without separation, between God's acts of grace in redemption and God's general providential care for creation must be upheld, just as must the distinction between justification and sanctification. Otherwise, the danger becomes that we serve the god of our imaginations rather than the God who addresses us in His Word in the concrete bodily form of Jesus of Nazareth.

God's Loving Provision for Pagans and Christians Alike

As we have seen, Herdt criticizes Luther for giving some place to civic virtue, but in such manner that it only serves to further entrench prideful self-deception. Nonetheless, she argues, for the sake of order, Luther supports the promotion of this type of virtue. In her view, then, Luther views politics in a wholly negative light as what ultimately proves to be a sinful response to sin, a view necessitated by his refusal of a place for graced human agency among the pagans. However, I will argue that Luther actually provides a more differentiated and subtle account of grace than Herdt ascribes to him. In fact, Luther does find God graciously at work among pagans,[70] but Luther's differentiated account of grace does not collapse this work straightforwardly into the work of God in the church. Luther's account, I argue, is theologically more faithful to the witness of Scripture and requires the distinctiveness that Herdt otherwise seeks to tame in thinkers such as Hauerwas. Nonetheless, for Luther, the distinctiveness lies not at the empirical level of the behavior, character, or action of the members of the church, either individually or communally, but instead in the distinctiveness of the address to which the church attends and witnesses to and the distinctiveness of the *one* addressing the church. As such, Luther stands alongside Hauerwas in upholding the particularity of the work of Christ in the church without thereby restricting God's work in Christ and the Holy Spirit to that location alone. Before turning to these larger questions, which are the questions of grace and its relation to nature in Luther's theology, and the questions of agency thereby entailed, it will be helpful to first address the specific place of pagan virtue in his thought.

Herdt finds no place for true pagan virtue in Luther's work, as outside of the activity of the Spirit in the church there is no grace. A graceless, and therefore necessarily virtue-less world outside the church, according to Herdt's Luther, requires the imposition of a falsely virtuous authoritarian order to reign in a totally depraved humanity. However, as demonstrated in the previous chapter, although Luther's political theology is clearly Augustinian, whereby authority serves to restrict sin, it is also true that Luther finds the political estate to be consistent with God's original will for creation, that is, politics still bears the promise, the promise

---

70. The title for the heading of this section follows Bonhoeffer's poem, "Christians and Heathens," in *Letters and Papers from Prison*, 461.

under which all humans, Christian or otherwise, stand. If this is the case, then, we can expect to find in Luther a place for God's gracious activity even among pagans. I argue that we can find such a place in Luther's thought, especially in his commentaries on the Psalms. A reading of Luther's 1534 commentary on Psalm 101 reveals that Luther does, in fact, find much place for God's gracious work in all the world, including among pagans and particularly in the instance of pagan government. Interestingly, in this account of government, Luther places focus on obedience in reception of the Word of God and its forming of human life in opposition to the imitative creativity which wants to "produce (*schaffen*) and make something new" in an attempt to be *sicut deus*.[71] Attentiveness to God's Word is being called out of oneself and one's self-chosen works and toward encounter with God and God's good works for one's neighbor. Luther finds that this Word, the Word found in the call of the needs of one's neighbor, is spoken and can be heard among the heathen too.[72]

Luther calls Psalm 101 "one of those which praise and thank God for the secular authorities."[73] As seen in the treatment of Psalm 127 in the previous chapter, here Luther insists that good government comes from the hand of God. "God distributes secular dominions (*weltliche herrschaft*) or kingdoms (*königreiche*) among the godless in the grandest and most wonderful way, just as He also lets the good sun and rain minister to the godless, without establishing the Word or worship of God among them or teaching or directing them through prophets as He did at Jerusalem among His people." Even if it is misused by the godless, Luther argues that God still "calls this secular government of the godless His ordinance (*ordnung*) and creation."[74] As such, Luther holds that Christians have much to learn from the heathen. As he argues, again with reference to government, on such matters they speak and teach very well. He states that God has made temporal government subject to reason, given that its concerns are properly those things that God has placed under human dominion (Gen. 2:8ff.). Since God establishes and preserves secular dominion, He "casts great intelligence, wisdom, languages, and oratorical ability" among the godless. Even fallen pagans hold onto reason. In fact, their reason is of such a sort as to make "Christians look like mere children, fools and beggars by comparison." As such, Luther encourages those who would learn to become wise in the affairs of government (*weltlichen Regiment*) to attend to "heathen books and writings," as they, like other temporal goods, have been given and preserved by God among the heathen "at all times."[75] In a remarkable passage, Luther writes:

> I am convinced that God gave and preserved such heathen books as those of the poets and the histories, like Homer, Vergil, Demosthenes, Cicero, Livy,

---

71. "Psalm 101 (1534–35)," LW 13:196.
72. On this point, see Stefan Heuser, "The Public Witness of Good Works: Lutheran Impulses for Political Ethics," *Journal of Lutheran Ethics* 6.7 (2006), 2.1, 5 and 3.1.3, 19.
73. He refers to Psalms 127 and 128 as among "many others" that do likewise.
74. "Psalm 101 (1534–35)," LW 13:193.
75. Ibid., 199.

and afterwards the fine old jurists—as He has also given and preserved other temporal goods among the heathen and godless at all times—that the heathen and godless, too, might have their prophets, apostles, and theologians or preachers for the secular government . . . Thus they had their Homer, Plato, Aristotle, Cicero, Ulpian and others, even as the people of God had their Moses, Elijah, Isaiah, and others; and their emperors, kings, and princes, like Alexander, Augustus, etc., were their Davids and Solomons.[76]

Luther has no qualms with these books as they are directed to "virtue, laws, and wisdom with respect to temporal goods, honor, and peace on earth." In this sense, contra Herdt, Luther's concern is not purity of intention, but rather making the proper distinctions within the one work of God in creation-salvation history. This logic allows Luther to keep the world always under the rule of Christ, without turning Christ into a principle or an ideal.

Luther likewise notes the possibility of pagan virtue in the third part of "On Councils and the Church (1539)." There he argues that although the second table of the Ten Commandments serves for the sanctification of the church, it is also the case that non-Christians too carry out these works. In fact, Luther warns against identifying the church by its obedience to the second table, given that "heathens too practice these works and indeed at times appear holier than Christians; yet their actions do not issue from the heart purely and simply, for the sake of God, but they search for some other end because they lack a real faith in and a true knowledge of God."[77] Nonetheless, God's works carried out in accord with the last seven commandments, which is to say, carried out within the institutions, can be implied to be understood by Luther as "means of grace."[78] God is graciously at work in pagan life.

The place that Luther gives to pagan virtue can also be understood in relation to the distinction he makes between the "holy" and the "blessed/saved" in the "Confession Concerning Christ's Supper (1528)." There, in a condemnation of the monasticism of his time, Luther argues that the "office of priest, the estate of marriage, [and] the civil government" are the only true holy orders and "religious institutions established by God."[79] All three are holy because they "are found in God's Word and commandment; and whatever is contained in God's Word must by holy, for God's Word is holy and sanctifies everything connected with it and involved in it."[80] However, although all of these are holy and good, none of them

---

76. Ibid., 198–9.
77. "On the Councils and the Church, 1539," LW 41:167.
78. So argues Bayer, "Nature and Institution," in *FR*, 112. Bayer suggest that Luther nonetheless adds the proviso quoted earlier, regarding this obedience as unreliable as a mark of the true church, in order to "establish a clear distinction between the creating and sustaining of the world, in which God makes use of the activity of the heathen, and its redemption, which is communicated to us in assurance and salvation through the word of Christ." I pick up this theme again in more detail in the following chapter.
79. "Confession Concerning Christ's Supper, 1528," LW 37:364.
80. Ibid., 365.

are a means of salvation, for salvation belongs to faith in Jesus Christ alone. Luther continues, "For to be holy and to be saved are two entirely different things. We are saved through Christ alone; but we become holy both through this faith and through these divine foundations and orders. Even the godless may have much about them that is holy without being saved thereby. For God wishes us to perform such works to his praise and glory."[81] In conflating holiness and salvation in her interpretation of Luther, Herdt fails to see that Luther does in fact give place for pagan virtue (or in his terminology, "good works"),[82] but virtue is not efficacious for salvation. That is the work of Christ alone, which must be passively suffered by the believer in faith. Reinhard Hütter, in distinguishing between saving knowledge of God and living in God's good world writes, "There might be potential and partial knowledge of God apart from these practices and from doctrine [i.e., the marks of the church], yet saving knowledge of God—the knowledge we suffer by being drawn into God's triune life—is the reception of the gospel through which the Holy Spirit recreates us."[83] So then, it is possible according to Luther for non-Christians to perform good works in politics and economics (i.e., in service to God's promise to care for and govern God's creatures) that bring "praise and glory"

81. Ibid. Bayer suggests that the meaning of the distinction between "holy" and "blessed" can be further elaborated with reference to Luther's exposition of Psalm 127 (1524), where he utilizes Aristotle's four causes, arguing that pagan thinkers can have genuine insight into the material and formal causes of politics and economics, but not the final and efficient cause. Bayer, "Nature and Institution," in *FR*, 114.

82. Luther favors the use of the language of good works over that of virtue, given that the former places more stress on activity in cooperation with God's own work, whereas the virtue discourse tends to speak of a *habitus* that belongs to the doer as a possession. See, for example, Luther's treatment of the "fruits of the spirit" in the 1519 lectures on Galatians, where he argues against those who interpret the fruits to be "qualities of their own that inhere subjectively in the soul," rather than "living works of the spirit that are spread out through the whole man." "Lectures on Galatians 1519," LW 27:373. Given his rejection of created grace, as discussed more fully later, Luther necessarily always sees good works as a response to the calling Word of God, not as propelled by a quest for virtue formation. Nonetheless, as Herdt is also keen to do, Luther does not denigrate pagan good works, but finds that even in the works of unbelievers God's gracious activity is present. Stefan Heuser, in describing Luther's understanding of good works, writes, "The citizen who is called to do good works does not have to be a Christian in the confessional sense. Indeed, he can be anything, or less than anything, like a Samaritan. God's justice reaches into the world though mouths and hands that it calls to service. In doing so, God's *verbum externum* (external word) makes all people equal . . . Good works are possible and real *extra muros ecclesiae*, not because they are the possibility of human beings, but because they are the possibility of God who makes human beings instruments to reach into the world." Heuser, "Public Witness," 1.1, 14.

83. Reinhard Hütter, "The Church: The Knowledge of the Triune God: Practices, Doctrine, Theology," in *Knowing the Triune God: The Work of the Spirit in the Practices of the Church*, ed. James Joseph Buckley and David S. Yeago (Cambridge: Eerdmans, 2001), 32-3.

to God. Luther certainly divorces such works from merit, as only Christ alone is worthy of salvation, but outside the language game of justification there is no reason to posit a strong distinction between the good works of Christians and non-Christians, as the works of the latter may often indeed be more virtuous, and in that sense, may testify to God's Word in creation more faithfully than the good works of the church. As such, good works as instituted by God, even when carried out by non-Christians, are "equivalent (not analogous) to God's people and its political worship."[84]

Even though political authority is a manifestation of God's gracious gift to pagans and Christians alike,[85] it is only the latter who can give appropriate articulation to this gift, even if the former still witness to this truth in deed. In the commentary on Psalm 101, Luther argues, given that the establishment of authority is by the will of God, the political authorities "should learn to know that this is a special gift of God and not a matter of their own wisdom or ability."[86] But here lies the greatest danger that Luther finds coming from those to whom authority has been given. While the "pagan prophets" or wisdom writers know the limits of human ability in matters of worldly affairs, they are not able to name the true source of the establishment and maintenance of the temporal regiment. He does not deny that pagans are capable of good works, that is, truly good works and not just mere semblances thereof. However, they are incapable of naming them correctly, which is a task that can only be carried out in the church where the Word is made articulate. Instead, the pagan philosophers call God's directing "fortune" or "luck," hence showing that "even they conclude that no one has ever become a great man through his own powers but only by a special secret inbreathing or imparting of the gods."[87] Without the

---

84. Hans G. Ulrich, "God's Commandments and Their Political Presence: Notes of a Tradition on the 'Ground' of Ethics," *Studies in Christian Ethics* 23.1 (2010), 50.

85. In an interesting "Table Talk," Luther was asked a question by his interlocutor concerning the difference between Samson, who was strong from the Spirit, and the great strength of a pagan like Julius Caesar. Luther answered, "The Spirit of Samson was the Holy Spirit, who makes holy and who produces actions which are obedient to God and serve him. We can also speak of the Spirit among the heathen; that is, God also acts among them, but this is not sanctifying action." LW 54:79. Here we see that Herdt's claim that Luther restricts the work of the Spirit to Word and sacrament in the church is inaccurate. Nonetheless, Luther does distinguish between the work of the Spirit in the church and the work of the Spirit in the wider preservation, care and governance of creation and history. As we show later, much of this distinction is necessitated by the dangers of Pelagian understandings of divine and human cooperation. See also Regin Prenter on Luther's understanding of the work of the Spirit: "When he reads the first chapter of the Bible the believer must be content to hear that this Spirit also has a work to do with God's other creation, with the grass in the field, with the birds under the heavens, and with all that exists." Prenter, *Spiritus Creator: Luther's Concept of the Holy Spirit*, trans. John M. Jensen (Philadelphia: Muhlenberg Press, 1953), 195.

86. "Psalm 101 (1534–35)," LW 13:147.

87. Ibid., 201.

articulating Word of the church, calling proper attention to the one Lord who alone is good, the danger is always near that those in authority will ascribe their success to their own wisdom and ability, or they may even acknowledge the dependency of their agency, but not rightly acknowledge the one on whom it depends. The call of the pagan prophets for acknowledgment of dependence on good fortune or the "imparting of the gods" will not prove sufficient to call those in authority back from arrogant self-attribution. This opens up the door to the whole problematic of original sin, whereby humans do not want to let God be God. Even though the "offices of princes and officials are divine and right . . . those who are in them and use them are usually of the devil." Luther continues, "This is caused by the evil, depraved nature, which cannot stand success; that is, it cannot use honor, power, and authority in a divine way." Instead, they "always want to be God themselves when they ought to be God's maid (*dienerin*)."[88] In Satanic fashion (Is. 14:12) the handmaid to God seeks to rule in God's place.[89] For Luther, the seriousness of this sin is such that it cannot be overcome by habit or the acquisition of virtues, even if understood in the context of dependence, but rather requires being subject to the yoke of discipleship to Christ. Without such discipleship, one remains a wanderer like Cain, and in the worst instances becomes "Belial," that is, one who refuses to be subjected to a yoke, "just as the Antichrist exalts himself and places himself over everything that is called God."[90] In light of the need to be under the yoke of Christ, Luther calls obedience (rather than Aristotle's magnanimity) "the crown and glory of all virtues."[91] In the chapter on the three institutions to follow, we will spell out the form of this obedience more concretely. First, however, we turn to Herdt's criticisms of Luther's understanding of agency.

Luther's Account of Agency: Progressive Transition or Disruptive Transformation?

So as not to be misled by the subtitle of this section, we first acknowledge that Luther does not have "the problem of agency" such as it is set up in Herdt's account. Luther's insistence on remaining concrete and avoiding abstraction ensures he does not set up the question of the relationship of God, the world, and humans in such manner that what is typically referred to as the "problem of agency" comes into play. Rather, we could say that Luther views these matters not in terms of subject and object, but rather in terms of a living interaction where none of the constitutive elements can be abstractly separated from one another. Rather than humans and the world as "objects" of the acting "subject,"

---

88. Ibid., 213; WA 51. 254, 20.
89. Cf. "Psalm 101 (1534–35)," LW 13:163, "The poison of original sin comes to us by birth; it stems from the bite of the apple, whereby the devil made us shrewd and like God. This is the reason why fools do not want to be fools . . . They run the world. God plagues us with such people." See also p. 196.
90. Ibid., 178.
91. Ibid., 176.

God, Luther views reality as God's address to creatures through creatures. God is never so transcendent from the world such that the world can be understood as a discrete entity alongside God, nor is God's immanence such that the absolute division between Creator and creation is lessened.[92] As such, it is simply inaccurate to ascribe the sort of univocalist relationship between God and the world that Herdt ascribes to Luther. Instead, Luther's thought is best understood according to a different grammar from that of agency and causality. To begin to understand this, we can turn to anthropologist Tim Ingold's treatment of creative activity. Against hylomorphic conceptions of making whereby an agent willfully imposes his or her intentions (form) on an inert, lifeless object (matter), Ingold seeks "an ontology that assigns primacy to the processes of formation as against their final products and to the flows and transformations of materials as against states of matter." He defines "things" as "a 'going on'—or better, a place where several goings on become entwined." In this specific sense, people too are things. Criticizing the transformation of things into objects, he writes,

> In the very first move that isolates these things [the materials used in building, gardening, cooking, painting] as objects . . . theorists of material culture have contrived to rupture the very flows that brought them to life. The "problem of agency" is thus one that they have created for themselves, born of the attempt to re-animate a world already rendered lifeless by an exclusive focus on the "objectness" of things. Theirs is a world not of things that exist in the throwing, but in which the die is already cast. It is indeed striking that the more theorists have to say about agency, the less they seem to have to say about life. To rewrite the life of things as the agency of objects is to effect a double reduction, of things to objects, and of life to agency. And the life of this reductive logic lies in the hylomorphic model.[93]

Ingold is insistent that things not become lifeless through a rendering of them in terms of a subject–object schema. Rather, both "agents" and "things" must be seen

---

92. See William Placher *The Domestication of Transcendence: How Modern Thinking about God Went Wrong* (Louisville, KY: Westminster John Knox Press, 1996), 119. Placher argues that Luther is in agreement with Aquinas regarding two different orders of causal efficacy. Further, he argues that for Luther, like Aquinas, there is never a question of *how* God's providence works. The relation between the two orders of causality for both theologians remains unknowable and unimaginable (126). As such, Placher argues, Luther does not view human and divine agency in competitive terms. Accordingly, "For Luther, God's grace was not one cause among others to be fit into a world-system philosophically understood" (148). Cf. Kathryn Tanner, *God and Creation in Christian Theology: Tyranny or Empowerment* (Oxford: Blackwell Publishers, 1988); and David B. Burrell, *Freedom and Creation in Three Traditions* (Notre Dame: University of Notre Dame Press, 1993).

93. Tim Ingold, "The Textility of Making," *Cambridge Journal of Economics* 34.1 (January 2010), 96-7. On the question of hylomorphism and a rejection of the Scotist *haeccitas*, see Milbank, *BSO*, 265-9.

in their interaction. To view either as they are in themselves is impossible, since such "in themselves" is an abstraction that necessarily distorts their reality.

In order that such ontology not lead to an impersonal God or a deification of the world, to God as a force or the world as necessary to God's becoming, it is requisite that Ingold's account be qualified theologically. Further, it is necessary to allow space for truly human passivity if one is to avoid meritorious accounts of justification that would at the same time be a denial of God's *creatio ex nihilo*. In turning to Luther's famous (infamous?) metaphor of the human as a "beast of burden," we find just such a theologically qualified account. The metaphor is found in "The Bondage of the Will (1526)," where Luther asserts, "The human will is placed between [God and the devil] like a beast of burden. If God rides it, it wills and goes where God wills . . . If Satan rides it, it wills and goes where Satan wills; nor can it choose to run to either of the two riders or to seek him out, but the riders themselves contend for the possession and control of it."[94] Although often interpreted in a deterministic fashion, Bernd Wannenwetsch has suggested that this metaphor can be fruitfully extended beyond its original soteriological context to include the framework of anthropology and ethics, thus providing illumination of Luther's understanding of divine and human cooperative interaction.[95] Wannenwetsch argues that Luther's understanding of will as presented here should not be viewed as "some kind of instance in man, but rather as a kind of medieval designation of human 'personhood'. The will stands *pars pro toto* for the human overall."[96] Given this interpretation, it is not inaccurate to suggest that in his use of this metaphor, Luther describes humans passively as the "things" wherein the "goings on" of history—God calling creation back in redemption against Satanic forces—occurs. In this sense, humans are the battlefield, the place of this going on. In Wannenwetsch's terms, the human is the "found-between-being" (Dazwischen-gestellt-sein).[97] However, for Luther the passivity of humans described in this metaphor results from their bondage to sin after the Fall. As such, the metaphor in this sense is limited to soteriology, from the hopeless situation of humans wherein their life *is* finally determined. But the promise of the Gospel is deliverance. Humans are in bondage until they are made cooperators of God, until they have been freed from enslavement to the devil. And it is in this sense, argues Wannenwetsch, as the metaphor extends out to the framework of anthropology and ethics, that its fruitfulness becomes evident. It is here that the focus is on the "mounted beast" who "wills and goes where God wills." As one freed to freely do the will of God, the mounted beast comes into view here as almost "the *telos* of Christian ethics and of the Christian

94. "The Bondage of the Will, 1526," LW 33:65–6.
95. Bernd Wannenwetsch, "Zwischen Schindmähre und Wildpferd: Luthers Reittier-Metapher ethisch betrachtet," *Zeitschrift der Luther-Gesellschaft* 65.1 (1994), 22–33. All translations in the text to follow are mine.
96. Ibid., 24.
97. Ibid., 25.

ethos."⁹⁸ Whereas soteriologically the focus is on the "becoming-possessed" of the mounted beast, ethically the focus is on the "'going-riding' (*Los-reiten*) as the specific context of action of the rider and horse."⁹⁹ But this refers to the art, as Wannenwetsch notes, of riding (Equestrik), in which the "mounted beast" is neither merely a nag who goes passively and inattentively to where she is led nor a wild horse who goes wherever she wills, purportedly determining her own course without noticing the rider mounted atop. Rather, "the constructive question can no longer be designated, whether the ethical practice (Praxis) of Christians results from a free will to the good, or whether it is constituted by the shape of the tutelage of the unfree will by God, but rather how man is therein guided by the free will of God, freely to will and to do, what he wills."¹⁰⁰ Importantly, the horse and rider always remain together in the art of riding. The rider does not simply indicate a direction or give instruction to the horse, leaving the latter free to then pursue her own course.¹⁰¹ Rather, the rider rides the horse, but in such a way that the horse freely moves and the rider responds to the movement of the horse. In an important sense, there is a free interplay between the two, such that neither is absorbed into the other, but also, at its height, the art of riding does not allow for a separation of one from the other either. For Luther, this sort of interaction of human and divine agency takes place paradigmatically in the sanctifying practices of the church as set forth in the second table of the Ten Commandments (which pagans, too, can also participate in).

It must be granted, the metaphor will not stand up to all criticism. Rather, the point is that Luther does not set up agency in terms of divine and human competition, but rather describes it in terms of an interplay that can never be fully grasped or mapped. Therefore, the proper grammar for the conception is metaphor, just as in the case of the union of the believer with Christ, Luther employs the bridal metaphor. Again, Luther's employment of metaphor proves capable of opening up paths that are not made available when the conceptuality employed is of a more ontological type. Importantly, this also reveals how the form of Luther's theology, his "method," follows the form of Scripture.¹⁰²

Elsewhere in "The Bondage of the Will" Luther describes the sense in which humans can cooperate with God, and he does not restrict such cooperation to instances in which the Spirit has been given to believers. He argues that humans have been left with their own choice concerning the things beneath humans, but

---

98. Ibid., 27.
99. Ibid., 28.
100. Ibid., 30.
101. "God does not come into consideration alone as the basis of a Christian ethos, as the setter of the norm and task; he is not only the goal in a teleologically oriented ethical practice, but is always constitutively involved as an agent of the interplay in its enactment." Ibid., 32.
102. On the metaphorical nature of Scripture, see Brian Brock, *Singing the Ethos of God*, 270–6.

even here humans can only act in cooperation with God. "Here he reigns and is lord, as having been left in the hand of his own counsel. Not that God so leaves him as not to cooperate with him in everything, but he has granted him the free use of things according to his own choice, and has not restricted him by any laws or injunctions."[103] So while acknowledging a sense in which humans and God always cooperate, Luther nonetheless restricts this language to "nature." But, as he writes, "We are not disputing about nature but about grace, and we are not asking what we are on earth, but what we are in heaven before God."[104] When it comes to grace, or more precisely, to the question of human agency being delivered from the powers of death, sin and evil and freed for a life that freely "wills and goes where God wills," then cooperation is the wrong grammar, as here, "no one can receive anything except what is given him from heaven (John 3:27)."[105] This life with Christ must not only begin with divine initiative, but requires the very presence of the Holy Spirit. Luther explains this in his refutation of Erasmus, who in an attempt to exegete Jesus's statement, "No one comes to me unless my Father draws him (John 6:44)," claims that God draws us like we draw a sheep, by holding out a green twig to it. Using this simile, Erasmus argues that there is a power in humans to follow God's calling. But Luther argues that the simile does not work when applied to this passage:

> For God holds out not only one of his good things, but all of them, and even Christ his Son himself, yet not a man follows unless the Father inwardly does something else and draws in some other way; instead, the whole world persecutes the Son whom he holds out to it. The simile fits very well the case of the godly, who are already sheep and know God their Shepherd; for they, living in the Spirit and moved by him, follow wherever God wills and whatever he holds out to them. But the ungodly does not come even when he hears the Word, unless the Father draws and teaches him inwardly, which He does by pouring out the Spirit. There is then another "drawing" than the one that takes place outwardly; for then Christ is set forth by the light of the Spirit, so that a man is rapt way to Christ with the sweetest rapture, and rather yields passively to God's speaking, teaching, and drawing than seeks and runs himself.[106]

Again, the emphasis on passivity here guards against Pelagian understandings of soteriology. However, this passive moment, where God through Christ in the Spirit comes to us is immediately followed (logically) by the highest activity, an activity that yet remains always a response to the ongoing activity of the present Christ mediating the Triune God to the believer in faith. In fact, according to Luther humans are created and re-created for the very purpose that God "might work

---

103. "The Bondage of the Will, 1526," LW 33:119.
104. Ibid., 284–5.
105. Quoted in ibid., 284.
106. Ibid., 286.

in us and we might cooperate with him." However that we cooperate with God does not negate that humans do not "do anything toward becoming a creature, and after [they] are created [they] neither do nor attempt to do anything toward remaining a creature." The same is true in the case of re-creation by the work of the Holy Spirit. But having been created/re-created, humans are then divine cooperators. Crucially, in both cases, whether the cooperation occurs according to God's "general omnipotence" (as according to the grammar of creation and preservation, i.e., "nature") or "by the special virtue of his Spirit" (as according to the grammar of justification and sanctification), for Luther the divine activity is always foregrounded, without obliterating human activity.[107] Further, this distinction between God's work in creation and preservation and God's work in redemption within the one activity of God is crucial in order that soteriology not be described falsely according to the grammar of cooperation and in order that the particularity of Christ not be idealized and principlized.

Creation and Redemption

Herdt, in seeking for a continuity of the self in the form of character, implicitly collapses (rather than distinguishing in an inseparable intertwining) creation and redemption. As we have seen, Luther's conception of human participation in the divine drama is not an experience of continuity, but rather one of rescue, characterized by rupture and discontinuity. Thus, we turn to Luther's anthropology in order to clarify how Luther can affirm pagan good works in a particular sense (as argued earlier), while simultaneously distinguishing and affirming the distinctiveness of the work of Christ among believers without either separating this saving work from Christ's work in creation and preservation or placing the two on a continuum such that the one is absorbed into the other.

Central to Herdt's argument is a denial of "a simple dichotomy between nature and grace" in favor of "manifold forms of grace-enabled human agency."[108] On one level, certainly Luther would want to say something like this. For him creation is an unmerited, gracious act of God, as is God's ongoing work of preserving God's creation. For Luther, human life is shot through by the present activity of the living God. Nothing could be more impossible to Luther than a realm of "pure nature." Furthermore, Luther posits no separation of the grace of God in creation from the grace of God in the sending of Jesus Christ to deliver the fallen creation (redemption). However, it would be a mistake to simply identify them. As Robert Jenson argues, in Scripture creation and grace are not simply the same thing.[109] However, when one follows Luther regarding the oneness of the Word of God, creation and redemption (nature and grace) can be inseparably joined

---

107. Ibid., 242–3.
108. *PV*, 97.
109. Robert Jenson, "Triune Grace," in *The Gift of Grace*, 29.

without identification. Jenson writes, "God's act to create us and his act of what the tradition calls 'grace' are but two addresses of one word, two utterances in a single conversation of God with his creature." The two "are related as events in a narrative."[110] In a decisive difference from Herdt, who follows Erasmus in viewing grace as working "through a process in which realities already present, though as yet unknown and unacknowledged, are gradually rendered explicit," Luther views the relation of creation and redemption, not as united in that the latter is the gradual "rendering explicit" of the former, but rather in terms of a massive rupture that is nonetheless not a tearing apart, because each remains circumscribed in the one story of God's dealing with God's creatures in both judgment and grace by means of his Word. Crucially, for Luther this one Word of God cannot be abstracted from the particular name Jesus Christ. As such, Luther avoids any talk of a general grace before Christ, or Christ himself as a special grace. Rather, God's gracious Word to humans, in creation and redemption, is always the same Word who is the Son. This unity is found only in the Word, not in the life of the believer. On the contrary, the believer experiences her life, the life of faith, as one of discontinuity, as one of death and resurrection, characterized by a continual return to baptism. This experience follows upon the fact for Luther that Satan and sin cannot be enfolded into a conceptuality aimed at the oneness and unity of God. Rather, again, this unity is something Christians have faith in, not something that can be grasped or possessed in experience. Further, it is crucial to maintain this distinction if redemption is not to fall under the capacity of any creature, such that salvation is a sort of creaturely self-realization. In other words, the distinction within the one Word between creation and redemption safeguards against Pelagian accounts of human agency and preserves the radicality of the Word that creates ex nihilo.[111]

An account of grace in Luther's theology helps to clarify these matters. Luther explicates grace in terms of its Trinitarian dimensions. It is in these dimensions, argues Regin Prenter, that God's one Word as the two addresses of creation and redemption can be seen in its contours. He writes, "That Luther speaks in Trinitarian terms about creation means first of all that creation and redemption to him are part of the same all embracing act of God."[112] However, Prenter argues, the unity of the act is a "testimony," and not a rational fact to be grasped and comprehended. The unity can only make any sense at all with reference to the living presence of the Holy Trinity in the midst of the world inhabited by human beings. As such, Luther centers his treatment of God's gracious activity toward us on the work of the Holy Spirit, who makes the Trinity present for us. In fact, for Luther, in speaking of the grace of God, he speaks of the Holy Spirit being given

110. Ibid., 30.
111. For treatment of this point, particularly with reference to the *nouvelle theologie*'s attempts at overcoming the distinction between nature and supernature, see Jenson, *Systematic Theology*, vol. 2, 68.
112. Prenter, *Spiritus Creator*, 194.

to the believer. In his "Confession Concerning Christ's Supper (1528)," Luther describes how the believer receives the Triune God:

> The Father gives himself to us, with heaven and earth and all the creatures, in order that they may serve and benefit us . . . The Son himself subsequently gave himself and bestowed all his works, sufferings, wisdom, and righteousness, and reconciled us to the Father, in order that restored to life and righteousness, we might also now have the Father and his gifts . . . But because this grace would benefit no one if it remained so profoundly hidden and could not come to us, the Holy Spirit comes and gives himself to us also, wholly and completely.[113]

So for Luther, the grace Christians receive is God Himself in all God's fullness. As such, Christian love is not a created habit, an effect of the work of the Spirit, but rather following Peter Lombard, Luther views the Christian's love as the Holy Spirit himself, the same Spirit who makes Christ present in faith.[114] In making this move, Prenter notes, "Luther no longer thinks of the Holy Spirit in terms of the scholastic tradition as a transcendent cause of a new (supernatural) nature in man producing infused grace (i.e. *caritas*—the sublimated idealistic urge). The Holy Spirit is instead proclaimed as the real presence of God."[115] For Luther then, the Christian life is not characterized by the development or mimetic putting into action of virtue graciously received in order to one day find oneself fit for God's presence, but rather is a suffering the Spirit's work of conformation to Christ by remaining in the places where the gracious presence of the Triune God has been promised to humans. This has massive implications for how one understands the divine and human relation, and the related question of their respective agencies. If the place of the Holy Spirit in the Christian life speaks of God's presence, then the Spirit can no longer be understood in terms of transcendental causality, undermining causal accounts of justification and sanctification. Instead, sanctification names the political significance of justification, or the form of justification in the institutions.[116]

Here is also the place to respond to Herdt's charge that Luther seems to be grasping after something like the infused virtues. On the contrary, Luther has no need for the infused virtues, not because he has no place for sanctification, but rather because of the sufficiency of Christ. The need for the infused virtues would suggest that something is still lacking and that Christ and his Spirit are insufficient and would improperly divide the giver and the gift, or to put it more precisely, to suggest that the gift is something other than the giver. For Luther, perfection attained through virtue is not the goal, but rather remaining in the

---

113. "Confession Concerning Christ's Supper, 1528," LW 37:366.
114. Simo Peura, "Christ as Favor and Gift," in *Union with Christ*, 48.
115. Prenter, *Spiritus Creator*, 18–19.
116. Wannenwetsch refers to sanctification as "the empowerment for political life." *Political Worship*, 11.

presence of Christ who has already accomplished everything. The goal for Luther is not so much something we move toward but someone we remain in. Humans are transformed as a result of being in the presence of Christ in the Spirit, not as a result of something other than Christ that the Spirit gives. That Christ has already given everything and is given to the believer for Luther means that there could be no possible need for infused virtues. Further, to affirm that God's grace in justification means God's presence eschews any neo-Platonic participationism whereby Christians partake in some idealistic aspect of the divine nature.[117] Instead, the Christian life takes the form of a continual return to one's participation in the death and resurrection of Jesus Christ, which is to say, to one's baptism.

There is certainly an eschatological immediacy here, which pushes against too strong a separation of the already being redeemed creation as we presently experience it and the promise of a new heavens and a new earth. Prenter captures this immediacy in Luther's eschatology well, writing, "In connection with this view of God salvation is understood as something present and immediate in the presence of God and not as a remote goal toward which one is gradually struggling by the aid of grace. Grace is the real presence of God himself. Where God is, there the whole salvation is already present."[118] As demonstrated so clearly in the promising command given at the Lord's Table to "take and eat," so in his understanding of the work of the Holy Spirit, Luther stresses that the advent is now, yet in such a way that the passing age has not yet disappeared. "The Spirit is the presence of the living God himself in his all-embracing, eschatological act, with man in Christ Jesus as the new sphere of life in the midst of our death."[119] The advent is now, but it is now in the midst of death. Without the continual presence of the Spirit, Christians would fall back into the bondage from which the completed work of Christ delivered them. And it is in learning to remain in the places of God's promised presence *for us* that one can speak of gradual progress in sanctification. However, the language of remaining suggests that for Luther the proper way to describe sanctification is not in terms of progress, but rather in terms of return.[120]

Agency and the Self

Central to the self in Herdt's conception, of course, is the underlying account of agency that attaches to it. Herdt argues throughout that a primary difficulty with the "hyper-Augustinian" tradition generally, and with Luther specifically, is the positing of a single order of causality in which divine and human activity stand

---

117. Jenson, "Triune Grace," 21.
118. Prenter, *Spiritus Creator*, 25.
119. Ibid., 191.
120. Hence Gilbert Meilaender's statement, "Life is not the gradual development of a virtuous self; it is a constant return to the promise of grace." *The Theory and Practice of Virtue*, 107.

in competition. However, in the case of Luther, Herdt's charge suggests a failure to take into account the particular language game under which Luther is giving an account of agency. When it comes to the language game of justification, as we have shown earlier, Luther does, in fact, stress divine agency to the exclusion of human agency (although, again, it is necessary to stress that his grammar is not one of cause–effect, agency, etc., but of narrative interactions). However, this is precisely because the act of justification is a uniquely divine act that Luther often parallels to the act of *creatio ex nihilo*. As Bayer argues, Luther does not include human agency in his account of justification because that would be to "ascribe one and the same level to human and divine acts."[121] For Luther, that humans cannot play a role in justification is not due to an assumption that such action would competitively encroach upon divine action, but rather that as an act exclusively of God's work, justification does not ever enter into the order of primary and secondary causality. Like creation, justification for Luther does not follow a cause–effect logic. To ask after the human being's role in justification is a grammatical error, just as it would be an error to ask about the role of humans in creating the heavens and the earth. Justification, like creation, is simply not the *kind* of thing humans do. In this, justification must be distinguished from other divine acts, such as preserving cities and households, in which God acts as a primary agent while humans act as secondary agents. Outside the language game of justification, Luther is happy to speak of divine and human cooperation,[122] but in such a manner that the respective agencies are not univocally predicated.

Luther brings in a third element notably absent from Herdt's account of agency, and that is the role of Satan, the realm of the demonic. This "third" necessarily complicates Luther's account of agency. It also places his anthropology squarely in the midst of the history of salvation, meaning he gives a dramatic–narrative account of humanity rather than a static and formal account. The difference between the two is mapped onto the difference between theology and philosophy in Luther's "Disputation Concerning Man (1536)." There, he argues that philosophy defines humans as "an animal having reason, sensation, and body."[123] However, philosophy fails to grasp the efficient and final cause. It mistakenly "posits no other final cause than the peace of this life, and does not know that the efficient cause is God the creator." Theology, on the other hand, "from the fullness of its wisdom defines man as whole and perfect."[124] It defines humans as made in the image of God, but subject to the devil, sin, and death after the fall, a subjection from which humans can only be freed by the Son of God. Therefore, theology, which is attentive to the story of God with God's creatures, arrives at the understanding, via the history of creation and redemption as given in the Word, which reads, "Man is justified

121. Bayer, "Freedom?: The Anthropological Concepts in Luther and Melanchthon Compared," *HTR* 91.4 (1998), 385.
122. Lohse, *Martin Luther's Theology*, 242.
123. "The Disputation Concerning Man, 1536," LW 34:137.
124. Ibid., 138.

by faith."[125] Hence, bondage to sin and the freedom of faith are core elements in Luther's anthropology. His understanding does not begin with the sole individual, or even humanity in community with itself, but rather is shot through by the awareness that humans stand always "between God and the devil."[126] This is a key element, especially the Scriptural witness to human enslavement to principalities and powers, and therefore the need for a deliverer, which is lacking in Herdt's account of mimetic virtue acquisition.

The depth of the problem of sin in Luther's understanding of humanity is also seen in the anthropological explication he gives in his "Lectures on Genesis": the human "is a rational animal which has a heart that imagines."[127] As Bayer demonstrates, in this definition we are dealing with the question of the unity of God and whether that unity is something that we can conceive, or rather if it is something that we presently can only confess in spite of our false imaginings. He argues that we can only confess this unity.

> But this can happen only in the sense of I Corinthians 8:4–6 and of the prayer of the Isaiah Apocalypse: "O Lord our God, other lords besides you have ruled over us, but we acknowledge your name alone" (Isa. 26:13; cf. Micah 4:5). Yahweh's lawsuit with the other gods must not be glossed over even by systematic theology through an abstract monism. At stake is the truth of the first commandment: "I am the Lord your God, you shall have no other gods besides me!" Nevertheless, the other gods have their reality in their promises and enticements, as either something fascinating (*fascinosum*) or frightening (*tremendum*), in the sense of a power that is given to them by the human fabricating heart (*cors fingens*).[128]

The human heart can only be delivered from the power of these gods, from the power of its own imagination, by means of an external deliverance. And this

---

125. Ibid., 139. Hans Ulrich writes, "There is no definition of us, human beings, but there is a defining story." Ulrich, "Bodily Life as Creaturely Life: The Ethical Coexistence of Humans Beings with Disabilities and Its Fulfillment," *Journal of Religion, Disability and Health* 15.1 (2011), 54.

126. To take the title from Heiko Oberman's biography, *Luther: Man between God and the Devil*, trans. Eileen Walliser-Schwarzbart (New Haven: Yale University Press, 1989).

127. "Lectures on Genesis, Chapters 6–14 (1535–38)," LW 2:123. "It is true that there is no desire for anything that is unknown. Hence our nature cannot love God, whom it does not know; but it loves an idol and the dream of its heart" (124). "Therefore *the virtues of the heathen must be distinguished from the virtues of Christians*. It is true that *the hearts of both are prompted by God*. But among the heathen the zeal and ambition for glory eventually corrupt these divine impulses in great men" (125–6, emphasis mine). Here again we find that for Luther God is always working both in Christians and non-Christians, but without a constant gaze on Christ, the danger is that one will attribute one's virtue and good works to oneself above all (or perhaps to one's community, mentors, even one's church and its practices) rather than to the reality of the presently acting Christ.

128. Bayer, *TLW*, 197–8.

deliverance requires more than a growing awareness of our dependent agency, more than a gradual transformation via imitation, more than an intensification in virtue (of which Christian and pagan virtues stand together on a continuum), more than a (possibly unrecognized) transformation by Christ's beauty. Rather, what is required is nothing less than death and resurrection. The human heart and its imaginings must be put to death and raised anew through participation in the death and resurrection of Jesus Christ via baptism. Rather than continuity, as is suggested by habituation into virtue, what is required is radical rupture, the sort of rupture Paul describes in his baptismal language in Romans 6:4: "Therefore we have been buried with him by baptism into death, so that, just as Christ was raised from the dead by the glory of the Father, so we too might walk in newness of life."[129] A transformation on the scale of death and resurrection is nothing less than a "new creation."[130] Luther does not refer to baptism simply in the sense of a one-time occurrence, but rather as something that continues throughout life. He writes

---

129. Bonhoeffer, in exegeting the call of the disciple Levi in the Gospel of Mark, describes the way in which the encounter with Christ is abrupt and responsive, not a gradual progress. In expositing the refusal of the call from the young man in Mark 10:21, he argues, "Discipleship would also be misunderstood if the young man were to view it as a final conclusion of his previous deeds and questions, as a summary of what went before, as a supplement, completion, or perfection of his past." What Jesus offers the young man "really is an addition, but one whose content abolishes everything of ones' past." Bonhoeffer, *Discipleship*, 57. Later, Bonhoeffer connects what the synoptic Gospels describe as the call to discipleship to what Paul calls baptism. Baptism is "suffering Christ's call." It means a rescue from the demonic rule of the present age. "Baptism thus implies a *break*. Christ invades the realm of Satan and lays hold of those who belong to him, thereby creating his church-community [Gemeinde]. Past and present are torn asunder. The old has passed away, everything has become new . . . The break with the world is absolute. It requires and causes our *death*. In baptism we die together with our old world. This death must be understood in the strictest sense as an event that is suffered" (207–208); emphases in the original.

130. "Lectures on Galatians 1535, Chapters 1–4," LW 26:392. Cf. "Lectures on Genesis, Chapters 1–5 (1535–36)," LW 1:17, where Luther argues that everything was made through Christ the Word, but "this point should also be noted: that Paul regards the conversion of the wicked—something which is also brought about by the Word—as a new work of creation." Here again we find Luther making a distinction without separation between the one Word of God in creation (original creation) and redemption (new creation). Luther derives the language of "new creation," of course, from Paul (see 2 Cor. 5:17 and Gal. 6:15). Moyer Hubbard argues that Paul's use of "new creation" language should be interpreted in connection with his soteriological language of "new birth," "resurrection," and the terminology of dying and rising with Christ. He locates the language doctrinally within Paul's pneumatology. Hubbard argues that the language points not to "ontological transformation," but rather "pneumatological restoration." Moyer V. Hubbard, *New Creation in Paul's Letters and Thought* (Cambridge: Cambridge University Press, 2004), 233–5.

in the *Large Catechism* that the "power and effect of baptism" is nothing other than "the slaying of the old Adam and the resurrection of the new creature, both of which must continue in us our whole life long. Thus a Christian life is nothing else than a daily baptism, begun once and continuing ever after. For we must keep at it without ceasing, always purging whatever pertains to the old Adam, so that whatever belongs to the new creature may come forth."[131]

In response to Herdt's concern for maintaining the identity of the self, we can affirm there is continuity within rupture. However, as with resurrection and the baptismal logic of death and new life, we hold that this continuity is not to be found at the empirical level such that it can be traced by human observation, but rather it is only found in the faith that God remembers. As our identity is hidden in God, it is only in faith that we can speak of our identity. Human continuity is not grounded in the human as such, but is rather only a result of the remembering God's promising Word.[132] Whereas Herdt, for philosophical reasons, seeks to provide for a more stable account of the self through time (although she does call for "porousness"), as she finds in Hauerwas's early utilization of the concept of "character," Luther, for theological reasons, insists on an unstable and hidden self, paralleling his insistence on the hiddenness of the church and of the reality of God and God's grace, a hiddenness corresponding with a *theologia crucis*. He writes, "A Christian is even hidden from himself; he does not see his holiness and virtue, but sees in himself nothing but unholiness and vice."[133] This hiddenness means a great

---

131. The Large Catechism IV, 65–6, in *BoC*:465. Prenter argues, "The death and resurrection of Christ do not for Luther become an objective satisfaction given once and for all time to the Father. But the death and resurrection of Christ are a present reality in the conformity to Christ which is man's condition in the Spirit's work." Prenter, *Spiritus Creator*, 25. Althaus argues that Luther's doctrine of baptism differs from Paul's at this point. Whereas for Paul, death and resurrection with Christ have already happened in baptism (and must continue), for Luther there is no sense that death and resurrection has happened in toto at baptism, but is rather an occurrence that will take an entire lifetime. Althaus, *The Theology of Martin Luther*, trans. Robert C. Schultz (Philadelphia: Fortress Press), 356–9. Cf. also Lohse, *Martin Luther's Theology*, 302. Perhaps these arguments might be nuanced with reference to Bonhoeffer, who stresses both the "once-and-for-allness of Christ's death" with the Christian's call to a "daily dying," the latter of which he refers to as the cross of Christ given to us in our baptism. Bonhoeffer argues of the baptized, "They know themselves only as those who have already died, as those who have already undergone everything that is necessary for salvation." Bonhoeffer, *Discipleship*, 211.

132. "Not in essence, but by promise, I have eternal life." WA 16:52, 19–21; translation Oswald Bayer, quoted in *Living by Faith*, 34–5. Elsewhere, Bayer writes, "From the outset, our relationship with God is enhypostatized in the word, so to speak, but we ourselves are anhypostatic . . . our essence is outside us, in God's word." *TLW*, 53.

133. "Prefaces to the New Testament," LW 35:411.

liberation, for the believer becomes self-forgetful, focusing on the will of God as expressed in the Word and in the needs of one's neighbor.[134] Further, it means that the Christian does not have to look inside herself to discern herself, but rather knows herself simply as one to whom God's Word is addressed. It is in attending to this Word, particularly in the worship of the church in Word and sacrament, in constant and recurrent attentiveness to Scripture, that the self is transformed. In describing this work that Christians suffer, Brian Brock writes, "The service of the church to the world is to bear within itself the painful grinding away of the idolatrous self."[135] Contrary to Herdt's focus on the infinite imitability of Christ, Luther argues that the otherwise wandering human heart must be drawn in and cling to the places where God has promised to encounter humans. Without such drawing in, without the given-ness and particularity of the Scriptures and the church that gathers around them, the human heart will encounter not the living God, but the god of the human imagination.

At this point, I would argue for the centrality of Scripture in the Christian life, as a Word that draws in and redirects the human imagination to Christ in the mode of receptive listening and praise, rather than in active imitation of the "infinite exemplarity" of Christ. Here it is also appropriate to reiterate the point made in Chapter 2 that for Luther it is not primarily we who interpret Scripture, but rather Scripture that interprets us. If God's grace in Christ through the Spirit is not given to specific promised places, in other words, if we operate with a wide-open account of grace, where is the human imagination, the "idol" factory, challenged? Christ as example is always in danger of becoming Christ as we imagine him. In a strange way, the infinitely imitable Christ, open to infinite interpretation, becomes domesticated under the human imagination. The objectivity of Word and sacrament and the external works of Christ that are inimitable are important for this very reason. This is also the reason for circumscription by the commandments and life in the institutions. Luther is not looking for the gracious God and assurance of salvation, but rather the place where he could assuredly meet the living God and not the idol god of his own imagination. The institutions and commandments lend this kind of assurance to the Christian life, freeing the Christian from anxieties about what is the work of God and what is the idolatrous works of one's own imagination. Rather than distancing from Scripture, as Herdt does,[136] Luther turns more fully to Scripture, to meditating on it and dwelling

---

134. For a poetical reflection on this truth, see Bonhoeffer's "Who am I?" in *Letters and Papers from Prison*, 459–60. See also Bayer, *Living by Faith*, 25–7. In his exposition of Hamann, Bayer says that the Christian is hidden from herself in a twofold manner: (1) as a sinner who is ignorant and is a restless wanderer like Cain (Gen. 4:12), and (2) as a justified person whose alien righteousness is hiddenness in Christ, *A Contemporary in Dissent: Johann Georg Hamann as a Radical Enlightener*, trans. Roy A. Harrisville and Mark C. Mattes (Grand Rapids, MI: Eerdmans, 2012), 57–8.

135. Brock, *Singing the Ethos of God*, 225.

136. See 128 n.67 earlier.

within it. The divine–human distinction is so important to Luther, not in order to ensure purity of intention or to protect respective agencies, but because of his concern for faithfulness to the true and living God who so often contradicts the god of our wandering imagination.

Given that the continuity in the Christian life, as in that between creation and redemption, is something that Christians confess in faith, not something that is empirically evident to the senses in the midst of the rupture between the ages, there cannot be an easy distinction between a "good Christian" and a "good pagan." There is much about Christians that remains non-Christian, much that awaits death at the Final Judgment, and much about "pagans" that shows God's loving care for God's creation, a care to which pagans too can respond. In this sense, we can agree with Herdt that it would be theologically unwise to suppose that Christians form a community that can be pointed to in stark contrast to the surrounding world. Nonetheless, the distinction of the Christian confession cannot be put aside. It is always a strong counterlogic to the logic organizing the present age, a particular counterlogic that must be stressed, confessed, and explored again and again as Christians seek to live faithful to Christ, while humbly acknowledging our continuing need to pray "forgive us our sins."[137] It must be encountered specifically in the places where Christ has promised to encounter us with certainty, namely, in Word and sacrament. It is as we attend to the living address of Christ in the worship of the church that the transforming Word that makes all things new claims us. Only here, where the church suffers the work of the living God can we speak of an unambiguous distinctiveness of the church over against the world, but this is the distinctiveness of Christ present in the Spirit, which also stands over against the church itself. It is in our confession, in faith and hope, that we belong to *this* One that distinctiveness is located. As soon as we turn to our practices and ourselves we are caught up in the ambivalence of the age, an age in which God's loving provision for Christians and pagans alike continues in the face of all of humanity's senseless rebellion. We forget that as humans we are "justified by faith," that we are defined by what God has spoken to us, not by the actions that we perform. This is not to say that this worship does not reconfigure Christian's relationship with other humans and the rest of creation—surely it does—but to say that this reconfiguration only comes about by continual return to worship. In continuing to listen and attend to the living Word, Christians learn to share in the affects of Christ, in his love of the world. However, this is not a disposition located within the believer, but rather is a result of the union with Christ in the Spirit that Luther points to when he speaks of justification and sanctification. Only as we live continually in the presence of Christ can we live in right relationship with the rest of creation. What matters is not simply doing good acts, but participating in the acts of God in the world. But this assumes that our life in the world is ordered under God's care and governance: heuristically, this

---

137. "Lectures on Galatians 1535, Chapters 5–6," LW 27: 85.

means looking for and cooperating with God's work in the church, city, and home/economy.

Concluding Reflections on the Importance of Luther's Account of the New Creation for Political Theology

In the resurrection, when the Word of redemption has come to consummation, earthly governments and their reliance on death to maintain their position will be done away with. The secular government, in this Augustinian sense, is a tragic result of the Fall that is destined to be done away. However, as we argued in the previous chapter, this sense of political order does not exhaust Luther's understanding of the "political." On the contrary, he sees another aspect of it that belongs to creation prelapsum. This is the account of government that we get from Luther when he is engaging the language game of sanctification, and it is in this game that he employs the terminology of the three institutions. The negative, Augustinian moment is followed, then, by a more Aristotelian moment. This tension, or refusal to simply stand on one side or the other, is an indication that theology, not philosophy is driving Luther. His response to the biblical Word requires this sort of political ambivalence precisely because humans "cannot find out what God has done from the beginning to the end" (Ecc. 3:11). An overarching political theory would require a philosophical—in Aristotle's terms a full understanding of all four causes—grounding, but Luther insists on grounding his understanding of politics in theology and hence requires a darkness around the edges appropriate to the life of faith. However, this is not tragic, again, because of resurrection. Yet it remains senseless given the senselessness of sin. When Luther speaks of justification, he necessarily speaks of the divine activity alone, and hence of faith, but when he speaks of sanctification, he speaks of humans as participating in God's care of creation, and hence he speaks of love. This discontinuity in Luther's account is a result of the disorder that is sin, a disorder beyond human rectification. Herdt's account is able to maintain such a seamless continuity because the disruptivity of the Fall never seems to fully enter in.

We must be more specific here than Herdt in the passage referenced earlier, where she writes, "We can affirm the redemptive activity of the Word at work throughout created-but-fallen nature while also insisting that the quality of that redemptive activity is transformed when the Word is known as Jesus Christ and His Spirit is known in the church."[138] Yes, the Word is at work throughout created-but-fallen nature. But this formulation is far too vague. It too easily collapses creation and redemption, providence and salvation, penultimate and ultimate. The latter terms are not merely qualitative increases along a continuum of the former terms. Instead, although it is correct to speak of the *one* Word of God, of the unity of God, we must hold with Bayer that this unity is a confession that remains contested by

---

138. *PV*, 97.

humanity's enslavement to the imagining of the human heart and the gods of the world.[139] An ideal Christ, serving as an exemplar, whose "ideal form" or essence can be found in any number of instances of "moral beauty," is not sufficient to overcome the *cors fingens*. The human heart must be re-created, it must be given the affections of Christ himself. And this, for Luther, means justification and sanctification, and a new politics.

---

139. Bayer writes, "Hegel and Barth have consistently tried to remove the difference between 'theology' and 'economy,' or more specifically, between a general experience of God and Christian experience of salvation . . . .If we speak of 'unity' in connection with law and gospel, life and death, judgment and grace, it must be clear that this is meant in a strictly eschatological sense." *TLW*, 196, 198.

Chapter 5

THE THREE INSTITUTIONS: A POLITICS FORMED BY GOD'S STORY WITH US

We concluded the previous chapter by emphasizing the need for the re-creation of the human heart in justification and sanctification. Herdt accuses Luther of too sharply separating justification and sanctification such that no room is left for human virtuous activity. However, as we saw in our discussion of Luther's challenge to the concept of *fides caritate formata*, Luther actually keeps the two closely together in that he describes both as naming human life as it is re-created and formed by the living Word. While clearly protecting the doctrine of justification from Pelagian incursion, Luther nonetheless does not separate sanctification, and the good works that characterize it, from justification. In the previous chapter we also indicated that the promise of a new politics is located doctrinally under sanctification. When Luther speaks of sanctification, he includes in this what has traditionally been referred to as the doctrine of the three estates. In sanctification our affections are conformed to Christ, and this formation occurs through suffering the divine activity in the estates of the *ecclesia*, *oeconomia*, and *politia*.[1] In sanctification our affections and perceptions are transformed so that we may come to recognize and explore the will of God.[2] Herein lies a major, and often overlooked, part of the topography of Luther's theology that presses back against the oversimplistic reduction of his thought to "justification by faith alone." Rather, in the estates we see that sanctification plays a significant role in the overall grammar of Luther's theology. As Bernd Wannenwetsch argues, "Sanctification for Luther is not just a matter of faith, but a matter of faith *and* created orders, or more precisely of *faith that is exercised in love within the divinely assigned spheres of social life*, politics, economics and religion (cf. WA16: '*in talibus ordinationibus exercere ceritatem*')."[3] It is inside of this grammar of sanctification by the forming

---

1. For the terminology of suffering God's work, see Reinhard Hütter, *Suffering Divine Things*.

2. Hans G. Ulrich, "Waiting for the other Word—God's advent in human preaching: Consideration for a theology of preaching," available at christenethik.de/God%20is%20different6.pdf, accessed March 8, 2016.

3. Wannenwetsch, "Luther's Moral Theology," 132; emphasis in the original. See also Bernd Wannenwetsch, "Wovon handelt die "material Ethik"? Oder: warum die Ethik der

Word of God that we can begin to fully explicate Luther's political understanding. In Christ, the justified believer is freed for a new politics, which it is the crucial task of this chapter to describe in its contours.

Further, in this chapter we continue to acknowledge the question of agency and the moral agent as raised by Herdt (a question that is central in most contemporary treatments of political ethics). However, we will quickly see that Luther moves the focus to the divine agent rather than describing the creaturely ethical agent (or the communities to which ethical agents belong). While Herdt seems primarily interested in giving a description of the workings of human moral agency, Luther is concerned with the quite different question of that to which the human heart clings, that is, with the locus of human faith, hope, and love and the places where the human heart can be conformed to Christ. Whereas Herdt's account of sanctification runs according to the grammar of virtue formation, Luther's follows the grammar of suffering the divine activity by carrying out the works that are pleasing to God. This may sound trite, but it is precisely this move that makes possible my contention that Luther's political ethics is a more fully *theological* political ethics. In Luther's teaching on the estates we encounter a genuinely theological politics, oriented by the continuous and consistent (not static or predictable) divine activity that makes all things new. This is in contrast to accounts in the theological tradition that base government on sin, such that politics is a necessary antidote (the more Augustinian tradition as represented in this book by Milbank) or that base government on an optimistic view of human nature, such that humans are naturally political animals (the more Aristotelian, Thomistic, or Erasmian traditions as represented in this book by Herdt). In turning to the institutions, Luther provides us with a framework enabling a genuine alternative to these two poles of the tradition, where politics begins in the rule of God, but is described differently according to the particular moment in the history of salvation.

The chapter is divided into four sections. First, we consider recent criticism of Luther's teaching on the three institutions as articulated by Karl Barth, whose concerns over the separation of law and gospel serve as the larger framework within which the various criticisms of Luther's political thought that we have already considered fall. Of particular concern in this section is countering the (rightful) negative reaction most have to the teaching given its perversion and abuse in the first half of the twentieth century. Next, we show how Luther's teaching on the institutions meets the criticisms of Barth, while also giving appropriate place to the doctrine of the Fall and sin. We do so by setting forth the "institutional" nature of the estates, showing how Luther understands the divine speaking to counter human presumption, and examining the relation of the estates and the sacraments. We will then turn to Luther's description of each of the three estates in turn, beginning by demonstrating their relation to Scripture and arguing that

elementaren Lebensformen ("Stände") einer "Bereichsethik" vorzuziehen ist Oswald Bayer zum sechzigsten Geburtstag, in *Kirche(n) und Gesellschaft*, eds. Andrease Fritzsche and Manfred Kwiran (Munich: Bernward, 2000), 128.

they are, in fact, part of the deep grammar of Scripture. In the final section of the chapter we look at the political significance of the estates (focusing, of course, on the *politia*) and their critically heuristic capacity in confronting the false grammars that would enslave human life by robbing it of its freedom under the rule of God. This chapter thus continues the constructive task of describing Luther's theological politics while furthering the response to Herdt's critique by challenging the more basic theological assumptions said to underlie Luther's moral theology. The former task is carried out explicitly; the latter implicitly.

Criticism of the Institutions as Orders of Creation (Schöpfungsordnungen): Karl Barth

Luther's teaching on the three estates has fallen into disrepute in recent generations given the distortion of the doctrine in some prominent late-nineteenth- and early-twentieth-century Lutheran theology. According to this interpretation of Luther's teaching, God created autonomous "orders of creation" (*Schöpfungsordnungen*), which are divorced morally from God's will in redemption and from the continuous divine address. One such interpreter belonging to this tradition was Paul Althaus, who argued regarding vocation (which he equates with the "orders"), "There is no special outward characteristic that distinguishes the Christian's activity in his vocation from that of other men. *Neither God's word nor faith tell him what to do.* Rather, he is directed by reason and the immanent law of his vocation."[4] Althaus included in his notion of the orders of creation the idea of a national people. As rulers are part of God's creation and order for Luther, so too, Althaus argues, "Luther explicitly asserts that this is also true of a people in the sense of a national group (Volk)."[5] Interpretations of this sort gave the state free reign to determine its morality according to the dictates of reason alone and separate from the morality of the church, which in the case of the Nazi period in Germany led to a theology idealizing the *Volk* and the German lands (*Blut und Boden*).[6] Politically,

---

4. Paul Althaus, *The Ethics of Martin Luther*, 40 (emphasis mine). Althaus argues that after 1522 Luther "uses *Beruf* synonymously with station (*Stand*), office or function (*Amt*), and duty (*Befehl*)" (39). For an extended account of Luther's teaching on this concept, see Gustav Wingren, *The Christian's Calling: Luther on Vocation*, trans. Carl C. Rasmussen (Philadelphia: Muhlenburg Press, 1957).

5. Althaus, *The Ethics of Martin Luther*, 112. James Stayer argues that including the nation (*das Volk*) among the orders of creation was a "modernizing" of Luther's teaching, which "offered a mock-Lutheran common platform for Elert, Althaus, Hirsch and Gogarten," that is, between the confessional Lutherans (like Althaus) and the German Christians. Stayer, *Martin Luther: German Saviour: German Evangelical Theological Factions and the Interpretation of Luther, 1917–1933* (Montreal: McGill-Queen's University Press, 2000), 120.

6. On Althaus's contribution to these developments, see in addition to Stayer, cited earlier, Christopher J. Probst, *Demonizing the Jews: Luther and the Protestant Church in Nazi Germany* (Bloomington: Indiana University Press, 2012), 27ff.

this perverted version of Luther's teaching proved disastrous as it lent support to the *Deutsche Christen*, the pro-Nazi German Christian movement, by proclaiming the autonomy of the political and the duty of the Christian to submit to political authority even in this case.[7]

Perhaps the most important twentieth-century critic of the Lutheran teaching on the orders of creation was Karl Barth, who carried out his attack on the doctrine largely in conversation with his contemporary, Emil Brunner. Before turning to the specific debate between the two theologians, however, it will be useful to place Barth's objections to the orders of creation within his larger political-theological resistance to the Nazi regime. In his 1935 essay "Gospel and Law," Barth argued against a false separation of the law and gospel, which the *Deutsche Christen* carried out in supposed faithfulness to Luther's own teaching on the relation of law and gospel. The separation of the two led to a false separation of divine and human activity, carving the world into autonomous spheres. Political ethics, then, are not determined by the gospel, but rather by the law as it is left to the interpretation of non-Scriptural sources, such as philosophy and natural theology. In contrast to such separation, Barth argued "that the Law is nothing else than the necessary form of the Gospel, whose content is grace."[8] In acknowledging that the content of the Law is grace, Barth refuses any other source such as "'natural law,' or an abstract 'reason,' or history, or, in these recent troubled times, the 'Volknomoi' (people's laws), so happily invented [and] undertake[n] to give to the Law of God the content usable and desirable" for the purpose of self-justification.[9] To counteract abuse of the law, Barth argues that both law and gospel are the Word of God, and this Word is *one*.[10] Again, the content of the one Word is grace, that is, Jesus Christ. If Christ is not seen as the goal of the law, the result is either a *nomianism* that uncritically obeys every authority as though this were obedience to God, or an essential *antinomianism* that finds faithfulness to the gospel in a pure inwardness unaffected by any commands. In the case of Luther, this leads to what Barth elsewhere refers to as "law-gospel quietism."[11] Instead of the law being "the prophetic witness *for* the will of God *against* all of men's sinful presumption,

---

7. On this paragraph, see William Lazareth, *Christians in Society: Luther, the Bible and Social Ethics* (Minneapolis: Fortress Press, 2001), 7–10. See also Robert P. Ericksen, *Theologians under Hitler: Gerhard Kittel, Paul Althaus and Emanuel Hirsch* (New Haven: Yale University Press, 1985).

8. Karl Barth, "Gospel and Law," in *Community, State, and Church: Three Essays by Karl Barth with a New Introduction by David Haddorff* (Eugene, OR: Wipf & Stock, 1960), 80. For an interpretation of the essay along the lines I set out here, see David Haddorff's introduction to this volume, esp. 28–31.

9. Ibid., 91.

10. Ibid., 72. Of course, Barth is careful to distinguish law and gospel while affirming their unity, as a failure to distinguish the two "would contradict the whole of Holy Scripture" (76).

11. Lazareth, *Christians in Society*, 10.

against all their lawlessness and unrighteousness," it becomes a justification for untethered governmental authority.[12] Barth wants to call all authority back to Christ, reminding us, "We are always concerned with faith in Jesus Christ, who is crucified and risen. Thus there can never be claims and demands which would have legal validity from another source or in themselves: there can only be *witnesses*" (emphasis in the original). These witnesses only have authority "to the extent that they proclaim the 'Law of Christ' (Galatians 6:2) and thus the 'Law of faith' (Romans 3:21), and thus the 'Law of the Spirit of life' (Romans 8:2)."[13] When the law and gospel are separated, that is, when there is a freestanding law emptied of the promise of the gospel, there is a "relapse out of belief in the one living God into the impoverished heathen worship of the elements."[14] Keeping them together means keeping together creation and redemption, society and church—in short, "the universal lordship of Jesus Christ."[15]

Barth's objection to an "orders of creation" theology is spelled out more specifically in his engagement with Brunner, first in "Nein!" written in response to Brunner's "Nature and Grace,"[16] and later in the *Church Dogmatics*.[17] In his essay, Brunner made a distinction between God's preserving grace and God's redeeming grace, arguing that human activity comes under the purview of the former alone. Therefore, the "ordinances"[18] fall under the sphere either of creation that precedes the Fall (e.g., marriage) or under the sphere of preserving grace that follows the Fall (e.g., the State).[19] In the distinction between saving and preserving grace, Brunner claims to be following Luther, whose "entire doctrine of vocation

---

12. Barth, "Gospel and Law," in *Community, State and Church*, 80; emphasis in the original.

13. Ibid., 83.

14. Ibid., 91.

15. This is Lazareth's terminology for his summary of Barth's argument, *Christians in Society*, 10. The separation of law and gospel also leads, Barth argues, to the Lutheran doctrine of "two kingdoms" understood as separate spheres, one a sphere of creation with a somewhat anonymous providence, the other a sphere of redemption, thus splitting the lordship of Christ. For the purposes of this chapter, however, I am restricting myself to Barth's treatment of the orders, as understanding Luther's grammar in this case will also address much of Barth's objection to his doctrine of the two regiments, a doctrine that must necessarily find its place within the teaching on the three estates. For Barth on the two kingdoms, see "Church and State" (*Rechtfertigung und Recht*), in *Community, State and Church*, 101–48.

16. See the English translation of Brunner, "Nature and Grace," and Barth, "No! Answer to Emil Brunner," in *Natural Theology*, trans. Peter Fraenkel (Eugene, OR: Wipf and Stock Publishers, 2002).

17. See especially *Church Dogmatics* III.4, 19–46.

18. In explicating Brunner's essay, I follow Fraenkel's translation of "Ordnung" as "ordinance."

19. Brunner, "Nature and Grace," in *Natural Theology*, 30.

and status is informed by the idea of preserving grace and of the ordinance of creation and preservation which are its instruments. The same is true of his clear distinction between Church and State."[20] Further, he argues that the Reformers (meaning specifically Luther and Calvin) held that the goodness and necessity of the ordinances can be recognized by natural men even if they do not know the God revealed in Jesus Christ.[21] While their full significance can only be understood in faith, they are nonetheless "divine ordinances of nature." Brunner specifically argues that they belong to a realm of preservation, separate from that of redemption and the church. Here, in the realm of preservation, nature and instinct are most important. In fact, Brunner goes so far as to argue that the ordinances "are created and maintained by instinct and reason."[22]

In his reply to Brunner, Barth asks where Brunner gets his notion of preserving grace. He wonders how preservation can be "grace" abstractly without reference to the grace of God in Jesus Christ. Without such reference, how do we know that for which we are being preserved? Perhaps this preservation is the "antechamber of hell."[23] According to Barth, a preserving grace as propounded by Brunner can certainly not be found in the Bible, which knows of no such severance of creation and reconciliation. Having called into question Brunner's separation, Barth turns specifically to the question of the ordinances. He grants the existence of "moral and sociological axioms" that underlie the laws and customs of various peoples, but he asks what these axioms are and who is to decide? Barth finds it dubious that instinct and reason could discern and determine these axioms, much less raise them to the level of binding and authoritative commandments, that is, divine ordinances.[24] At best the result would be arbitrary.[25] Further, if they are ordinances of God, how could they be realized to any extent by humans outside of Christ, given that humans are thoroughly sinners. Rather, Barth argues, it is impossible to realize the law to any extent outside of God's grace in Christ. To suggest otherwise would mean that "it is now purely arbitrary to continue to say that only holy Scripture may be the standard of the Church's message, that man can do nothing

---

20. Ibid., 52.

21. Referring to Calvin's understanding of the *lumen naturale*, Brunner writes, "Wherever a man of science investigates the divine laws of the starry heavens, wherever an artist creates any great works, there the Spirit of God is active in him, there he is in relation with divine truth." Ibid., 42.

22. Ibid., 30. "For it is peculiar to the preserving grace of God that he does his preserving work both by nature acting unconsciously and by the reason of man" (31).

23. Barth, "No!" 84.

24. Ibid., 86.

25. In his *Church Dogmatics*, Barth likewise criticizes Bonhoeffer's "mandates" for being somewhat arbitrary, asking why there are only four mandates and not others. Their arbitrariness can be seen in what Barth detects as their "suggestion of North German patriarchalism." Barth, *Church Dogmatics* III.4, 22.

for his salvation, that it takes place sola gratia, that the Church must be free from all national and political restrictions!" Obviously, the point here is that the place given to a natural theology in Brunner means a repudiation of the central elements of Reformation theology. With characteristic fervor, Barth argues that at this point the "pot is boiling over."[26] Barth says that theological ethics will remain on firm ground if, instead of these "mythical ordinances," it always remembers the commandments of God.[27]

Barth spells out his criticism of the "orders of creation" with more specificity in the *Church Dogmatics*. He takes issue with Brunner's explication of the orders, which reads, "Therefore God's command for the actual moment reaches us through the world around us, with all its pressure and its restrictions. Even the historically 'given' must be regarded primarily as God's Command, telling us to adjust ourselves to it."[28] Brunner calls these "divine orders" given that in them God's will meets humans. While Barth agrees that the command of God meets us in our actual human existence, and not in some realm above it, his earlier question remains, namely, "From what source and in what way do we hear a divine command?"[29] He thinks it is pretty clear that Brunner grounds the orders on a natural law understood in an Aristotelian manner and restricts the gracious commands of God to the realm of individual rather than social ethics. Barth wants to make clear that we are to learn what is to be done from God's Word alone, but from the Word understood in a comprehensive sense and not limited to the specifically ethical sayings of Scripture. Brunner, as the "outstanding representative" of the view that God's command is to be heard in the created orders by means of natural reason, is found wanting for Barth. He gives three specific reasons for rejecting a theology of created orders. First, he finds the orders to be an abstraction from the revealed Word of God that, rather than giving useful knowledge of the commanding Creator and the confronted human creature, instead reverts to an "obscure magnitude 'reality'" leaving the ethical encounter between God and man shrouded in uncertainty. Second, it divides the command of God by positing an order that is separate from the command of God the Redeemer. Over against this move, Barth again stresses the oneness of the command of God. There cannot be a separate command of God the Creator alongside the command of God the Reconciler and God the Redeemer. Rather, "always in the ethical event God commands and man acts in all three spheres at once."[30] The third objection, which Barth calls perhaps "the most weighty of all," is that the concept of orders of creation requires neither revelation nor faith, and thus it is a conceptuality divorced from the true Creator–creature

---

26. Barth, "Nein!" 87.
27. Ibid., 128.
28. Brunner, *The Divine Imperative: A Study in Christian Ethics*, trans. Olive Wyon (London: Lutterworth Press, 1949), 125; quoted in Barth, *Church Dogmatics* III.4, 19.
29. Barth, *Church Dogmatics* III.4, 20.
30. Ibid., 33.

relationship. The concept stands intermediary between the command of God and the human beings to whom it is addressed, thus putting God's command at the handling and disposal of human creatures.[31] In opposition to this splitting of the commands of God and distorting the Creature–creator relationship, Barth speaks of the eternal divine decree of election which precedes creation and which makes possible a unity of the commands and preserves the proper relation of Creator and creatures in Jesus Christ.[32]

In setting out Luther's teaching on the three institutions, we will show how such an account is actually more consistent with Barth and is not subject to his criticisms in the same way that is the case for Brunner and other late-nineteenth- and early-twentieth-century interpreters of Luther.[33] For Luther, the estates refer to the deep grammar of Scripture and cannot in any way be abstracted from revelation or faith. In fact, I show that for Luther the doctrine of the estates is not a subset of the doctrine of creation, but rather belongs more properly to the doctrines of God and revelation. Further, part of the attraction of the estates for Luther is precisely that they give humans confidence and certainty that their obedience is pleasing to God, and this because they are a hermeneutic of Scripture and not a natural theology. The estates speak of the socially formed life of humans following from either obedience or disobedience to the commands, and thus are not an entity alongside the commands. Before making these arguments, however, I will consider the oneness of the command of God for Luther by briefly examining his understanding of the law and gospel relationship, an understanding that is dramatic, although subsequent readers of Luther have all too often interpreted it in a static-systematic fashion.[34]

---

31. Ibid., 37–8. Paul Nimmo describes these three objections to the orders of creation as (1) ethical, (2) theological, and (3) epistemological. See his "The Orders of Creation in the theological ethics of Karl Barth," *SJT* 60.1 (2007), 24–35.

32. Ibid., 39–40.

33. I should make clear at the outset that the commonality I find between Luther and Barth is the prominence that both give to the Word of God, not what has come to be called "divine command" theory. As Wannenwetsch argues, Luther's "commandment ethics is an ethics anchored in worship, not a pure commandment ethics." Wannenwetsch, *Political Worship*, 61. In his argument that Barth's assessment of Luther was not mostly negative, as commonly assumed, George Hunsinger writes, "Like Luther, and in his footsteps, Barth is preeminently a Word of God theologian." Further, "perhaps one way to appreciate the powerful impact on Barth of the primacy Luther assigned to God's Word would be to say that it led Barth, almost alone among modern theologians, to grant uncompromising precedence to the Reformation over modernity itself. Barth took Luther extremely seriously that apart from God's Word ultimate reality cannot possibly be known, and that it can be apprehended by faith alone." Hunsinger, "What Karl Barth Learned from Martin Luther," *LQ* 13.2 (Summer 1999), 151, 137.

34. On this point, see Bernd Wannenwetsch, "Luther's Moral Theology," 124–6.

The Commandments of God as an Invitation to Formed Creaturely Life: The Three Institutions

As we saw earlier, Lazareth describes Barth's overall criticism of Luther's theological ethics as being "law–gospel quietism." This is the view that Luther understands the law only in its accusing (theological) and restricting (political) function, which is to say as a mirror for sin and in its political sense as a duty of passive obedience qua Romans 13 given that politics is simply a remedy for sin. When framed this way, the law is simply placed in opposition to the gospel, ultimately to be negated. However, David Yeago has shown, based on Luther's exegesis of Genesis, that Luther's understanding of the law follows a narrative form that is viewed differently under different salvation–historical circumstances. By placing the law–gospel distinction within a wider narrative frame, the oppressiveness of the law and its opposition to the gospel is not grounded in the law itself, but rather in human disobedience.[35] In Yeago's formulation, "the negativity of the law is not located in its formal character as commandment, as proposal of form and order; its ground is rather in our *disorder*, our sin, our non-conformity to Christ."[36] The original context of the law as command of God was not one of sin, so that its proper function cannot refer to either accusation or restraint of chaos. Rather, the first command of God to Adam was concerning eating the fruit of the tree of the knowledge of good and evil. Here, for Luther, is the first instance of the law, and it comes at a time while Adam was "intoxicated with rejoicing toward God," that is, in a state of innocence prior to the Fall.[37] As Yeago interprets this passage, Luther affirms "that there was law and commandment, properly so-called, in the state of innocence, before sin's entry on the scene."[38] The purpose of the command not to eat from the tree was that Adam would praise and thank God and have a place for rendering concrete obedience.[39] As such, Luther calls for a distinction between the law as it stands before sin and as it stands after. In either case the law remains, but the one to whom it is addressed changes. Adam is a different person before and after the Fall, which results in the fact that the "Law before sin is one thing and the Law after sin is something else."[40] Yeago refers to Luther's notion of the law as being analogical—that is, while properly called law in both cases, its meaning is not equivalent before and after sin.[41]

---

35. David Yeago, "Gnosticism, Antinomianism, and Reformation Theology: Reflections on the Costs of a Construal," *Pro Ecclesia* 2.1 (1993), 40.

36. Ibid., 48.

37. "Lectures on Genesis, Chapters 1–5 (1535–36)," LW 1:94.

38. Yeago, "Martin Luther on Grace, Law and Moral Life: Prolegomena to an Ecumenical Discussion of *Veritatis Splendor*," *The Thomist* 62.2 (1998), 175.

39. "Lectures on Genesis, Chapters 1–5 (1535–36)," LW 1:106.

40. Ibid., 109–10.

41. Yeago, "Martin Luther on Grace, Law and Moral Life," 176.

So what is the meaning of the law in its original sense? As Wannenwetsch argues, the law or commandments of God, outside the soteriological language game (i.e., outside of the accusing/restraining sense of the law) is to give "concrete form and order to the joy of a life in Christ."[42] According to Reinhard Hütter, Luther understands the proper function of God's commandment to be its offer of "concrete guidance, the concrete social practice that allows us as believers to embody our communion with God in concrete creaturely ways."[43] It is within this context of the commanded law, the context of the law that follows from the promise contained in the preface to the Decalogue ("I am the Lord, your God"), that we find the proper setting for Luther's doctrine of the three estates. As such, the estates do not fall under the doctrine of the law in antinomy to the gospel, but rather articulate the continuity of the divine claim across the whole biblical witness. Already in the garden, Luther sees the instituted Word of God making good works possible. Without the Word, there could be no obedience. "The first thing to know is that there are no good works except those works God has commanded, just as there is no sin except that which God has forbidden."[44] When interpreted in this way, we find that Luther is not so far from Barth and that the institutions are quite different from what Brunner posits in the orders of creation.[45] In his exegesis of Genesis 2, Luther finds that the giving of the law to innocent Adam corresponds with the institution of the first estate, the *ecclesia*. Therefore, the estates first come

---

42. Wannenwetsch, "Luther's Moral Theology," 126. Yeago calls this the "original and proper function" of the law, "Martin Luther on Grace, Law and Moral Life," 177.

43. Reinhard Hütter, "The Twofold Center of Lutheran Ethics: Christian Freedom and God's Commandments," in *The Promise of Lutheran Ethics*, ed. Karen L. Bloomquist and John R. Stumme (Minneapolis: Fortress Press, 1998), 43. Hütter, following Paul Althaus, makes a distinction between "commandment" and "law," arguing that the first and second uses of the law (restraining and convicting) remain given the *simul*, although this character of the law is not inherent to it but rather the result of sin estranging humans from God (182, n. 16). When I speak of the law in its positive sense in this section (i.e., *not* as it appears under the conditions of sin), I intend what Hütter means by commandment or what is meant by the term Torah. Ulrich writes that law understood as Torah is "the reliable context of living and living together articulated in God's commandments . . . Commanded law is not established because of the fall." Ulrich, "God's Commandments and their Political Context," 46. None of this, of course, is meant to suggest that the *simul* has been left behind. Therefore, as Hütter notes, we must continue to stress the importance of the political and theological use of the law in Luther's teaching.

44. "Treatise on Good Works, 1520," LW 44:23.

45. In fact, Yeago writes, "In a surprisingly 'Barthian' turn of phrase, Luther says that the commandment was 'gospel and law' for Adam and Eve in the state of innocence." Yeago, "Martin Luther on Grace, Law and Moral Life," 178; Albrecht Peters, referring to the same passage in Luther's "Lectures on Genesis," writes, "Here we still have the order Gospel—commandment." Peters, *Commentary on Luther's Catechisms: Ten Commandments*, trans. Holger K. Sonntag (Saint Louis: Concordia Publishing House, 2009), 206.

to light not under a general or abstract providence, much less under a doctrine of preservation in the light of sin, but rather as enabling humans to respond in concrete, social fashion to the unmerited promise of life with God.

Having set out the context (state of innocence) in which Luther grounds the estates, it will be helpful to give attention to the actual terminology Luther uses before continuing on to a more precise definition and description of the estates. He employs a broad range of terminology in describing what we are here calling the estates, including the Latin terms *ordinationes*, *ordo*, and *hierarchia*, and the German terms *Stand* (estate/station), *Stiften* (institutions), *Hierarchie* (hierarchy), *Ordnung* (orders), and *Amt* (office).[46] Bernhard Lohse argues that although the precise historical background for the concept cannot be determined with certainty, likely Luther is following the Aristotelian division of his time in conceiving of ethics in three areas.[47] However, the important point is that Luther's underlying concept remains constant even if his terminology changes. So, Lohse says, it is significant that early on Luther prefers the terms "estates" and "offices," only later and rarely using the term "hierarchies."[48]

Despite the varied terminology Luther utilizes in his teaching on the "estates" of *ecclesiae*, *oeconomia*, and *politia*, the single term that best captures his overall sense is "institutions" (*Stiften*). Here we cannot avoid the connection to the words of institution in the Sacrament. Oswald Bayer argues that the theme of institution, or of God's giving of "categorical gift," characterizes the whole of the Christian life. He cites J. G. Hamann in explaining the meaning of this gift: "Woe to us if we should be found to be our own creator, inventor, and author of our own future well-being. The first command in the Bible says: 'Eat!' and the final one says: 'Come, all is ready!' "[49] In these words we have command, but it is a command that permits, that gives an unconditional promise.[50] We hear these words of the living God in the words of institution at the Lord's Table, "Take, eat; this is my body" (Matt. 26:26). God thus gives Godself to us "in the midst of life, not in some way that is separate from our daily bread." The proper human response to this grace is discernment of the gift in faith and praise to the Creator who has so freely given us all good things. Understood as such, faith means tasting and seeing the goodness of the Lord, while sin is not transgression of the eternal order, but rather "a failure to discern

---

46. Luther's terminology on the three estates is summarized in Bernhard Lohse, *Martin Luther's Theology*, 322; see also Althaus, *The Ethics of Martin Luther*, 36, and Wannenwetsch, "Wovon handelt die "material Ethik"?," 123.

47. For the historical background of Luther's teaching on the three institutions, see Reinhard Schwarz, "Luthers Lehre von den drei Ständen und die drei Dimensionen der Ethik," *Lutherjahrbuch* 45 (1978), 15–34; and Risto Saarinen "Ethics in Luther's Theology: The Three Orders," 195–215.

48. Bernhard Lohse, *Martin Luther's Theology*, 322.

49. J. G. Hamann, letter to F. H. Jacobi, December 5, 1784, quoted in Bayer, "Categorical Imperative or Categorical Gift," in *FR*, 13.

50. Bayer, "Categorical Imperative or Categorical Gift," in *FR*, 14.

and appreciate that we have been charged with a command as gift and opportunity. Sinners are above all those who despise good things."[51] For Luther the testing of faith in response to the promise of God finds its proper locus in the Word and sacrament and in life as lived in the three estates, while unbelief (i.e., sin) names the refusal to attend to the places of promise and receive the gifts given there.

Hans Ulrich, who likewise favors the term "institutions," calls them spheres of interaction and living proactively established, which signify "the explicitly marked place of living within God's governance and government insofar as this expresses God's promise to His people and is embedded within the story of God's interaction with His people. This establishment of a context of living is given in that particular commanded and taught 'law' which is the Greek translation of 'Torah' (Ps. 19:8)."[52] In an explication of Ulrich's argument at this point, Brian Brock argues that the nomenclature "institution" proves helpful in that it "best preserves Ulrich's interest in the estates as descriptions of the new patterns of social life that God has promised to found and secure."[53] Accordingly, the institutions are not to be understood as created orders or in an individualistic fashion. Rather, the institutions are descriptions of the shape and form of the divine promises found in Scripture regarding the establishment of and provision for creaturely human life. They are "an invitation to explore God's will and to receive God's cooperation."[54] The stress on the divine Word that establishes the estates is crucial in that their institution by God means they stand against the human propensity to understand social formations in self-referential and immanent fashion, closed off to the way that human action must always be related to God's work. In instituting these forms of life, Luther argues that God confronts human pride in its claims of sufficient knowledge and wisdom for self-justification, in its claims to generate and exercise power according to human will alone, and in its claim to provide for the necessities of life out of its own resources. Luther's "institutional" understanding of divine activity in social formation, which is to say, his understanding of the grammar of the estates, is laid out clearly in his commentary on "The Magnificat (1521)," where he describes the way the works of God form human life, providing the means for knowing God in faith and counteracting the strife of unbelief.

---

51. Ibid., 15.

52. Ulrich, "God's Commandments and their Political Presence," 45–6.

53. Brian Brock, "Why the Estates? Hans Ulrich's Recovery of an Unpopular Notion," *Studies in Christian Ethics* 20.2 (2007), 180.

54. Hans Ulrich, "On the Grammar of Lutheran Ethics," in *Lutheran Ethics at the Intersection of God's One World*, ed. Karen L. Bloomquist (Geneva: The Lutheran World Federation, 2005), 35. In the "Treatise on Good Works, 1520," Luther argues that although God could work on God's own, God does us the honor of wanting to work through and with us. If God were to work alone, "his commandments would be given us in vain, because nobody would have occasion to exercise himself in the great works of these commandments, nor would anyone test whether he regards God and his name as the highest good and would sacrifice everything for his sake." LW 44:52.

In his exegesis of Mary's song, Luther identifies three works of God, which are opposed to the works of the proud and worldly. The works of the latter consist of wisdom, power, and riches; whereas God's proper works are his mercy, judgment, and justice. These three works (which Luther divides into their negative and positive form depending on whether they are carried out among the godly or the wicked—thus rendering six works of God) can be mapped onto the institutions, such that mercy belongs to God's work in instituting *ecclesia*, judgment belongs to God's work in instituting *politia*, and justice belongs to God's work in instituting *oeconomia*. For Luther, God is to be found in these works and in these places, again demonstrating that his understanding of the institutions belongs most properly to the doctrine of God and revelation. ' "In these things," says He (i.e., God), 'I am to be found; indeed, I practice them, so near am I to them; nor do I practice them in heaven, but in the earth, where men may find Me.' "[55] Luther does not set out an ontology or epistemology of the works of God, but rather, following the biblical teaching on God's creation *ex nihilo*, he likewise understands the continuing works of God as "such that out of that which is nothing, worthless, despised, wretched, and dead, He makes that which is something, precious, honorable, blessed, and living."[56] Access to these works is not by speculation or reflection, for they cannot be taught in words, but rather one must "taste and see" (Ps. 34:8) the works of God by experience.[57] Only the one who "trusts in God with his whole heart when he is in the depths and in sore straits" can attain to such experience.[58] That is, the works of God are only known in faith, a faith that is required for recognizing them, and hence for doing God's will, given that they are so often hidden under their opposite and not determinable in advance via reduction to principles for application that can be abstracted from the ongoing divine activity. Thus, Luther insists on a continual listening to the divine address and the call to do God's will in concrete and particular attentiveness to one's neighbor.

The call for continual attentiveness in faith follows from Luther's refusal to seek God outside of the Incarnate Suffering One. Christ is the demonstration of the ways of God's working. "Christ was powerless on the cross; and yet there He performed His mightiest work."[59] The cross reveals the nature of the divine activity,

---

55. "The Magnificat, 1521," LW 21:332. "How can one know God better than in the works in which He is most Himself? Whoever understands His works correctly cannot fail to know His nature and will, His heart and mind. Hence to understand His works is an art" (331).

56. Ibid., 299.

57. Ibid., 302. In his scholia on Romans 12:2, Luther says that understanding of the divine will requires a transformed mind, which is "something even more profound than can be expressed in written words, something which can only be understood by experience." "Lectures on Romans (1515–16)," LW 25:437.

58. "The Magnificat, 1521," LW 21:302–203. "He must and will be known by faith; hence our sense and our reason must close their eyes" (341).

59. Ibid., 340.

where strength and weakness are so easily confused. When "God Himself works," then "a thing is destroyed or raised up before one knows it, and no one sees it done." Here Luther speaks of the hiddenness of God, namely, the hiding of God's strength in weakness.[60] The presence of God's strength in the despised, foolish, and poor, and in God's bringing down the noble, true, good, strong, and resplendent—this describes the nature of the divine activity for Luther and explains why recognition (though not necessarily comprehension) of such activity is only open to the eyes of faith.[61] As stated earlier, Luther describes the divine activity in terms of God's work among the godly and the wicked.

> He lets the godly become powerless and to be brought low, until everyone supposes their end is near, whereas in these very things He is present to them with all His power, yet so hidden and in secret that even those who suffer the oppression do not feel it but only believe. There is the fullness of God's power and His outstretched arm. For where man's strength ends, God's strength begins, provided faith is present and waits on Him.
>
> ... On the other hand, God lets the other half of mankind become great and mighty and exult themselves. He withdraws His power from them and lets them puff themselves up in their own power alone. For where man's strength begins, God strength ends.[62]

The institutions describe the places where the divine activity can be awaited in faith and recognized such that humans do not attempt to live out of their own resources.[63] Luther fleshes out what God's work looks like in exalting the lowly and bringing down the proud by implicitly linking it to the form it takes in each of the institutions. That is, he describes the difference that faith or unbelief makes in the institution of social forms of life, upon which depends the distinction between divine and human institutions.

---

60. In describing Luther's understanding of the hiddenness of God, Robert Jenson writes, "God's hiddenness is an impenetrability of his moral agency in his history with us ... rather than a correlate of God's ontological uniqueness or our creaturely epistemic limitations." Jenson, "The Hidden and Triune God," *International Journal of Systematic Theology* 2.1 (March 2000), 5.

61. In his "Sermon on the Faith of the Syrophenician Woman," Luther says that we must "learn firmly to cling to the Word, even though God with all his creatures appears different than his Word teaches." *The Complete Sermons of Martin Luther*, Vol. 2, ed. John Nicholas Lenker (Grand Rapids, MI: Baker Book House, 1983), 150. Luther also makes the famous assertion in this sermon that God often hides God's "Yes" in God's "No."

62. "The Magnificat, 1521," LW 21:340.

63. "It is because of our lack of faith that we cannot wait a little, until the time comes when we, too, shall see how the mercy of God together with all His might is with those who fear Him, and the arm of God with all severity and power against the proud." Ibid., 341.

The work of unbelief in the *ecclesia* is a proud wisdom, which "includes all spiritual possessions and gifts." Such gifts are "knowledge, piety, virtue, a godly life, in short, whatever is in the soul that men call divine and spiritual."[64] However, none of these good creatures of God are themselves God. In their idolatry, those who are "proud in the imagination of their hearts" confuse the creature for the Creator, elevating human work above the divine activity. Such "scholars and saints," Luther argues, appear to be in the right in that they "are not proud of their dress or conduct; they pray much, fast much, preach and study much; they also say Mass, go meekly with bowed head, and shun costly clothes."[65] Such as these are convinced that they have truth and right on their side. In fact, Luther admits that sometimes such proud people do actually have the right on their side, but that they negate it by wrongly asserting their right without setting God before their eyes. Rather than faith in the living God, they have faith in the right and in their desire to carry out the right by their own power. In spite of all appearances, however, Luther argues that such wise ones "are the most venomous and pernicious men on earth, their hearts abysses of satanic pride." The spiritually proud make the error of putting the right and the true above the living God, and in so doing "vent their pride on those who fear God," that is, on the poor in spirit.[66] Luther does not deny that the right and true are good, for God's Word itself says such, but he insists on a distinction between seeking to obtain such good by one's effort and patiently waiting in the fear of the Lord and refusing to do anything apart from God's will.[67]

Another way Luther puts the distinction is in terms of confessing and obtaining. He argues that the human work is to confess, but the obtaining must be left to God.[68] Luther offers Abraham and David as examples of those who faithfully followed this distinction. When they went into battle, he argues, they did so not for the sake of the goods (i.e., because they had the right on their side), but rather because they had a command from God. While they confessed that the right was on their side, they were willing to dispense with securing it so long as God's will was not for them to obtain it. Luther's distinction between confessing and obtaining is a powerful indictment of the rights based interest politics characteristic of our own times. "Oh," writes Luther, "this is a thing that ought to be known to all princes and rulers who, not content with confessing the right, immediately want to obtain it and win the victory, without the fear of God; they fill the world with bloodshed and misery, and think what they do is right and well done because they have, or think they have, a just cause."[69] For Luther, the justness of the cause is not determinative,

---

64. Ibid., 332.
65. Ibid., 342.
66. Ibid., 343.
67. Relatedly, Luther makes the point in his "Admonition to Peace, 1525" "that no one may sit as judge in his own case or take his own revenge." LW 46:25. For more on this theme, see Piotr J. Malysz, "*Nemo iudex in causa sua*," 370–3.
68. "The Magnificat, 1521," LW 21:336.
69. Ibid., 336–7.

but rather clinging to the promises of divine activity that makes possible a doing of the divine will in its confrontation of our idolatry.

God's work of mercy stands in opposition to the wisdom of the proud. The poor in spirit, who fear God, who await God's good giving in God's time, and who refuse to act apart from God's will, are the recipients of God's mercy. Recognition of God's mercy does not mean a denial of God's good creatures, but a refusal to cling to them rather than to God alone. It also does not mean the end of sorrow over the loss of temporal goods, but instead is capable of enduring such loss in the mode of a lament that refuses to deny the confession of God's goodness. The negative side of God's mercy is his work in "scattering the proud in the imagination of their hearts."[70] Although this work is "done quietly and in secret," it can nonetheless "be known and understood" by faith.[71]

The work of unbelief in the *oeconomia* is characterized by trust in riches, by which Luther means "good health, beauty, pleasure, strength, and every external good that may befall the body."[72] This unbelief refuses to cling to God's promise to feed human beings and thus "our wretched unbelief always hinders God from working such works in us, and ourselves from experiencing and knowing them."[73] While we should "make a trial, and venture out on His words," instead we store up provision to secure our own future, asserting that we no longer have need of God and God's works. Such activity, Luther argues, is tantamount to calling God a liar and a refusal to probe God's will in faith that God will provide all necessary things. For Luther, what is called for is not merely an "attitude" of poverty, but in a quite straightforward way, he argues that only those who have "actually come to be in a low estate and caught in it, without any human aid" can experience the work of God's justice in this respect. Without such experience of being brought low and delivered we would misread the divine work on our behalf. "If God were to fill you before you were hungry or to exalt you before you were brought low, He would have to sink to the level of a wizard or conjurer," and "such works would be altogether unworthy of His divine power and majesty."[74] In contrast to such wizardry, Luther points to the Scriptural promises that God in God's work of justice will fill the hungry while sending the rich away empty, reversing the ways of merely human *oeconomia* with the promise of the institution of divine *oeconomia*.

The work of unbelief in the *politia* is characterized by trust in might, by which Luther understands "authority, nobility, friends, high station, and honor."[75] The

---

70. Luke 1:51, quoted in ibid., 339.
71. Ibid., 339.
72. Ibid., 332.
73. Ibid., 347.
74. Ibid., 348.
75. Ibid., 332. In parallel to the works of unbelief as manifested in each of the institutions laid out in Luther's treatment of the *Magnificat* are the three "adversaries" of calling upon God and trusting God that he posits in the "Treatise on Good Works." The three are: (1) the flesh, which seeks pleasure and repose; (2) the world, which seeks riches, favor, power, and

work of God's judgment in instituting this estate takes the form of exalting the lowly while putting down the mighty. "But this, too, must all be known and waited for in faith."[76] In explicating this work of God, Luther is careful to make a distinction between the person and the office. He says that although Mary confesses here that God "casts the mighty from their seats," she does not say that God destroys their seats. "For while the world stands, authority, rule, power, and seats must remain. But God will not long permit men to abuse them and turn them against Him, inflict injustice and violence on the godly, and enjoy it, boast of them, and fail to use them in the fear of God, to His praise and in defense of righteousness."[77] Luther finds instances of God instituting God's judgment in the long history of the decline and fall of once seemingly eternal world empires. In God's rejection of the mighty of the world and in God's choosing of "those whom the world rejects, the poor, lowly, simplehearted, and despised" (1 Cor. 1:28), it becomes possible "that men may know that our salvation consists not in man's power and works but in God alone." Again, it is important not to falsely spiritualize Luther's understanding of the "lowly." By those of "low degree," Luther explicitly says that he does not mean those who are humble, "but all those who are contemptible and altogether nothing in the eyes of the world."[78] Luther's point in this is that God rules by God's Word, but this cannot be internalized or spiritualized. Rather, the institutions alert us to the way that God's Word concretely encounters, forms, and reforms the material creation, including the social forms in which human life is to be found and is made possible.

In addition to the way Luther understands God's activity through God's Word in the three estates, the fittingness of the terminology of "institutions" in describing his teaching is further brought out by displaying the connection of the estates and the sacraments. We have already discussed the "institutional" nature of the both the sacraments and the estates. The estates are conceptually quite close to the sacraments for Luther, but with an important difference that must be stressed if the teaching on the estates is not to lead to a false sacramentalization of all creation. We begin with a brief quote from Wannenwetsch, which we will then unpack to show the similarity and difference between the sacraments and the estates:

> What is essential is the relation of these constitutive forms of life to the creative Word. First, they need to be considered in the sense of their establishment (*Einsetzung*) by God, "that those three institutions (*Stifte*) or orders (*Orden*) are apprehended (*gefasst*) in God's Word and Commandment." Although the estates (*Stände*) are not *media salutis*, they are nevertheless "holy" by the Word (WA

---

honor; and (3) the wicked spirit, which seeks pride, glory, to think well of itself and to despise others. "Treatise on Good Works, 1520," LW 44:49.
   76. "The Magnificat, 1521," LW 21:343.
   77. "The Freedom of a Christian, 1520," LW 31:344.
   78. "Treatise on Good Works, 1520," LW 21:345.

26, 504, 30). As the proving ground (*Bewährungsraum*) of sanctification, they likewise describe the calling/vocation (*Beruf*) of a Christian person.[79]

The quote from Luther's "Confession Concerning Christ's Supper (1528)" embedded here, which we already brought up in the previous chapter, is key: "these three religious institutions or orders are found in God's Word and commandment; and whatever is contained in God's Word must be holy."[80] In their connection with the Word comes their quasi-sacramental character. Like baptism and the Supper, the estates are "a word to which God has bound himself."[81] In his exposition of Psalm 82, Luther writes, "The Word of God hallows and deifies everything to which it is applied. Therefore those estates that are appointed in God's Word are all holy, divine estates."[82] Speaking of the entangling of Word and element in the "Lectures on Genesis," of the logic of the material apprehended by the Word, though here with specific reference to the sacraments, Luther writes:

> Therefore the Word must always be taken into consideration and honored as that by which God takes hold of and, as it were, clothes the creatures; and a difference must be made between the creature and the Word. In the Sacrament of the Altar there are bread and wine; in Baptism there is water. These are creatures, but creatures apprehended by the Word . . . Consider only whether there is a promise and a command; for this is what imparts to the creatures a new power beyond that power which they have through their nature.[83]

As I indicated Chapter 2, it is the intermingling of the Word with the elemental world, the mediating of the spiritual by the worldly, the new conception of Word and sacrament, that constitutes Luther's discovery of the positive meaning of worldly reality and its spiritual importance. For Luther, the sacraments are spiritual because they are based on God's Word of institution. Remarkably, Luther views the estates according to the same logic, as means of God's self-giving, that is, as means of grace, although not as means of salvation.[84] Here again we see that Luther refuses a separation of the spiritual and the worldly, of a sacred and a secular realm, of nature and grace. We see this with particular clarity in his understanding of the

---

79. Wannenwetsch, "Wovon handelt die "material Ethik"?" 123 (my translation).

80. "Confession Concerning Christ's Supper, 1528," LW 37:365. Cf. 1 Timothy 4:4–5: "For everything created by God is good, and nothing is to be rejected, provided it is received with thanksgiving; for it is sanctified by God's word and by prayer." Bayer argues that Luther consciously follows this text in his explication of the three estates in the "Confession Concerning Christ's Supper." Bayer, "Nature and Institution," in *FR*, 107.

81. Ulrich, *Wie Geschöpfe leben: Konturen evangelischer Ethik*, 2nd ed. (Berlin: Lit Verlag, 2007), 112 (my translation).

82. "Psalm 82 (1530)," LW 13:71.

83. "Lectures on Genesis, Chapters 1–5 (1535–36)," LW 1: 228–9.

84. Bayer, "Nature and Institution," in *FR*, 112.

sacraments and the three estates as institutions of the Word. Human creatures are called to a wholly spiritual/wholly worldly life, because human life in its sociality is constituted at the coming together of the Word (spiritual) and the element (estate). A secular and spiritual divide supposes that we can arrange and order the world (even if only theoretically) from an autonomous standpoint outside the creation, but for Luther, the Word actively orders the world, an ordering that comes to light in the Word's self-giving always by means of the creaturely, material, and elemental. Understood in this way, "the estates contrast with every attempt to capture and classify outside of the economy of God."[85] Instead, the institutions affirm that there is no reality outside of the reality of the one Word of God who continually gives Godself to God's creatures. In fact, Luther can even say that the "creatures [are] only the hands, pipes, and means through which God gives everything."[86] The institutions are an embodiment of God's will found in God's command, and not of an abstract "divine" law somehow lying behind them, just as there is not an abstract "Word" behind the Word who is Jesus Christ given in Scripture and the sacrament of the Table. This is the common logic of the institutions and the sacraments. Both follow the logic of the *communicatio idiomatum*, Luther's conviction that God really gives Godself to us through bodily means. However, whereas in the Eucharist God gives Godself to us for our justification (the particular work of the Son), in sanctification, through the estates, God gives Godself to us to transform us, but also to preserve us as bride for Christ the bridegroom (the particular work of the Spirit). But, since for Luther God is one, these two aspects of God's giving cannot be separated and divided any more than the Triune God can be separated and divided. What God gives us is the whole of God's Triune self, but in such a way that it is not beyond what we should grasp. In God's instituting Word, humans are given what is necessary for human life. The command of God is grace in that it makes possible simple obedience without having to get all of our conceptuality in order first. The command is grace because it makes a right human relationship with God possible without the necessity of speculation into the Godhead. God meets humans here on the earth in such a way that it is enough. Human strife can find itself at rest and accept the gift of the gracious God without first setting out a comprehensive ontology or description of the Triune God.

In saying that God gives Godself to the believer in justification and in sanctification, we also mean that we can make a distinction between the sacraments and the institutions, which Luther does by distinguishing between "holy" and "saved." We refer back to our discussion of pagan virtue in the previous chapter, where we showed that Luther holds to the possibility of pagan goodness, but that such goodness is never a means of justification, for salvation belongs to faith in Jesus Christ alone. There we quoted Luther, who writes, "For to be holy and to be saved are two entirely different things. We are saved through Christ alone; but we become holy both through this faith and through these divine foundations and

---

85. Ulrich, *Wie Geschöpfe leben*, 112 (my translation).
86. BSLK, 566.20, quoted in Peters, *Ten Commandments*, 125.

orders. Even the godless may have much about them that is holy without being saved thereby. For God wishes us to perform such works to his praise and glory."[87] This distinction is vital if we are not to misunderstand Luther as sacramentalizing creation or minimizing Scripture's teaching concerning the Fall and sin, and all the ambiguity the latter lends to our judgments concerning human life in the world. The distinction makes it possible to hold both to the traditional Christian teaching that salvation is found very particularly in Christ alone without any human contribution, for the need for repentance and recognition of sin and brokenness permeating creation, while at the same time affirming the goodness of God's material creation such that we "do not call anything impure that God has made clean."[88] The distinction warns us against assuming the seat of judgment while at the same time providing the certainty of the confession that our salvation is in Christ. In other words, believers are freed for life in the estates without hindrance by the never-ending quest for justification. The locus for holiness is taken off of the works themselves and relocated in Christ. Human works are therefore holy, not because they are done in imitation of the works of Christ according to a logic of analogy, or because they correspond to a moral law that determines the relative holiness of actions based on eternal principles, but rather they are holy insofar as they are the works of God that have been "prepared in advance for us to do."[89]

Luther's utilization of the distinction between "holy" and "saved" and its attendant grammar occurs also in the concluding section of "On the Councils and the Church (1539)." Having discussed the seven *notae ecclesiae*, Luther writes, "In addition to these seven principal parts there are other outward signs that identify the Christian church, namely, those signs whereby the Holy Spirit sanctifies us according to the second table of Moses." He argues that as the seven marks of the church, including the sacraments proper (baptism and Lord's Supper) belong to the first table of the Decalogue, so these too could be divided into seven marks, "seven holy possessions or seven principal parts, according to the seven commandments."[90] Therefore, as Word and sacrament belong to the first table, the three estates belong to the second table as the place of obedience to the commandments.[91]

87. "Confession Concerning Christ's Supper, 1528," LW 37:365.
88. Acts 10:15.
89. Eph. 2:10.
90. "On the Councils and the Church, 1539," LW 41:166–7. Luther's makes a similar division in the "Treatise on Good Works, 1520," stating that the fourth through tenth commandments correspond to the petition in the Lord's prayer, "Thy will be done" (LW 44:80). The first table enables exercise of faith in action toward God, while the second table enables faith in action toward the neighbor.
91. Ulrich writes, "'Institutions' signify a reality equivalent to the commandments." Ulrich, "God's Commandments and their Political Presence," 52. This point marks an important difference between the "traditional" Lutheran understanding of the estates as "orders of creation" and Ulrich's interpretation of the estates that we follow in this chapter. Likewise, Wolf argues that the estates place "obedience to the commandments of God at the

Having stressed the distinction between the sacraments and the estates, which corresponds to the distinction between justification and sanctification, or between the first and second tables of the Decalogue, it is important to stress a further similarity between the two, and that is that both provide believers with the certainty of being within God's will. In the assurance that the works performed in these places are pleasing to God, these works are properly described as worship.[92] Worship according to both tables is centered on the Word, whether in attending to the Word as preached, as instituted in baptism and the Supper, or as instituted in the estates. As in the sacraments, so in the institutions, the certainty comes not from the elements considered in themselves, but from the instituting Word. As Bayer puts it, although the element is itself already a word, it remains ambiguous and uncertain without a definite word of institution.[93] Again, we make the point that the estates provide the certainty and concrete definiteness of institutions that counteracts the wandering heart of Cain with its impulse to flee.

A brief aside is in order at this point to show how an interpretation of the three estates according to the logic of "institutionality" such as we set out earlier differs from the many modern interpreters and reinterpreters of Luther's teaching on the three estates. We have already discussed the use of "orders of creation" (*Schöpfungsordnungen*) by theologians such as Paul Althaus.[94] Interpretations along similar lines see the estates as structures of life given as part of God's common grace or as "places of responsibility" giving moral context within which to live.[95] Our differences from these interpreters are clear. Much closer to our view is the interpretation of Dietrich Bonhoeffer. In his *Ethics*, Bonhoeffer argues that

---

forefront." Ernst Wolf, "Die Institutionen als von Gott angebotener Ort der Bewährung in Verantwortung," in *Sozialethik: Theologische Grundlagen*, 3rd ed. (Göttingen: Vandenhoeck & Ruprecht, 1975), 178 (my translation). Wolf takes aim at Brunner for tearing apart the unity of order [*Ordnung*] and the commandment of God (173).

92. Wannenwetsch, *Political Worship*, 60.

93. Bayer, "Nature and Institution," in *FR*, 110; cf. also Bayer, "I Believe that God Has Created Me with all that Exists. An Example of Catechetical-Systematics," *LQ* 8.2 (Summer 1994), 146: "The element without the word of institution would be blind; the word of institution without the element would be empty." This speaks to Luther's insistence on not separating the Spirit and the Word.

94. For Althaus's interpretation along these lines, see his chapter "Stations and Vocations (The Orders)," in his *The Ethics of Martin Luther*, 36–42. This view tends to see the orders as structures within creation or in somewhat static fashion as stations (*Ständen*) in society to which individuals belong as a result of being placed within them by God. On this interpretation, individuals have a duty to remain within their station (whether as parent, spouse, ruler, servant, etc.) for the preservation of society.

95. For an important articulation of this view, see Robert Benne, "Lutheran Ethics: Perennial Themes and Contemporary Challenges," in *The Promise of Lutheran Ethics*, 13–17 and Benne, *Ordinary Saints: An Introduction to the Christian Life* (Minneapolis: Fortress Press, 2003), 69–83.

the Lutheran doctrine of the three estates "must be replaced by a doctrine which is drawn from the Bible."[96] He develops his doctrine with use of the term "mandates" and extends Luther's three to four: the church, marriage and the family, labor and government.[97] Bonhoeffer describes these as the places where God's commandment comes to us.[98] In the mandates, God deputizes an actor or representative in his place and assigns her a commission. Significantly, Bonhoeffer argues, "The divine mandates depend solely on God's *one* commandment as it is revealed in Jesus Christ."[99] They do not come from history or "arise out of the created world," but rather come from above.[100] With these statements, Bonhoeffer makes clear that his conception of the mandates is centered on Christology. In fact, Brian Brock describes Bonhoeffer's mandates as "christologically keyed descriptions of the features of reality which allow us to encounter Christ."[101] While agreeing with Bonhoeffer about the centrality of Christology and distancing from nature and history in explicating the estates, I argue that it is better to follow Luther's lead in restricting their number to three, rather than the expansion Bonhoeffer carries out. I will make this argument under the treatment of the estate of *oeconomia* later.[102]

96. Dietrich Bonhoeffer, *Ethics*, Dietrich Bonhoeffer Works 6, ed. Clifford J. Green, trans. Reinhard Krauss, Charles C. West, and Douglas W. Stott (Minneapolis: Fortress Press, 2009), 389n. 2.

97. That there are four thus comes from Bonhoeffer's splitting the *oeconomia* into marriage/family and labor. Ibid., 68. Bonhoeffer says that his purpose in using the term "mandate" is "to contribute to renewing and reclaiming the old concepts of order, estate, and office" (390).

98. Ibid., 388.

99. Ibid., 390; emphasis in the original.

100. Ibid., 380.

101. Brian Brock, "Bonhoeffer and the Bible in Christian Ethics," 24.; cf. Jordan J. Ballor, "Christ in Creation: Bonhoeffer's Orders of Preservation and Natural Theology," *The Journal of Religion* 86.1 (January 2006), 1–22

102. Another important interpreter of the institutions worthy of a note is Ernst Wolf, "Die Institutionen." He speaks of "occasions for good works" which he says are partly analogous to concepts like orders of creation, orders of preservation, and Bonhoeffer's mandates. Wolf holds that in these places one sees the foundations (*Stiftungen*) of God that require the acceptance of humans for their realization. As such, they are not merely a state or condition (*Zurstand*), but rather a process. They are the place where God "offers humans the place of probing in responsibility," which means that at the same time he puts them under his command. Wolf thus offers an initial summary of these places: they are "the social structures of existence (*Daseinsstrukturen*) of the created world as an invitation of God to ordered and formed activity (*Tat*) in the freedom of the obedience of faith towards his command" (173, my translation). They provide space for the reality of life and are properly located in God's covenant with his people, to which God remains faithful. In them God's people are proved in partnership with God within God's eschatological history.

Luther's Description of the Three Institutions

Having set out in outline form the way in which Luther understands the estates as instituted by divine activity in contrast to "orders of creation" interpretations, we now turn to Luther's fuller description of each of the three. However, in presenting this description, it is useful first to highlight the relative importance of the doctrine in relation to Luther's thinking as a whole before turning to each of the three in turn. Oswald Bayer has provided textual evidence for the centrality of the teaching in Luther's theology and for its greater weight in his thinking than the doctrine of the two governments.[103] The teaching is found in most concentrated form in Luther's 1535 commentary on Genesis, but Bayer shows that precedent for his handling of Genesis here can be seen as far back as 1520, including in "The Freedom of a Christian,"[104] Luther's commentaries on the Psalms,[105] and in his sermons on John.[106] The centrality of the institutions can be seen in Luther's own summations of his theology and his own understanding of the significance of the Reformation. This includes his mention of the key importance of this doctrine in his preface to the Smalcald Articles,[107] in his 1528 "Confession Concerning Christ's Supper,"[108] at the conclusion of his 1539 "On Councils and the Church,"[109] and in his table talks.[110] Importantly, in these self-summations of Luther's theology, the doctrine of the two governments is absent.[111] This is not to discount the latter doctrine, but simply to acknowledge the need to contextualize and relate it to the more important doctrine of the three estates.

Bayer describes the doctrine as "a way of expounding [the primeval history in the book of Genesis] which appropriates *the social dimensions of creation and sin* for Luther's contemporary setting."[112] The doctrine provides "a narrative of origins" with implications for all later social development, as "these estates continue and abide throughout all kingdoms, throughout the wide world and unto the world's end."[113] They are both necessary and inescapable for human life. They should

---

103. Oswald Bayer, *MLT*, 122–5; "Nature and Institution," in *FR*, 94.
104. LW 31:360.
105. LW 13:44ff.
106. LW 22:477.
107. The Smalcald Articles (Preface), 10, in *BoC*: 299. For Luther's understanding of this document as an important summary of his theology, see William R. Russell, "The Smalcald Articles, Luther's Theological Testament," *LQ* 5.3 (Autumn 1991), 277–96.
108. LW 37:364–5.
109. LW 41:176–7.
110. See, for example, LW 54:42–3.
111. Bayer, "Nature and Institution," in *FR*, 94.
112. Ibid., 92 (emphasis mine). I would perhaps sharpen Bayer's statement to reflect not only creation and fall, but also new creation. These three dramatic settings, corresponding to Luther's understanding of the law, must always be taken into account when considering Luther's specific comments on the estates.
113. "Psalm 111 (1530)," LW 13:369.

not be viewed in sociological terms as straightforwardly applicable to different levels within any given political or social order. Rather, they are "con-creatures" of humankind, "created together with man in order to provide the social spheres that are necessary for a flourishing and obedient life."[114] As such, they are neither eternal static entities preceding the creation of humans, nor are they merely the result of human invention. Instead they are given together with humans at the time of the creation of humans. This is an important point to make if the institutions are not to fall victim to "right- and leftwing idealist accounts."[115] They do not follow the eternal dictates of a universal reason, nor are they properly subject to a never-ending deconstructive politics according to the hermeneutics of suspicion.

In addition to opening up the narrative of origins in Genesis, the three institutions further provide Luther with a hermeneutic key for the interpretation of Scripture and the divine activity more generally. He writes,

> The Bible speaks and teaches about the works of God. About this there is no doubt. These works are divided in three hierarchies [*hierarchias*]: the household [*Oeconomiam*], the government [*politiam*], the church [*ecclesiam*]. If a verse does not fit the church, we should let it stay in the government or the household, whichever it is best suited to.[116]

It is essential to stress the Scriptural basis of the teaching on the three estates in Luther's theology. As we noted previously, "These three religious institutions or orders are found in God's Word and commandment."[117] The focus on the need for the Word distinguishes our interpretation of the estates from renderings that find them immediately open to human reason and instinct. Rather, our argument is that the estates can be accessed only in the Word of God.[118] They are not sociological constructs, philosophical categories, or mediating concepts, but a way of drawing together Scripture's emphasis on the aspects of human life to which God has attached God's promise. Although the relationships in the estates "may also belong to natural life, 'recognition' (*Erkenntnis*) of them is not revealed by rational contemplation itself."[119] As such, Wannenwetsch notes that for Luther marriage, as a paradigmatic illustrative example, is a specific task of recognition (*Erkenntnisaufgabe*). Such recognition can happen only by listening to the Word. Luther says that those who recognize it "believe steadfastly that God himself instituted it (*Eingesetz*). For they have the surety of God's word that it pleases him in all that they do and suffer."[120] The point here is that it is not the will of the

114. Wannenwetsch, "Luther's Moral Theology," 130.
115. Ibid., 131.
116. "Table Talk," LW 54:446; WATR 5.218, 12–18. See also LW 54:42.
117. "Confession Concerning Christ's Supper, 1528," LW 37:365.
118. See Brian Brock, *Singing the Ethos*, 220–1.
119. Wannenwetsch, 'Wovon handelt die "material Ethik"?" 124 (my translation).
120. WA 10.2, 294, 27–32, quoted in Wannenwetsch, "Wovon handelt die 'material Ethik'?", 124 (my translation).

couple coming together or the sanction of the community that makes a marriage (important as these may be), but rather the very Word of God who joins the two together. This being joined by and in the Word *is* marriage. The task of marriage is to recognize this Word, the word that tells me that this one and no other is my husband/wife, who God has brought to me just as he brought Eve to Adam.

An understanding of the institutions as the provision of God in God's ongoing activity in God's Word does not entirely rule out anything like a natural law, but it does say that it is not immediately available to us. It is only as our perception is conformed to Christ through meditation on the Word of God that the creation is freed once again (or rather, our perception is freed) to address us as a word from the Creator. Central here is not the establishment of universal moral principles or dictates of practical reason, but rather being properly attuned to the world by means of Scripture. The institutions are a hermeneutic for interpreting both the world and Scripture, and for seeing the Word in the words.[121] As an aid in interpreting Scripture, they are also descriptions of the material content of Scripture; they are the "deep grammar of Scripture."[122] Creation and its meaning are found only within the realm of the Word, a realm outside of which there is only death and nothingness. So Luther does not look to nature or creation in the abstract to tell us about the "orders," but rather he finds them running throughout the Word of God as revealed in Scripture. For Luther, the Word is more fundamental than natures. He makes this point when considering the death causing function of the tree of the knowledge of good and evil. He argues that it was not the intrinsic nature of the tree that made it deadly, but that the Word of God made it so. This same Word enables the preservation and "endless propagation" of all creatures.[123]

As places where human beings encounter the concrete command of God as God addresses them even today, the estates belong, in an ultimate sense, not to the doctrine of creation (although, of course, creation is not excluded), but rather to the doctrine of revelation. They are instituted by the divine address. They speak of God's revelation of God's will to and for God's human creatures, the creatures who, being made in God's image, are God's counterpart (*Gegenüber*).[124] They are guidance to the places of God's promise, places God gives to humans in order that God's will may be done.[125] For Luther, this means that the command and obedience or disobedience, faith or unbelief, is a more basic reality than morality. The institutions give us direction as to where to await the divine activity in faith

---

121. Brock, "Bonhoeffer and the Bible," 14.

122. As Brock describes Ulrich's "re-expression" of the three estates teaching, "Ulrich sees the theory of the *Stände* as encapsulating a deep grammar of Scripture in the recurring biblical emphasis on the divine provision for human *salvation, co-operation, feeding, and governance*." Brock, "On Generating Categories in Theological Ethics: Barth, Genesis and the *Ständlehre*," *TynBul* 61.1 (2010), 66.

123. "Lectures on Genesis, Chapters 1–5 (1535–36)," LW 1:95.

124. On humans as God's *Gegenüber*, see Wolf, "Die Institutionen," 175.

125. Brock, "On Generating Categories," 67.

of divine advent, which is the basic reality. As Ulrich puts it, the institutions are concerned with "the way in which what humans do (working, praying, ruling) remains present to the many different ways in which God's activity shapes and bears human life."[126] We now turn to a closer examination of each of three as understood by Luther.

Ecclesia

Luther's fullest treatment of the estates comes in his "Lectures on Genesis." Here, as elsewhere, the centrality of the Word is evident. Luther asks, "What else is the entire creation than the Word of God uttered by God, or extended to the outside?"[127] As God created by the Word, so God's activity in governing and preserving the world continues by God's efficacious Word.[128] The church (*ecclesia*) is the fundamental estate, whose establishment (*institutio*) comes before the household or the state.[129] The church was founded upon the occasion of God's first address to mankind in Genesis 2:16–17: "You may freely eat of every tree of the garden; but of the tree of the knowledge of good and evil you shall not eat, for in the day that you eat of it you shall die." The command to eat is the primal institution (cf. Matt. 26:26), in which Luther says the Lord is preaching the Word to Adam. Had Adam remained in paradise, Luther argues, this preaching would have served as a Bible and as the sum of wisdom for Adam and for all who followed after him.[130] In addressing this word to humans, God provides humans with the concrete possibility for worshipping the Creator. In fact, Luther suggests that without the Fall, Adam and all his descendants would have gathered on every Sabbath around the tree of the knowledge of good and evil, which provided an outward form for worship of God.[131] As we noted earlier, Luther calls this giving of an outward form of worship "Law," hence, the law understood in this sense precedes the Fall.[132] Speaking of this gift of the law, Luther writes, "God gave Adam Word, worship, and religion in its barest, purest and simplest form." This command was given for Adam in order that humankind would have an outward and concrete focus for worship and obedience.[133] Again, we note the importance of the entangling of the Word and

---

126. Ulrich, *Wie Geschöpfe leben*, 110 (my translation).
127. "Lectures on Genesis, Chapters 1–5 (1535–36)," LW 1:22.
128. Ibid., 75.
129. Ibid., 103. However, it may be more accurate, theologically speaking, to refer to a simultaneity of the three estates, rather than a temporal ranking. They all follow from the prior rule of God and the stability of God's purpose for human flourishing before any human response.
130. Ibid., 105. Luther offers that Psalms 148 and 149 would have provided the liturgy for worship in the garden.
131. Ibid., 106.
132. Ibid., 101.
133. Ibid., 109.

the material world for Luther, a definite turn away from false spiritualization and inwardness.

The *ecclesia* is, as Bayer writes, "the estate of the human being who is addressed by God, who is furnished with the ability to respond freely in thankfulness."[134] As such, every human being belongs to the church by definition, for to be human is to be addressed by God and to be created for worshipful response to this address. In fact, Luther points to the Sabbath as revealing that knowledge and worship of God is the end for which humans were created. He writes, "On the seventh day [God] wanted men to busy themselves both with His Word and with the other forms of worship established by Him, so that we might give first thought to the fact that this nature was created chiefly for acknowledging and glorifying God."[135] Given that it is the common vocation of all human beings to worship God, this is a church "established without walls."[136] The institution of the church is concerned with the relationship between God and humans and is fundamentally about faith or unbelief. Including the *ecclesia* within the estates in this way has important implications for our understanding of natural religion.[137] Insofar as religion is a part of creation, even religions other than Christianity maintain something of the truth of creatureliness in relation to the Creator.[138] Luther's statement in the Large Catechism should be considered in this respect: "All who are outside this Christian people [i.e., those who confess the Creed], whether heathen, Turks, Jews or false Christians and hypocrites" nonetheless can be described as believing in and worshipping "the one, true God," but without the confidence that comes from having Christ and the gifts of the Holy Spirit.[139] That is, there is a general faith that there is a good and gracious God, but not that God's goodness is *pro me*. In other words, non-Christians seem to have some form of the *ecclesia*, but without certainty, similar to Cain's experience of the institutions, which we will discuss in more detail later when we further clarify the institutions as places of remaining in God's will.

---

134. Bayer, *MLT*, 122.
135. "Lectures on Genesis, Chapters 1–5 (1535–36)," LW 1:80.
136. Ibid., 103.
137. Bayer, *MLT*, 126–39. Bayer interprets Luther's "natural theology" through the lens of the latter's "Lectures on Jonah, 1526," LW 19.
138. Cf. Bernd Wannenwetsch, "'Christians and Pagans': Towards a Trans-Religious Second Naïveté or How to be a Christological Creature," in *Who Am I?*, 175–96. Wannenwetsch argues that Bonhoeffer views religion along the same lines as Luther treats the law, that is, "religion must be narrated as a plot featured within God's salvific story, in which the meaning of individual concepts change as they relate to each respective act within the divine play" (180). Wannenwetsch then spells out Bonhoeffer's understanding of religion according to this dramatic, and as such, he provides us with an instructive account of the way the estates are to be interpreted according to the story of God with God's people—that is, according to creation, fall, and new creation.
139. The Large Catechism II, 66, in *BoC*:440.

More importantly, the *ecclesia* is the paradigmatic estate in that it shows clearly the nature of human social life as established by the divine speech. Ulrich writes, "The grammar of cooperation and living with God is to be found paradigmatically within the church, the Christian congregation and community. Here is the place where people learn to be aware of God's presence." It is at the place where God establishes *ecclesia*, where hearts and minds are transformed, that human beings learn what it means to live life under the rule of the Spirit. In being so ruled, "the Church is set free for the contradictory witness of God's governance and God's work. The church is the paradigmatic institution for this very political task."[140] Ulrich highlights here the way in which the divine working counters human presumption, as articulated in Luther's interpretation of the *Magnificat*. Humans become attuned to this working as they learn attentiveness in the practice of the worship of the church—that is, as the Spirit rules God's people. In the experience of the divine rule, in Word and sacrament, Christians are sensitized to the ways in which God's activity as promised in economic and political life can be experienced as well and further learn what it means to respond in faithful praise for the Creator's goodness.[141]

Oeconomia

The household, or *oeconomia*, is the second estate in Luther's articulation of the doctrine. The household is understood here to include marriage and the family, business and work (trade, husbandry, manufacture, etc.), and education. In his "Exposition of Psalm 127," Luther notes that he understands "'managing the household' [*haushallten*] in the same manner that Aristotle employs the concept of the 'oeconomia.'"[142] Again, the household estate is instituted in God's Word, "It is not good that the man should be alone" (Gen. 2:18), and in His declaration that a man should leave his mother and father and cleave to his wife, "and they become one flesh" (Gen. 2:24). Christ confirmed this divine institution when he said, "Therefore what God has joined together, let no one separate" (Mark 10:9). God joins the married couple together; the relationship is based not on a mere act of the human will. Rather, as we mentioned above, the marriage tie is constituted by the Word of God. Given Luther's conception of marriage, Bayer writes, "We cannot understand our marriage solely as the result of our own will by seeing it as nothing more than a contract, which either one can dissolve by mutual consent."[143] Rather, those with a proper understanding of marriage are those, in Luther's words, "who firmly believe that God himself instituted it, brought husband and wife together,

---

140. Ulrich, "On the Grammar of Lutheran Ethics," 41.

141. Bayer argues that in baptism and the Eucharist a "second naivety" is communicated to the participants, allowing experience of the new creation and disclosing the goodness of the Creator God, "Categorical Imperative or Categorical Gift?" in *FR*, 16.

142. "Exposition of Psalm 127, 1524," LW 45:322.

143. Bayer, *MLT*, 145.

and ordained that they should beget children and care for them. For this they have God's word, Genesis 1, and they can be certain that he does not lie."[144] In addition to once again stressing the centrality of the Word, this passage shows that Luther views marriage as part of the divine provision for the sustenance of human life. The institution of marriage also gives to each spouse a "dwelling place," a place that calls in the restless human heart and its idolatrous wanderings.[145] Just as the promise and command in the *ecclesia* gives humans a definite place and form for worship, so too does the establishment of *oeconomia* by the divine Word give humans a definite place and form for labor and sustenance.

In that Psalm 127:1 declares, "Unless the Lord builds the house, those who build it labor in vain," it is the case that the household and economy cannot be separated from the ongoing activity of God. As in the *ecclesia*, so also in the *oeconomia*, human life is properly characterized by faith in which human work is always responsive to the prior divine initiative. "So we see that the managing of a household should and must be done in faith—then there will be enough—so that men come to acknowledge that everything depends not on our doing, but on God's blessing and support."[146] When humans begin to believe that their sustenance is a result of their own efforts rather than the goodness of God, their labor becomes vain and is characterized by anxiety and covetousness. Humans take unto themselves the responsibility for producing a world in which they can live, leading to exploitation, the subjection of humans to the utilitarian calculus of other humans,[147] and the subjection of the creation (understood as "environment") to false gods made in the image of humans.[148] In opposition to this idolizing of work, Luther argues that "all our labor is nothing more than the finding and collecting of God's gifts; it is quite unable to create or preserve anything."[149] Instead of the ceaseless acquisition

144. LW 45:38; quoted in Bayer, *MLT*, 146.
145. "Lectures on Genesis, Chapters 1–5 (1535–36)," LW 1:136, cf., 132.
146. "Exposition of Psalm 127, 1524," LW 45:324.
147. Paul Lehmann, in a similar context, captures such exploitation in his quotation of Norbert Wiener's phrase: "the human use of human beings." Lehmann, *The Decalogue and a Human Future: The Meaning of the Commandments for Making and Keeping Human Life Human* (Grand Rapids, MI: Eerdmans, 1995), 19.
148. See Oliver O'Donovan, *Resurrection and Moral Order: An Outline for Evangelical Ethics*, 2nd ed. (Grand Rapids, MI: Eerdmans, 1992), 52. Hamann writes, "If the belly is your god, then even the hairs on your head are under its guardianship. Every creature will alternately become your sacrifice and your idol—Subject against its will—but in hope, it groans beneath your yoke or at your vain conduct." J. G. Hamann, "Aesthetica in nuce," in *Writings on Philosophy and Language*, ed. Kenneth Haynes (Cambridge: Cambridge University Press, 2007), 78.
149. "Exposition of Psalm 127, 1524," LW 45:327. Ulrich, in "On the Grammar of Lutheran Ethics," writes, "Nothing that anyone produces originates entirely from human work, but human production is created out of the wealth that is given to all humanity" (39). In addition to opposing an assumption of scarcity, Ulrich argues that Luther's conception of the economy is essentially based on a communal model, not a liberal individual model.

that drives those who take total responsibility for sustenance unto themselves, Luther calls for a laboring that rests secure in trust that God alone establishes and maintains households by God's instituting Word. Luther does not deny human work or activity in the household and economy, but insists that it can only take its proper form if it follows first from trust in God's own work and activity.

We noted earlier that in his reworking of the Lutheran teaching on the three estates, Dietrich Bonhoeffer split the *oeconomia* in two, separating marriage and family from labor. At first glance, this seems to be a reasonable move given the fact that in the modern developed world the home and the "place of business" have become increasingly distinct and separate. However, the estates, conceived as places indicated in the promises of Scripture, preclude such expansion following upon historical–sociological developments. The estates serve a critically heuristic role in asking whether any given social arrangement is consistent with trust in the divine promise to provide for human life (i.e., they unmask the faith lying at the root of any given social order). If estates are expanded following upon sociological developments, then they become simply sociological descriptors that come dangerously close to reading divine revelation off of history. Of course, this would be exactly contrary to Bonhoeffer's insistence that the mandates are found in Scripture, not nature or history. Nonetheless, in allowing for an expansion that follows historical development, in this case, the separation of the "economy" from the life of the "household," such developments are in danger of being seen as a given rather than being questioned for their underlying presuppositions about what it takes to sustain and nourish human life. This is not to say that such separation is precluded a priori. Such preclusion would be to falsely assume that the estates refer ontologically to structures within creation rather than as descriptors of the shape of the divine promise. The estates do not seek to be an exhaustive description of the form of human social existence, but are instead a means for attuning our discernment in the direction of the specific promises in Scripture for places where human life can be lived.[150] However, a multiplication of the estates will at some point begin to exclude some human beings from particular estates. For example, if labor is defined more and more in terms of present social practice, such that it is finally separated in a totalized way from the life of the household, then those who do not engage directly in the activities of a highly specialized "workforce" come to be excluded. For Luther, however, all human beings belong to all three estates. God has promised to encounter *all* humans there, so that any move toward exclusion necessarily violates the grammar of the estates. At the point in which social formations begin to exclude certain persons, the critically heuristic nature of Luther's teaching on the estates will prove most forceful, challenging both our conceptions of what constitutes "human being" and our assumptions about proper forms of social activity for humans in light of what God has promised to provide for human life.

---

150. For this paragraph, see Brian Brock, "Why the Estates?" 198.

Politia

The political estate (*politia*) is the third in Luther's teaching. However, a question immediately arises as to the political estate's creational status in Luther's thinking: was the political estate present at the original creation, or is it instituted only after the Fall as an emergency measure necessary to keep a reign on sin? Luther's thought on this question seems rather unclear. In fact, Luther scholarship has long been divided on the question of the status of politics within Luther's thinking itself. Paul Althaus and George Forell have argued that Luther assumed a kind of governmental order in the primitive state,[151] while Heinrich Bornkamm has rejected this assumption.[152] Meanwhile, W. D. J. Carghill Thompson remains ambivalent given the ambiguity of Luther's account.[153]

First, the evidence in Luther's writing for politics being but a response to the effects of the Fall. In the "Lectures on Genesis," Luther argues that the state is a necessary response to the depravity of nature consequent upon the Fall.[154] Likewise, in his treatise on "Temporal Authority (1523)," Luther argues that God ordained the temporal government to restrain "the un-Christian and wicked."[155] Thus, we see in Luther an account of government as an emergency measure that seems to correspond fairly closely with both Milbank and Augustine as interpreted by Milbank. However, even understood in this manner, for Luther government is still a divine institution expressive of God's rule in the world.

---

151. Paul Althaus, *The Ethics of Martin Luther*, 47–8; George Forell, *Faith Active in Love: An Investigation of the Principles Underlying Luther's Social Ethics* (Minneapolis: Augsburg Publishing House, 1954), 15.

152. See Heinrich Bornkamm, *Luther's Doctrine of the Two Kingdoms in the Context of His Theology*, trans. Karl H. Hertz (Philadelphia: Fortress Press, 1966), 34–5. Bornkamm acknowledges that leading Luther scholars have been divided on this question. He cites Werner Elert, Gustav Törnvall, and Franz Lau as proponents of the view that Luther assumed a prelapsum politics. On the other hand, Harald Diem and Johannes Heckel rejected this assumption.

153. W. D. J. Carghill Thompson, *The Political Thought of Martin Luther* (Brighton, Sussex: Harvester Press, 1984), 66–7. Thompson ultimately argues, "For Luther there is a clear distinction between government before and after the Fall. Before the Fall government, at least among persons, was essentially non-coercive, Adam's rule being limited to the beasts." Bayer in his constructive work chooses "a third option, which makes use of and applies an element of truth that is to be found in each." He argues that support for both positions can be found in Luther's writings, particularly in the way Luther roots the political in the economic estate. See Bayer, *MLT*, 147–9. Cf. Bayer, "Law and Morality," *LQ* 17.1 (Spring 2003), 63–76. While arguing that the *politia* was called into existence with humans according to Luther, Wannenwetsch acknowledges that Luther "did not always express himself unambiguously" on this question. *Political Worship*, 62.

154. "Lectures on Genesis, Chapters 1–5 (1535–36)," LW 1:104.

155. "Temporal Authority, 1523," LW 45:91.

However, the case for a different understanding of politics can also be found throughout Luther's writings.[156] Perhaps the best way to resolve this difficulty in Luther's writings would be, following Yeago's dramatic account of the law in Luther's theology, to say that the political changes form *pre-* and *postlapsum*, but there is only one political, that is, only one rule of God, which is experienced differently depending on the human subject of this rule, whether as innocent Adam, fallen humans, or reconciled in Christ to receive the gift of God's rule in its proper and original sense. Warrant for proposing this parallel between the law and politics comes from Luther himself, who writes that one "may correctly call civil government the rule of sin (*regnum peccati*) . . . This is the one and foremost function of government, to hold sin in check."[157] Here government corresponds to the first use of the law, but this is not the whole story of politics for Luther, just as the political and theological uses of the law are not the whole story. It has already been noted that Luther speaks of the political estate as a "con-creature" of humankind, brought into being with humankind before the Fall into sin.[158] In the "Lectures on Genesis" Luther calls the Garden of Eden a "royal headquarters" (*sedem regiam*) from which humans are to "rule (*imperium*) over all the beasts."[159] Of course, here, we have something very close to Augustine's understanding of *prelapsum* rule, in which humans ruled over animals, but not over other humans. However, it is also clear that Luther recognized relationships of authority between human beings even in the primeval state. George Forell argues, from Luther's "Lectures on Genesis," that even between Adam and Eve there was an authority structure. Forell writes, "The woman does not hear God's word directly but learns from Adam. This shows that even before the Fall the rule and authority was in the hands of men . . . Authority is also a divine order which precedes the Fall."[160] While Forell is correct in noting that authority is present *prelapsum* according to Luther's reading of the text, this does not necessarily indicate an assumption of patriarchy. Rather, Luther attributes to both Adam and Eve the priestly office of preaching and teaching.[161] In either event, however, human being is constituted by its being always in relations of authority, by always being in a state of hearing (either God or one's fellow humans) and responding (i.e., speaking). As Bayer argues, the ability to hear and speak makes human life possible. He writes:

> Whoever can hear places himself under the power of the one to whom he listens, into the power of the one who speaks. The one who speaks, who addresses another, positions that person, deals with that person in relation to himself, and even exercises authority over him . . . As one who hears and speaks, like every

---

156. In addition to the passages considered here, see those treated in Chapter 3.
157. "Lectures on Genesis, Chapters 1–5 (1535–36)," LW 1:104; WA 41, 79, 11.
158. See Wannenwetsch, *Political Worship*, 62, quoting Luther WA 40 III, 222, 35ff.
159. "Lectures on Genesis, Chapters 1–5 (1535–36)," LW 1:101; WA 41, 77, 24–6.
160. Forell, *Faith Active in Love*, 146.
161. "Lectures on Genesis, Chapters 1–5 (1535–36)," LW 1:246.

other human being, I am one who has power over others and one over whom others have power. Only within this relationship between having power and needing to respond—and not somehow outside of it—does the human being have dignity and his freedom.[162]

Human existence is rooted in human responsiveness to the address of God, but also to the address of one's fellow humans. Human existence is defined by it responsibility to both. As Gerhard Ebeling writes, "Man exists *coram mundo* and *coram Deo*. This fact of being addressed by another party, of being dependent on an *extra se*, this openness of his existence, is not something tacked on to his human nature, but constitutes his human nature as a nature called to responsibility."[163] Fundamentally, human existence is not individualistic for Luther, but is always a matter of relation to God and one's fellow creatures. Human existence is by definition social, and therefore political. Political structures make possible human responsiveness to the address of others. They mediate speech to one another. Therefore, the most unpolitical act imaginable is to silence another's voice, which is to say, to evade our responsibility to the other, to fail to respond to her address.

In addition to acknowledging relations of authority among human beings even before the Fall, Luther also envisions the *politia* as flowing from the *oeconomia*, the latter of which is clearly given with humanity before the Fall. As we noted in Chapter 3, Luther writes, "For a whole community is nothing other than many households combined. By this term we comprehend all manner of principalities, dominions, and kingdoms, or any other grouping of people."[164] He draws out the relationship between the estate of the household and the first (church) and third estate (temporal authorities) in his exposition of the fourth commandment's exhortation to honor mother and father. "From this commandment," Luther writes, "we teach that after the excellent works of the first three commandments there are not better works than to obey and serve all those who are set in authority over us."[165] The honor owed one's mother and father is to be extended to "temporal lords" and "spiritual fathers," for "everybody must be ruled and subject to other men."[166] As such, this commandment extends to all relationships in which

---

162. Bayer, *MLT*, 149–50. Oliver O'Donovan also comments on the centrality of speech to politics: "At the heart of politics is true speech, divine speech, entering into conflict with the false orders of human society, the guarantor of the only true order that the universe can ever attain." O'Donovan, "History and Politics in the Book of Revelation," in *Bonds of Imperfection*, 47.

163. Gerhard Ebeling, "The Necessity of the Doctrine of the Two Kingdoms," in *Word and Faith*, 401–402.

164. "Exposition of Psalm 127, 1524," LW 45:328.

165. "Treatise on Good Works, 1520," LW 44:80.

166. Ibid., 82. It is important to note that in his exhortation to honor Luther draws the limits of obedience to matters which do not violate the first three commandments. He writes, "Therefore, our first task it to take a firm hold of the first three commandments and the First Table, and be quite certain that no man, neither bishop, pope, nor even angel,

authority is present. And, as we have just seen, in every relationship in which a human being is involved, authority is present. Obviously, honor to one's natural parents comes first in this command. The second work of this command, however, is to pay honor and obedience to one's "spiritual mother, the holy Christian church, and [its] spiritual authorities."[167] The third work of the fourth commandment "is to obey the temporal authority, as Paul teaches in Romans 13, and Titus 3, and St. Peter in I Peter 2."[168] It is decisive that honor is due those in authority in all three estates because of the function assigned those in authority in each estate, namely, the duty to orient those under their authority properly to the first three commandments and also the last six. It is through this commandment—that is, through the observance of proper relationships within the institutions—that one is able to stand correctly in relation both to God and to one's neighbors. Parents are to teach their children "by words and works to serve God in the first three commandments" and to "exercise [themselves] in good works toward men" in the last seven commandments. The fourth commandment is the key to upholding the others. As such, Luther argues, "there is no greater, nobler power on earth than that of parents over their children, since they have spiritual and temporal power over them."[169] Here it can be seen how both spiritual and temporal authority flow forth from the original parental relationship. In this way, the political estate follows from the household estate. Thus Luther's statement: "The household is the source of all public affairs."[170]

Given the close tie between the household and the political order, I would argue that the overall thrust of Luther's writings, and especially the logic of his theology, tends toward an understanding of the political institution as a con-creature alongside the other two institutions.[171] Again, what we have is not a temporal ranking, but a change in form following a change in the subject of God's rule. After the Fall, coercion becomes a tragic part of politics, just as the law takes on a restraining and accusing function. But a true politics, as a response to the divine call, obedience without command, becomes possible among the community of the church whose hearts are transformed by the rule of the Spirit. Further, if we are to appropriate Luther's doctrine of the estates for contemporary theological purposes, it is strategically best to interpret the doctrine in such a way as to acknowledge the

---

may command or prescribe anything contrary to these three commandments and their works" (89).

167. Ibid., 87.
168. Ibid., 91.
169. LW 45:46; quoted in Bayer, *MLT*, 142.
170. "Notes on Ecclesiastes," LW 15:5. Bayer notes that on this point Luther "is at one with St. Thomas's reworking of the Aristotelian doctrine of society, which proceeds from the household outwards." Bayer, "Nature and Institution," in *FR*, 103.
171. In his "Lectures on Zechariah (1527)," Luther actually argues that the secular government comprehends the rule of the home and the authority of parents over their children. LW 20:171.

political as present even *prelapsum*. Bayer is surely correct when he states, "If the state is responsible solely for dealing with sinfulness, and not with what the human being was like originally, that has disastrous consequences for one's understanding of the state: the state will tend toward being purely a police state."[172] In any case, it is unquestionable that for Luther the political order is an ordinance of God by which He exercises His unitary rule in the world. God has ordained all three estates, and as such, all three are holy. That the estates are holy, even if the persons within them are not, makes it possible for Luther to argue that even among non-Christians God's hand can be at work in the establishment of political authority:

> We see very well that God distributes secular dominions or kingdoms among the godless in the grandest and most wonderful way, just as He also lets the good sun and rain minister to the godless, without establishing the Word or worship of God among them or teaching or directing them through prophets as He did at Jerusalem among His people. Still He calls this secular government of the godless His ordinance and creation, though they may abuse it as badly as they can. [173]

Luther's doctrine of the three institutions provides important insight into his understanding of the nature and status of the created world in relationship to the Creator. Returning to a theme of the early chapters of this book, contrary to Milbank's reading, it can be argued that Luther views the world, even in its political aspects, as God-infused. It is not an "alien locality" that God starkly confronts in God's simplistic unity. God's reality is mediated concretely and worldly, not via an otherworldly inner spirituality. This is expressed clearly by Luther when he writes, "One could very well say that the course of the world, and especially the doing of his saints, are God's mask, under which he conceals himself and so marvelously exercises dominion and introduces disorder in the world."[174] There is no aspect of the world free from God's rule. Everything, even disorder, ultimately submits to His rule. Humans can found nothing of themselves. Neither self-love, nor pride, nor false ontologies can bring about human societies or political arrangements. All are the work of God, their existence and continuance lay entirely in God's hands. Societies are not most fundamentally agreements of love, or contracts to bring stability out of the violent chaos underlying reality, even if those within these societies misunderstand them as such, even when "the blind world, because it does not know God and his work, concludes that it is owning to its own cleverness, reason, and strength that a community or dominion endures and thrives."[175] Rather, all communities reveal something of the hand of God at work in the world. They are "masks" that express his dominion. This of course, does not mean that

---

172. Bayer, *MLT*, 149; cf. "Social Ethics and Responsibility," in *FR*, 250.
173. "Psalm 101 (1534–35)," LW 13:193.
174. "Exposition of Psalm 127, 1524," LW 45:331.
175. Ibid., 328.

sin has not infected what God has ordained. On the contrary, political orders can become so corrupt as to no longer be properly considered as political societies at all. Rather, they become destructive to the very estates that God has instituted. And in these cases, they are brought down by God. Once again, we return to Luther's comments on Psalm 127:1, which reads, "Unless the Lord keeps the city, the watchman guards in vain." Luther writes:

> If you look at the history of the kingdoms of Assyria, Babylon, Persia, Greece, Rome, and all the rest, you will find there exactly what this verse says. All their splendor is nothing more than God's little puppet show. He has allowed them to rise for a time, but he has invariably overthrown them, one after the other. As they gained a brief ascendancy, through human wit and arrogance, so much the more quickly did they fall again; not because they lacked manpower, money, goods, and all manner of resources, but because the true watchman had ceased to uphold them, and caused them to see what human wit and power could accomplish without his watchful care and protection. So it turned out that their cause was nothing but vain counsel and a futile undertaking which they could neither uphold nor carry out.[176]

By rooting all political orders in the work of God in history, Luther takes politics, in a certain sense, radically out of the hands of humankind. What we, in our idolatrous pride, attribute to human wisdom, strength, or resources is really but the result of the continually creative Word of God. Luther could not be further from opening the door to, much less providing for a separate, autonomous, political sphere.[177] Unfortunately, most accounts of Luther's political thinking fail to pay proper heed to the teaching on the three institutions, resulting in an oversimplified understanding of his teaching on the two governments. Thus, the common prejudice according to which Luther sets up a false dualism between private and public morality and paves the way for the modern separation of Church and State with its attendant conception of an autonomous political sphere.

Conclusion: A Politics of Remaining in the Good Will of God

In an earlier chapter, in relation to the two *ecclesiae*, I showed the nature of Cain's punishment according to Luther, which involved a loss of promise, blessing, and

---

176. Ibid., 329.

177. In *Faith Active in Love*, Forell writes that for Luther, God's "secular realm is not at all secular in the modern sense of this word. There is no realm of being which is 'autonomous' and not ultimately God's realm" (131). Speaking of Luther in this respect, Anders Nygren writes, "No-one fought as he did against the secularisation of society. No-one so vigorously affirmed that earthly government is as much God's own rule as is spiritual, and that God never drops the reins from His own hands." Nygren, "Luther's Doctrine of the Two Kingdoms," *Ecumenical Review* 1.3 (Spring 1949), 307.

certainty in the estates. In this concluding section, we show how the estates name the place where Cain's wandering can cease, and spell out the logic of a politics of remaining as opposed to a politics of wandering. Having discussed Cain's loss in *ecclesia* and *oeconomia*, Luther speaks of Cain's wandering as a punishment that "involves civil government (*politica*)."[178] Luther describes Cain as an exile who has been excluded "from association with his fellow men (*civil consortio*)."[179] Even though Cain is the first person who builds a city, he nonetheless lacks "settled habitation" and is thus a wanderer.[180] In answering how these two statements go together, Luther notes that although Cain does build a city, he does not know how long it will last. When Cain is sent away from the place of promise that God gave to Adam and Eve after their expulsion from the garden, he is sent without direction, with no order as to where he should go. In speaking God's word, Adam sends Cain out with "no promise of a protector." Cain has no certainty that God will care for and defend him. Luther describes the very "different and better" situation that Adam found himself in after being expelled from the garden he had initially been placed (instituted) into.[181] In contrast to Cain, God gave Adam "a definite work of tilling the ground in a certain place and clothed him with a garment of skins . . . [as] a sign that God would take care of him and would defend him."[182] But Cain is given no such sign.

Central to Cain's uncertainty and roaming is that he does not have a Word from God or a command directing him to the places where he could be sure of encountering God turned toward him in grace and mercy. Luther writes, "Unsettled and roaming in this way are all those who do not have a Word and command of God designating a definite place and a definite person." To live without the Word is for Luther the true trial of Cain, which is "not to know what to believe, hope, or endure, but to do and undertake everything with no certainty as to the outcome."[183] Such uncertainty, as Bayer notes, leads to "lust for future things (*concupiscentia futurorum*), from an unhealthy domination by the future and the flight from the present that accompanies such preoccupation."[184] Without the assurance that allows one to remain in the estates marking out the places of God's good will, humans find themselves grasping after a self-grounding dominion and protection, which characterizes a life according to an anti-institutional logic, leading to the founding of antiestates in flight from the promises of God.

178. "Lectures on Genesis, Chapters 1–5 (1535–36)," LW 1:294; WA 42.217, 16–17.
179. "Lectures on Genesis, Chapters 1–5 (1535–36)," LW 1: 298; WA 42.220, 14.
180. "Lectures on Genesis, Chapters 1–5 (1535–36)," LW 1:295.
181. See Bayer's translation of Genesis 2:15: "And God the Lord took the man and put him [instituted him] in the Garden of Eden, that he might cultivate it and take care of it." Bayer, "Poetical Theology: New Horizons for Systematic Theology," 156.
182. "Lectures on Genesis, Chapters 1–5 (1535–36)," LW 1:300.
183. Ibid.
184. Bayer, "I am the Lord your God . . .," in *FR*, 58. The reference to *concupiscentia futurorum* is from Luther's commentary on Ecclesiastes, LW 15:50.

In his discussion of the descendants of Cain, Luther provides examples of the way that unsettled wandering leads to the establishment of anti-institutions, or antiestates. Cain, misreading the success he experienced in having children and establishing a city, saw his achievement as self-grounded rather than the result of God's "accidental mercy."[185] Puffed up by this mercy, Cain found an opportunity for prominence and seized it out of pride and a lust for ruling. His descendants would repeat this basic pattern, although not always in identical form. In his exegesis of Genesis 4:19 concerning Lamech's taking of two wives, Luther hints that it was uncertainty that caused Lamech's innovation in violating the institution of marriage. He did not practice polygamy out of sexual lust, Luther suggests, but rather his desire to increase his family was based on his desire to increase his rule, that is, to secure his "household" and his "government."[186] The error in this practice is twofold, at least. First, and most basically, it shows a faith falsely located. Rather than a faith in God's economy and rule, it is a faith in human effort and achievement. Rather than trusting God's faithful Word, it seeks to reorder human life such that human effort alone can achieve the blessings of creaturely life. Second, it shows the way that the estates are necessarily distorted when one is used to the advantage of the other. Rather than each institution being accorded its own proper dignity and understood as an end in itself, they become means to another end. That is, instead of viewing life in the institutions as the form of life with God in accordance with God's will, a life that is its own end, human faith in its own achievement too often manipulates the institutions for self-serving ends, resulting in setting the estates against one another, or falsely subordinating one to the other. Luther calls the arrogating by one estate of all life in the other two to itself the work of anti-Christ.[187] At this point what is found is life entirely outside of the estates, life in the form of anti-institution.[188]

Here is an appropriate place to stress the critical and heuristic nature of the institutions. As a hermeneutic of attentiveness, the institutions direct believers

---

185. "Lectures on Genesis, Chapters 1–5 (1535–36)," LW 1:315.

186. Ibid., 316–17.

187. No one estate has a monopoly on the Word. In the Word's freedom, the Word cannot be restricted to a single estate (*politia* and *oeconomia* are also "holy"), which serves against self-justification (i.e., using the Word for one's particular advantage or for the advantage of one's office at the expense of others). This does not, of course, take away the particular clarity and "promety" of the Word as encountered in the preaching and administering of the sacraments in the church.

188. For Luther's argument to this effect, see his 1539 "Die Zirkulardisputation über das Recht des Widerstands gegen den Kaiser (Matth. 19, 21)," WA 39.II, 34–52. Famously, Luther argued that in his time the anti-Christ took the form of the papacy, which is to say that the ecclesial estate had absorbed the other two. He claims that the ecclesial estate of his day assumed that faithfulness to the gospel meant destruction of the second table of the Decalogue (i.e., the monastics turned their back on economic and political life, while still living parasitically off of the work of these estates) (44–5).

to the places of hearing the Word always anew in the midst of the various opposing words that seek to structure and manipulate human life. In this sense, they serve a predominantly critical role, but it is a criticism that opens up to and frees those who hear for free response to the call of God. They clear space for genuine human life in response to the promise of the divine advent. An account of the institutions construed conservatively as telling people to remain within their socially constructed place exactly misses the point of the estates. Such an interpretation derives the estates sociologically, rather than theologically. It sees them as the result of some form of human effort (contract making, generative love, etc.), instead of seeing them as *God's* promise of places of pleasing worship where God's care and governance can be received in faith. The institutions shine a light on those social formations grounded in false faith and call back to Christ and to the social formations that God brings about by such faith. The institutions speak to the truth that God in God's Word has promisingly bestowed a place on every human being within each of these places that are constitutive of human life, such that any activity that deprives people of worship, of the means of sustenance and life in the family, and of their political status as human beings (a status bestowed by God, not created by humans)[189] must be named an anti-institution and called the work of anti-Christ.

In contrast to the anti-institutions, a politics according to the grammar of the estates is a politics of "the good works, which God prepared beforehand that we should walk in them."[190] Such a politics finds its home in a freedom from self-justificatory pressures and dissolution into the unending quest to establish and secure oneself and one's interests in futile self-chosen works undertaken with a fixed gaze toward an uncertain future. A politics of remaining in the place of God's will, in the works God has prepared, is a politics of assurance that it is God in God's faithfulness who rules human life, freeing our gaze for the need of the neighbor in the present. The human task is never to create or establish justice or peace, but rather to be attuned to God's work of reconciling the world in Christ. Such a politics is not concerned with defining itself over against the world (e.g., by understanding the church as a contrast or countersociety), nor is it concerned with meeting the demands for rule in human life via the development of virtue

---

189. On the *status politicus*, see Wannenwetsch, "Ruled by the Spirit: Hans Ulrich's Understanding of Political Existence," *Studies in Christian Ethics* 20.2 (2007), 257–72.

190. Ephesians 2:10. Cf., Ulrich, "God's Commandments and their Political Presence," 53. Expositing the apostle's appeal to God's "mercies" in Romans 12:1-2, Ulrich writes, "The main theological concern therefore, which arises from the experience of God's mercies, concerns how God's people are to *remain* in God's 'mercies,' i.e. in His good government, governance and salvation, how they remain in that way God's people" (47). For the relationship of "remaining" and the "estates," see Wannenwetsch, "Political Love," in *"You Have the Words of Eternal Life": Transformative Readings of the Gospel of John from a Lutheran Perspective*, ed. Kenneth Mtata (Geneva: The Lutheran World Federation, 2012), 97–8.

or character. Instead, a politics according to the grammar of Luther's theology is single-mindedly focused on the Word, the Word that is the means by which God forms and rules the world in and for Christ.

To remain in a creaturely life in the estates requires above all obedience to the First Commandment—that is, to "fear, love, and trust God above all things."[191] As we have shown earlier in relation to *ecclesia*, all human beings necessarily experience life in the institutions to some extent. The question is whether they experience them in faith or in unbelief. To live in unbelief, to sin, is not to violate the "order" of the created world, but rather to "go astray" instead of remaining.[192] As Ulrich puts it, "sin is disregard for God's work." Its opposite is found in worship: "The turn away from sin is public, liturgical praise of God (*öffentliche, gottesdienstliche Gotteslob*)."[193] Luther's is a Word-centered rather than an ecclesiocentric political theology. However, for Luther the Word can never be abstracted from the elemental forms in which it is given or from the people (*ecclesia*) to whom it is given. Thus, our access to the Word is always in political worship. Here we note the interrelation of the institutions. It is only as those who belong to the *ecclesia* in faith that we can recognize and so properly receive in faith God's sustenance and governance in the *oeconomia* and the *politia*. It is only as those who have been attuned to the receipt of God's justice as received with assurance in the Word preached and in the Supper that we become attentive to God's justice as it is enacted on behalf of the neighbor. As those who have experienced the hope of new creation in the death and resurrection of baptism, Christians are sensitized to God's work of making all things new as it takes form in creaturely life in the estates. To put this in explicitly political terms, it is in political worship that we come to experience human life as ruled by the Spirit.[194]

At this point, virtue-driven accounts of the Christian life stand on uncertain ground. The problem with such accounts is that the most significant aspect of reality is located *within*, either within the ethical agent as *habitus* or within the traditioned moral community and its practices. However, the difficulty with placing the locus of Christian ethics in the human agent/s understood in these ways is that there seems to be little or no room left for the Spirit—which is to say, for the places in between communities and in between individuals themselves. No space is left for Christ as the mediator of reality *in* whom we can take our *real* place as creatures and as neighbors, in whom we can be turned outward to face reality in faith toward God and love toward neighbor, such that we are a Christ to our neighbor. Rather than focusing on virtuous agency, we suggest that what is needed is a politics of obediently waiting on the Spirit by doing what lays at hand in faith that God is actively at work in giving political shape to human life. The institutions provide the grammar for such a waiting. They give an indication of

---

191. The Small Catechism, I, 2, in *BoC*:351.
192. Wannenwetsch, "Political Love," 99.
193. Ulrich, *Wie Geschöpfe leben*, 111 (my translation).
194. See Wannenwetsch, "Ruled by the Spirit."

the shape of human life as willed by God without providing an overdetermined blueprint or too narrowly defined overarching vision or master pattern such that a Christian imagining of the world could be imposed on those deemed to be on the outside, or such that an ideal is enacted. Rather, a life according to the institutions is a life of dispossession in the sense that it seeks all good things from God alone, rather than from human constructions of space, time, and material. Rather than the colonialist enactment of Western-conceived virtue, an ethics of the institutions is aimed at unmasking the various ways in which human life loses its freedom in receipt from God due to human manipulation and control (i.e., exploitation) of creation and fellow creatures in the name of humanly conceived images and ideals.[195] The institutions point to places where encounter with God can be expected, but without determining the shape of such encounter in advance. Importantly, it should also be stated that the institutions are not the preserve of any segment of humanity alone, but belong to all humans qua humanity as the good gift of the Creator given along with human life. As such, they render a critical heuristic for discerning and naming the demonic, but are not overset such that anything outside the community of the church is by definition "non-Christian." Rather, a grammar of the institutions expects to find God's good work present even among "pagans," and in such a way that Christians are willing to learn humbly from "non-Christians" without assuming a superior epistemic vantage point. Nonetheless, Christians will never forego the confession that the justification of human life is found in Christ alone and that the good works that are "holy and acceptable" (Rom. 12:1) to God can only be exercised in faith.[196]

In a culture under constant temptation to flee—whether in momentous ways, such as the temptation to abandon one's marriage, to seemingly more minor fleeing, such as to the "world" of virtual reality or simulated sociality—Luther's teaching on the estates encourages remaining and abiding in trust that life will be found in these places alone, and that it will be found there as the abundance of God's good provision. In this way, the estates counter Cain's fleeing impulse[197] and instead extend an invitation to remain involved in the reality of the world.[198] Media politics, with its sound bytes and banalities, too often is a fleeing from genuine politics into the virtual world of the screen. Luther's teaching calls us back to concrete, embodied politics. To a concern for concrete neighbors and to a search

---

195. Willie James Jennings, *The Christian Imagination: Theology and the Origins of Race* (New Haven: Yale University Press, 2010), 68–72.

196. "But works that are done apart from faith, no matter how holy they seem in appearance, are under sin and the curse." "Lectures on Galatians 1535, Chapters 1–4," LW 26:334–5. Elsewhere, Luther writes, "Doing the works of the law and fulfilling the law are two very different things." "Prefaces to the New Testament," LW 35:367.

197. Luther writes of those without faith that "their fleeing shows the infinite hatred of the human heart against the Law and, as a consequence, against God Himself." "Lectures on Galatians 1535, Chapters 1–4," LW 26:320.

198. On the significance of "reality" for Christian ethics, see Bonhoeffer, *Ethics*, 47–75.

for reconciliation among actual people and peoples, not a flight into ideologies that seeks such abstractions as "helping the poor" (understood as a statistical entity) or "defending against the enemies of freedom." Instead, a political perception attuned by the hermeneutics of the institutions will give attention to the needs of others without first "interpreting" them according to an overarching ideology. In this way, political responsibility has the same shape and form as response to the divine call—that is, it is either obedient or disobedient, carried out in faith or unbelief that God will provide God's governance. Ideology is but a way of circumventing the call of God, of putting it under our control, which means politically putting our neighbors under our hand and determining our willingness to help them based on criteria such as their "worthiness" or "desert," and of interpreting our "good deed" as but a means to some further end. But as fellow-citizens, as fellow members of the household of God, our relations to one another, as mediated by Christ, means an immediate willingness to meet the neighbor's need—and to accept their help in meeting our need. That this is a Christ-mediated immediacy means that we are not simply absorbed into the other, but on the other hand, it means that the other is never a "stranger," but always to the extent that their call in need reaches us, already a neighbor. Luther's institutions provide the grammar for living in this kind of Christ-mediated immediacy to our neighbors, where "ideology," "identity-politics," and the protective quest for self-preservation and the construction of temples to human glory no longer stand in between. Such a life must begin with trust that all has already been given and that we live by the unceasing faithfulness of the Word. Our faith is our politics.

BIBLIOGRAPHY

Martin Luther's Works

Luther, Martin. "85. Philip Melanchthon: Wartburg, July 13, 1521." In *Luther's Works 48: Letters I*. Edited and translated by Gottfried G. Krodel, 256-63. Philadelphia: Fortress Press, 1963.

Luther, Martin. "Admonition to Peace, 1525." In *Luther's Works 46: Christians in Society III*. Edited by Robert C. Shultz. Translated by Charles M. Jacobs and revised by Robert C. Shultz, 3-43. Philadelphia: Fortress Press, 1967.

Luther, Martin. "Against the Heavenly Prophets, 1525." In *Luther's Works 40: Church and Ministry II*. Edited by Conrad Bergendoff. Translated by Bernhard Erling and Conrad Bergendoff, 73-223. Philadelphia: Fortress Press, 1958.

Luther, Martin. "Auslegung des 101. Psalms. 1534/35." In *D. Martin Luthers Werke: Kritische Gesamtausgabe. Band 51*, 197-264. Weimar: H. Böhlau, 1914.

Luther, Martin. "The Babylonian Captivity of the Church, 1520." In *Luther's Works 36: Word and Sacrament II*. Edited by Abdel Ross Wentz. Translated by A. T. W. Steinhäuser and revised by Frederick C. Ahrens and Abdel Ross Wentz, 1-126. Philadelphia: Fortress Press, 1959.

Luther, Martin. "The Blessed Sacrament of the Holy and True Body of Christ, and the Brotherhoods, 1519." In *Luther's Works 35: Word and Sacrament I*. Edited by E. Theodore Bachmann. Translated by Jeremiah J. Schindel and revised by E. Theodore Bachmann, 45-73. Philadelphia: Fortress Press, 1960.

Luther, Martin. "The Bondage of the Will, 1526." In *Luther's Works 33: Career of the Reformer III*. Edited and translated by Philip S. Watson. Philadelphia: Fortress Press, 1972.

Luther, Martin. "A Brief Instruction on What to Look For and Expect in the Gospels, 1521." In *Luther's Works 35: Word and Sacrament I*. Edited and translated by E. Theodore Bachmann, 113-24. Philadelphia: Fortress Press, 1960.

Luther, Martin. "Concerning Rebaptism, 1528." In *Luther's Works 40: Church and Ministry II*. Edited and translated by Conrad Bergendoff, 225-62. Philadelphia: Fortress Press, 1958.

Luther, Martin. "Confession Concerning Christ's Supper, 1528." In *Luther's Works 37: Word and Sacrament III*. Edited and translated by Robert H. Fischer, 151-371. Philadelphia: Fortress Press, 1961.

Luther, Martin. *D. Martin Luthers Werke: Kritische Gesamtausgabe. Schriften*. 65 Vols. in 127. Weimar: H. Böhlau, 1912-21.

Luther, Martin. *D. Martin Luthers Werke: Kritische Gesamtausgabe. Tischreden*. Weimar: H. Böhlau, 1912ff.

Luther, Martin. "Der 127. Psalm ausgelegt an die Christen zu Riga in Liesland." In *D. Martin Luthers Werke: Kritische Gesamtausgabe. Band 15*, 348-79. Weimar: H. Böhlau, 1899.

Luther, Martin. "Disputation against Scholastic Theology, 1517." In *Luther's Works 31: The Career of the Reformer I*. Edited and translated by Harold J. Grimm, 3–16. Philadelphia: Muhlenberg Press, 1957.

Luther, Martin. "The Disputation Concerning Man, 1536." In *Luther's Works 34: Career of the Reformer IV*. Edited and translated by Lewis. W Spitz, 135–44. Philadelphia: Muhlenberg Press, 1960.

Luther, Martin. "Expostion of Psalm 127, For the Christians at Riga in Livonia, 1524." In *Luther's Works 45: Christian's in Society II*. Edited by Walther I. Brandt, 317–37. Philadelphia: Muhlenberg Press, 1962.

Luther, Martin. "The Freedom of a Christian, 1520." In *Luther's Works 31: Career of the Reformer I*. Edited by Harold J. Grimm. Translated by W. A. Lambert and revised by Harold J. Grimm, 327–77. Philadelphia: Fortress Press, 1957.

Luther, Martin. "Genesisvorlesung (cap. 1–17) 1535/38." In *D. Martin Luthers Werke: Kritische Gesamtausgabe. Band 42*. Weimar: H. Böhlau, 1911.

Luther, Martin. "Kirchenpostille 1522. Epistel in der Früh: Christmeß. Titus 3, 4–7." In *D. Martin Luthers Werke: Kritische Gesamtausgaber. Band 10/1*, 94–128. Weimar: H. Böhlau, 1910.

Luther, Martin. "The Large Catechism." In *The Book of Concord: The Confessions of the Evangelical Lutheran Church*. Edited by Robert Kolb and Timothy J. Wengert. Translated by Charles Arand et al., 377–480. Minneapolis: Fortress Press, 2000.

Luther, Martin. "Lectures on Galatians 1535, Chapters 1–4." In *Luther's Works 26*. Edited and translated by Jaroslav Pelikan. Saint Louis, MO: Concordia Publishing House, 1963.

Luther, Martin. "Lectures on Galatians 1535, Chapters 5–6." In *Luther's Works 27: Lectures on Galatians 1535, Chapters 5–6; Lectures on Galatians 1519, Chapter 1–6*. Edited and translated by Jaroslav Pelikan, 1–149. Saint Louis, MO: Concordia Publishing House, 1964.

Luther, Martin. "Lectures on Galatians, Chapters 1–6, 1519." In *Luther's Works 27: Lectures on Galatians 1535, Chapters 5–6; Lectures on Galatians 1519, Chapter 1–6*. Edited and translated by Jaroslav Pelikan, 151–410. Saint Louis, MO: Concordia Publishing House, 1964.

Luther, Martin. "Lectures on Genesis, Chapters 1–5." In *Luther's Works 1*. Edited by Jaroslav Pelikan. Translated by George V. Schick. Saint Louis, MO: Concordia Publishing House, 1958.

Luther, Martin. "Lectures on Genesis, Chapters 6–14." In *Luther's Works 2*. Edited by Jaroslav Pelikan. Translated by George V. Schick. Saint Louis, MO: Concordia Publishing House, 1960.

Luther, Martin. "Lectures on Genesis, Chapters 21–25." In *Luther's Works 4*. Edited by Jaroslav Pelikan. Translated by George V. Schick. Saint Louis, MO: Concordia Publishing House, 1964.

Luther, Martin. "Lectures on Jonah." In *Luther's Works 19: Lectures on Minor Prophets II*. Edited by Charles D. Froehlich. Translated by H. C. Oswald, 1–104. Saint Louis, MO: Concordia Publishing House, 1974.

Luther, Martin. "Lectures on Romans." In *Luther's Works 25*. Edited by Hilton C. Oswald. Translated by Walter G. Tillmanns and Jacob A. O. Preus. Saint Louis, MO: Concordia Publishing House, 1972.

Luther, Martin. "Lectures on Zechariah." In *Luther's Works 20: Minor Prophets III*. Edited by Hilton Oswald. Translated by Richard J. Dinda. Saint Louis, MO: Concordia Publishing House, 1973.

Luther, Martin. *Luther's Works*. American Edition. 55 Vols. Edited by Jaroslav Pelikan and Helmut T. Lehman. St. Louis, MO, and Philadelphia: Concordia and Fortress Press, 1958–66.

Luther, Martin. *Luther's Works 46: The Christian in Society III*. Edited by Robert C. Schultz. Philadelphia: Fortress Press, 1967.

Luther, Martin. *Luther's Works 54: Table Talk*. Edited and translated by Theodore G. Tappert. Philadelphia: Fortress Press, 1967.

Luther, Martin. "The Magnificat, 1521." In *Luther's Works 21*. Edited by Jaroslav Pelikan. Translated by A. T. W. Steinhaeuser, 295–358. Saint Louis, MO: Concordia Publishing House, 1956.

Luther, Martin. "Notes on Ecclesiastes." In *Luther's Works 15*. Edited and translated by Jaroslav Pelikan, 1–187. Saint Louis, MO: Concordia Publishing House, 1972.

Luther, Martin. "On the Councils and the Church, 1539." In *Luther's Works 41: Church and Ministry III*. Edited by Eric W. Gritsch. Translated by Charles M. Jacobs and revised by Eric W. Gritsch, 3–178. Philadelphia: Fortress Press, 1966.

Luther, Martin. "Prefaces to the New Testament." In *Luther's Works 35: Word and Sacrament I*. Edited by E. Theodore Bachmann. Translated by Charles M. Jacobs and revised by E. Theodore Bachmann, 355–411. Philadelphia: Fortress Press, 1960.

Luther, Martin. "Prefaces to the Old Testament." In *Luther's Works 35: Word and Sacrament I*. Edited by E. Theodore Bachmann. Translated by Charles M. Jacobs and revised by E. Theodore Bachmann, 233–333. Philadelphia: Fortress Press, 1960.

Luther, Martin. "Psalm 82." In *Luther's Works 13: Selected Psalms II*. Edited by Jaroslav Pelikan. Translated by C. M. Jacobs, 39–72. Saint Louis, MO: Concordia Publishing House, 1956.

Luther, Martin. "Psalm 101." In *Luther's Works 13: Selected Psalms II*. Edited by Jaroslav Pelikan. Translated by Alfred von Rohr Sauer, 143–224. Saint Louis, MO: Concordia Publishing House, 1956.

Luther, Martin. "Psalm 111." In *Luther's Works 13: Selected Psalms II*. Edited by Jaroslav Pelikan. Translated by Daniel E. Poellot, 349–87. Saint Louis, MO: Concordia Publishing House, 1956.

Luther, Martin. "Psalmus CXXVII." In *D. Martin Luthers Werke: Kritische Gesamtausgabe. Band 40/III*. 202–69. Weimar: H. Böhlau, 1930.

Luther, Martin. "The Sacrament of the Body and Blood of Christ against the Fanatics, 1526." In *Luther's Works 36: Word and Sacrament II*. Edited by Abdel Ross Wentz. Translated by Frederick C. Ahrens, 329–61. Philadelphia: Fortress Press, 1959.

Luther, Martin. "The Sacrament of Penance, 1519." In *Luther's Works 35: Word and Sacrament I*. Edited by E. Theodore Bachmann. Translated by E. Theodore Bachmann, 3–22. Philadelphia: Fortress Press, 1960.

Luther, Martin. "Sermon on the Faith of the Syrophenician Woman." In *The Complete Sermons of Martin Luther, Volume 2*. Edited by John Nicholas Lenker, 148–54. Grand Rapids, MI: Baker Books, 1983.

Luther, Martin. "Sermons on the Gospel of Saint John, 1–4." In *Luther's Works 22*. Edited by Jaroslav Pelikan. Translated by Martin H. Bertram. Saint Louis, MO: Concordia Publishing House, 1957.

Luther, Martin. "The Smalcald Articles." In *The Book of Concord: The Confessions of the Evangelical Lutheran Church*. Edited by Robert Kolb and Timothy J. Wengert. Translated by Charles Arand et al., 295–328. Minneapolis: Fortress Press, 2000.

Luther, Martin. "The Small Catechism." In *The Book of Concord: The Confessions of the Evangelical Lutheran Church*. Edited by Robert Kolb and Timothy J. Wengert. Translated by Charles Arand et al., 345–75. Minneapolis: Fortress Press, 2000.

Luther, Martin. "Temporal Authority: To What Extent It Should be Obeyed, 1523." In *Luther's Works 45: The Christian in Society II*. Edited by Walther I. Brandt. Translated by J. J. Schindel and revised by Walther I. Brandt, 75–129. Philadelphia: Muhlenberg Press, 1962.

Luther, Martin. "That These Words of Christ, 'This is My Body', etc., Still Stand Firm Against the Fanatics, 1527." In *Luther's Works 37: Word and Sacrament III*. Edited by Robert H. Fischer. Translated by Robert H. Fischer, 3–150. Philadelphia: Fortress Press, 1961.

Luther, Martin. "To the Christian Nobility of the German Nation Concerning the Reform of the Christian Estate, 1520." In *Luther's Works 44: The Christian in Society I*, Edited by James Atkinson. Translated by Charles M. Jacobs and revised by James Atkinson, 115–217. Philadelphia: Fortress Press, 1966.

Luther, Martin. "Treatise on Good Works, 1520." In *Luther's Works 44: The Christian in Society I*. Edited by James Atkinson. Translated by W. A. Lambert and revised by James Atkinson, 15–114. Philadelphia: Fortress Press, 1966.

Luther, Martin. "A Treatise on the New Testament, that is, the Holy Mass, 1520." In *Luther's Works 35: Word and Sacrament I*. Edited by E. Theodore Bachmann. Translated by Jeremiah J. Schindel and E. Theodore Bachmann, 75–111. Philadelphia: Fortress Press, 1960.

Luther, Martin. "Two Kinds of Righteousness, 1519." In *Luther's Works 31: Career of the Reformer I*. Edited by Harold J. Grimm. Translated by Helmut T. Lehman, 293–306. Philadelphia: Fortress Press, 1957.

Luther, Martin. "Von ehelichen Leben." In *D. Martin Luthers Werke: Kritische Gesamtausgabe. Band 10/II*, 267–304. Weimar: H. Böhlau, 1907.

Luther, Martin. "Von weltlicher Oberkeit, wie weit man ihr Gehorsam schuldig sei." In *D. Martin Luthers Werke: Kritische Gesamtausgabe. Band 11*, 229–80. Weimar: H. Böhlau, 1900.

Luther, Martin. "Whether Soldiers, Too, Can Be Saved, 1526." In *Luther's Works 46: The Christian in Society III*. Edited by Robert C. Schultz. Translated by Charles M. Jacobs and revised by Robert C. Schultz, 87–137. Philadelphia: Fortress Press, 1967.

Luther, Martin. "Die Zirkulardisputation über das Recht des Widerstands gegen den Kaiser (Matth. 19, 21)." In *D. Martin Luthers Werke: Kritische Gesamtausgabe. Band 39/II*, 34–52. Weimar: H. Böhlau, 1932.

Other Works

Althaus, Paul. *The Ethics of Martin Luther*. Translated by Robert C. Schultz. Philadelphia: Fortress Press, 1972.

Althaus, Paul. *The Theology of Martin Luther*. Translated by Robert C. Shultz. Philadelphia: Fortress Press, 1966.

Arendt, Hannah. *The Human Condition*. 2nd Edition. Chicago: University of Chicago Press, 1958.

Arendt, Hannah. *On Violence*. London: Penguin Press, 1970.

Aristotle. *The Politics*. Translated by Carnes Lord. Chicago: University of Chicago Press, 1984.

Augustine. *The City of God against the Pagans*. Edited and translated by R. W. Dyson. Cambridge: Cambridge University Press, 1998.

Augustine. *The Enchiridion on Faith, Hope and Charity*. Edited by Boniface Ramsey. Translated by Bruce Harbert. Hyde Park, NY: New York City Press, 1999.

Ballor, Jordan J. "Christ in Creation: Bonhoeffer's Orders of Preservation and Natural Theology." *The Journal of Religion* 86, no. 1 (January 2006): 1–22.

Barth, Karl. "Church and State." In *Community, State, and Church: Three Essays by Karl Barth with a New Introduction by David Haddorff*, 101–48. Eugene, OR: Wipf & Stock, 1960.

Barth, Karl. *Church Dogmatics*, I.1. Edited by G. W. Bromiley and T. F. Torrance. Translated by G. W. Bromiley. London: T&T Clark, 2004.

Barth, Karl. *Church Dogmatics*, III.4. Edited by G. W. Bromiley and T. F. Torrance. Translated by A. T. Mackay, T. H. L. Parker, Harold Knight, Henry A. Kennedy, and John Marks. Edinburgh: T&T Clark, 1961.

Barth, Karl. "Gospel and Law." In *Community, State, and Church: Three Essays by Karl Barth with a New Introduction by David Haddorff*, 71–100. Eugene, OR: Wipf & Stock, 1960.

Barth, Karl. "No! Answer to Emil Brunner." In *Natural Theology*. Translated by Peter Fraenkel, 65–128. Eugene, OR: Wipf & Stock, 2002.

Bartholomew, Craig, Jonathan Chaplin, Robert Song, and Al Wolters, eds. *A Royal Priesthood? The Use of the Bible Ethically and Politically: A Dialogue with Oliver O'Donovan*. Grand Rapids, MI: Zondervan, 2002.

Bauerschmidt, Fredrick Christian. "The Word Made Speculative? John Milbank's Christological Poetics." *Modern Theology* 15, no. 4 (October 1999): 417–32.

Bayer, Oswald. "The Being of Christ in Faith." *Lutheran Quarterly* 10, no. 2 (Summer 1996): 135–50.

Bayer, Oswald. "Categorical Imperative or Categorical Gift?" In *Freedom in Response: Lutheran Ethics: Sources and Controversies*. Translated by Jeffrey F. Cayzer, 13–20. Oxford: Oxford University Press, 2007.

Bayer, Oswald. *A Contemporary in Dissent: Johann Georg Hamann as a Radical Enlightener*. Translated by Roy A. Harrisville and Mark C. Mattes. Grand Rapids, MI: Eerdmans, 2012.

Bayer, Oswald. "The Ethics of Gift." *Lutheran Quarterly* 24, no. 4 (Winter 2010): 447–68.

Bayer, Oswald. *Freedom in Response: Lutheran Ethics: Sources and Controversies*. Translated by Jeffrey F. Cayzer. Oxford: Oxford University Press, 2007.

Bayer, Oswald. "I Believe that God Has Created Me with All That Exists. An Example of Catechetical-Systematics." *Lutheran Quarterly* 8, no.2 (Summer 1994): 129–61.

Bayer, Oswald. "Justification as the Basis and Boundary of Theology." *Lutheran Quarterly* 15, no. 3 (Autumn 2001): 273–92.

Bayer, Oswald. "Law and Morality." *Lutheran Quarterly* 17, no. 1 (Spring 2003): 63–76.

Bayer, Oswald. *Living by Faith: Justification and Sanctification*. Grand Rapids, MI: Eerdmans, 2003.

Bayer, Oswald. "Luther as Interpreter of Holy Scripture." In *The Cambridge Companion to Martin Luther*. Edited by Donald K. McKim. Translated by Mark C. Mattes, 73–85. Cambridge: Cambridge University Press, 2003.

Bayer, Oswald. "Luther's View of Marriage." In *Freedom in Response: Lutheran Ethics: Sources and Controversies*. Translated by Jeffrey F. Cayzer, 169–82. Oxford: Oxford University Press, 2007.

Bayer, Oswald. *Martin Luther's Theology: A Contemporary Interpretation*. Translated by Thomas H. Trapp. Grand Rapids, MI: Eerdmans, 2008.
Bayer, Oswald. "Nature and Institution: 'Luther's Doctrine of the Three Estates.'" In *Freedom in Response: Lutheran Ethics: Sources and Controversies*. Translated by Jeffrey F. Cayzer, 90–118. Oxford: Oxford University Press, 2007.
Bayer, Oswald. "Poetical Theology: New Horizons for Systematic Theology." *International Journal of Systematic Theology* 1, no. 2 (1999): 153–67.
Bayer, Oswald. "Social Ethics and Responsibility." In *Freedom in Response: Lutheran Ethics: Sources and Controversies*. Translated by Jeffrey F. Cayzer, 245–58. Oxford: Oxford University Press, 2007.
Bayer, Oswald. *Theology the Lutheran Way*. Edited and translated by Jeffrey G. Silcock and Mark C. Mattes. Grand Rapids, MI: Eerdmans, 2007.
Beiner, Ronald. "Machiavelli, Hobbes and Rousseau on Civil Religion." *The Review of Politics* 55, no. 4 (September 1993): 617–38.
Benne, Robert. "Lutheran Ethics: Perennial Themes and Contemporary Challenges." In *The Promise of Lutheran Ethics*. Edited by Karen L. Bloomquist and John R. Stumme, 11–30. Minneapolis: Fortress Press, 1998.
Benne, Robert. *Ordinary Saints: An Introduction to the Christian Life*. Minneapolis: Fortress Press, 2003.
Billings, J. Todd. "John Milbank's Theology of the 'Gift' and Calvin's Theology of Grace: A Critical Comparison." *Modern Theology* 21, no. 1 (January 2005): 87–105.
Bloomquist, Karen L. and John R. Stumme. *The Promise of Lutheran Ethics*. Minneapolis: Fortress Press, 1998.
Bonhoeffer, Dietrich. *Christ the Center*. Translated by Edwin H. Robertson. San Francisco: Harper, 1960.
Bonhoeffer, Dietrich. *Discipleship*. Dietrich Bonhoeffer Works 4. Edited by Geffrey B. Kelly and John D. Godsey. Translated by Barbara Green and Reinhard Krauss. Minneapolis: Fortress Press, 2003.
Bonhoeffer, Dietrich. *Ethics*. Dietrich Bonhoeffer Works 6. Edited by Clifford J. Green. Translated by Reinhard Krauss, Charles C. West, and Douglas W. Stott. Minneapolis: Fortress Press, 2009.
Bonhoeffer, Dietrich. *Letters and Papers from Prison*. Dietrich Bonhoeffer Works 8. Edited by John W. De Gruchy. Translated by Isabel Best, Lisa E. Dahill, Reinhard Krauss, and Nancy Lukens. Minneapolis: Fortress Press, 2010.
Bornkamm, Heinrich. *Luther's Doctrine of the Two Kingdoms in the Context of His Theology*. Translated by Karl H. Hertz. Philadelphia: Fortress Press, 1966.
Braaten, Carl E. "The Doctrine of the Two Kingdoms Re-examined." *Currents in Theology and Mission* 15, no. 6 (1988): 497–504.
Braaten, Carl E. and Robert W. Jenson. *Union with Christ: The New Finnish Interpretation of Luther*. Grand Rapids, MI: Eerdmans, 1998.
Bretherton, Luke. *Christianity and Contemporary Politics: The Conditions and Possibilities of Faithful Witness*. Chichester: Wiley-Blackwell, 2010.
Breyfogle, Todd. "Is There Room for Political Philosophy in Postmodern Critical Augustinianism?" In *Deconstructing Radical Orthodoxy: Postmodern Theology, Rhetoric and Truth*. Edited by Wayne J. Hankey and Douglas Hedley, 31–48. Hants: Ashgate, 2005.
Brian, Rustin E. *Covering Up Luther: How Barth's Christology Challenged the Deus Absconditus that Haunts Modernity*. Eugene, OR: Cascade Books, 2013.

Brock, Brian. "Bonhoeffer and the Bible in Christian Ethics: Psalm 119, the Mandates, and Ethics as a 'Way.'" *Studies in Christian Ethics* 18, no. 3 (2005): 7-29.

Brock, Brian. "On Generating Categories in Theological Ethics: Barth, Genesis and the Ständlehre." *Tyndale Bulletin* 61, no. 1 (2010): 45-67.

Brock, Brian. *Singing the Ethos of God: On the Place of Christian Ethics in Scripture*. Grand Rapids, MI: Eerdmans, 2007.

Brock, Brian. "Why the Estates? Hans Ulrich's Recovery of an Unpopular Notion." *Studies in Christian Ethics* 20, no. 2 (2007): 179-202.

Brunner, Emil. *The Divine Imperative: A Study in Christian Ethics*. Translated by Olive Wyon. London: Lutterworth Press, 1949.

Brunner, Emil. "Nature and Grace." In *Natural Theology*. Translated by Peter Fraenkel, 15-64. Eugene, OR: Wipf & Stock, 2002.

Burrell, David B. *Freedom and Creation in Three Traditions*. Notre Dame: University of Notre Dame Press, 1993.

Cavanaugh, William. "Eucharistic Sacrifice and the Social Imagination in Early Modern Europe." *Journal of Medieval and Early Modern Studies* 31, no. 3 (Fall 2001): 585-605.

Cavanaugh, William. *Migrations of the Holy: God, State, and the Political Meaning of the Church*. Grand Rapids, MI: Eerdmans, 2011.

Cavanaugh, William. *Theopolitical Imagination*. London: T&T Clark, 2002.

Cavanaugh, William. *Torture and Eucharist: Theology, Politics, and the Body of Christ*. Oxford: Blackwell Publishers, 1998.

Chambers, Katherine. "Slavery and Domination as Political Ideals in Augustine's 'City of God.'" *Heythrop Journal* LIV (2013): 12-28.

Chester, Stephen. "It Is No Longer I Who Live: Justification by Faith and Participation in Christ in Martin Luther's Exegesis of Galatians." *New Testament Studies* 55 (2009): 315-37.

Chester, Stephen. "Paul and the Introspective Conscience of Martin Luther: The Impact of Luther's *Anfechtungen* on his Interpretation of Paul." *Biblical Interpretation* 14, no. 5 (2006): 508-36.

Coakley, Sarah. "Why Gift? Gift, Gender and Trinitarian Relations in Milbank and Tanner." *Scottish Journal of Theology* 61, no. 2 (May 2008): 224-35.

Connolly, William. "Politics and Vision." In *Democracy and Vision: Sheldon Wolin and the Vicissitudes of the Political*. Edited by Aryeh Botwinick and William Connolly. Princeton: Princeton University Press, 2001.

Cranz, F. Edward. *An Essay on the Development of Luther's Thought on Justice, Law, and Society*. Cambridge: Harvard University Press, 1959.

Deutscher Evangelischer Kirchenausschuß. *Die Bekenntnisschriften der evangelisch-lutherischen Kirche*. 9th Edition. Göttingen: Vandenhoeck & Ruprecht, 1982.

Duchrow, Ulrich. "Introduction." In *Lutheran Churches—Salt or Mirror of Society?: Case Studies on the Theory and Practice of the Two Kingdoms Doctrine*. Edited by Ulrich Duchrow, 12-17. Geneva: Lutheran World Federation, 1977.

Ebeling, Gerhard. *Word and Faith*. Philadelphia: Fortress Press, 1963.

Ebeling, Gerhard. *The Word of God and Tradition: Historical Studies Interpreting the Divisions of Christianity*. Translated by S. H. Hooke. Philadelphia: Fortress Press, 1968.

Elshtain, Jean Bethke. *Public Man, Private Woman: Women in Social and Political Thought*. Oxford: Robertson, 1981.

Ericksen, Robert P. *Theologians under Hitler: Gerhard Kittel, Paul Althaus and Emanuel Hirsch*. New Haven: Yale, 1985.

Estes, James M. "Luther on the Role of Secular Authority in the Reformation." *Lutheran Quarterly* 17, no. 2 (Summer 2003): 199–225.

Estes, James M. *Peace, Order and the Glory of God: Secular Authority and the Church in the Thought of Luther and Melanchthon, 1518-1559*. Boston: Brill, 2005.

Figgis, J. N. *Studies of Political Thought: From Gerson to Grotius, 1414–1625*. Cambridge: Cambridge University Press, 1907.

Forell, George. *Faith Active in Love: An Investigation of the Principles Underlying Luther's Social Ethics*. Minneapolis: Augsburg Publishing House, 1954.

Gregersen, Niels Henrik, ed. *The Gift of Grace: The Future of Lutheran Theology*. Minneapolis: Fortress Press, 2005.

Gregersen, Niels Henrik. "Grace in Nature and History: Luther's Doctrine of Creation Revisited." *Dialog* 44, no. 1 (Spring 2005): 19–29.

Gregory, Eric. "Christianity and the Rise of the Democratic State." In *Political Theology for a Plural Age*. Edited by Michael Jon Kessler, 99–107. Oxford: Oxford University Press, 2013.

Gregory, Eric. *Politics and the Order of Love: An Augustinian Ethic of Democratic Citizenship*. Chicago: The University of Chicago Press, 2008.

Gunton, Colin. *A Brief Theology of Revelation: The 1993 Warfield Lectures*. London: T&T Clark, 1995.

Habermas, Jürgen. "Hannah Arendt's Communications Concept of Power." *Social Research* 44, no. 1 (Summer 1977): 3–24.

Haddorff, David. "Introduction." In *Community, State, and Church: Three Essays by Karl Barth with a New Introduction by David Haddorff*. Edited by Karl Barth, 1–69. Eugene, OR: Wipf & Stock, 1960.

Hagen, Kenneth. *Luther's Approach to Scripture as Seen in His "Commentaries" on Galatians, 1519-1538*. Tübingen: J.C.B. Mohr, 1993.

Hamann, J. G. "Aesthetica in Nuce." In *Writings on Philosophy and Language*. Edited by Kenneth Haynes, 60–95. Cambridge: Cambridge University Press, 2007.

Hamm, Berndt. *Reformation of Faith in the Context of Late Medieval Theology and Piety: Essays by Berndt Hamm*. Edited by Robert J. Bast. Leiden, NLD: Brill, 2003.

Hauerwas, Stanley. "Democratic Time: Lessons Learned from Yoder and Wolin." *Cross Currents* 55, no. 4 (Winter 2006): 534–52.

Hauerwas, Stanley. *The Peaceable Kingdom: A Primer in Christian Ethics*. 2nd Edition. Notre Dame: SCM Press, 2003.

Hauerwas, Stanley. "Remembering How and What I Think: A Response to the *JRE* Articles on Hauerwas." *Journal of Religious Ethics* 40, no. 2 (June 2012): 296–306.

Hays, Richard B. *The Faith of Jesus Christ: The Narrative Substructure of Galatians 3:1–4:11*. 2nd Edition. Grand Rapids, MI: Eerdmans, 2002.

Heckel, Johannes. *"Lex Charitatis": A Juristic Disquisition on Law in the Theology of Martin Luther*. Edited and translated by Gottfried G. Krodel. Grand Rapids, MI: Eerdmans, 2010.

Helmer, Christine. *The Trinity and Martin Luther: A Study on the Relationship between Genre, Language and the Trinity in Luther's Works (1523-1546)*. Mainz: Verlag Philip von Zabern, 1999.

Herdt, Jennifer. "Affective Perfectionism: Community with God without Common Measure." In *New Essays on the History of Autonomy: A Collection Honoring J.B. Schneewind*. Edited by Natalie Brender, 30–59. Cambridge: Cambridge University Press, 2004.

Herdt, Jennifer. "Back to Virtue." *Scottish Journal of Theology* 65, no. 2 (2012): 222–6.

Herdt, Jennifer. "Hauerwas among the Virtues." *Journal of Religious Ethics* 40, no. 2 (June 2012): 202–27.

Herdt, Jennifer. "The Invention of Modern Moral Philosophy: A Review of 'The Invention of Autonomy' by J.B. Schneewind." *Journal of Religious Ethics* 29, no. 1 (Spring 2001): 147–73.

Herdt, Jennifer. *Putting on Virtue: The Legacy of the Splendid Vices.* Chicago: The University of Chicago Press, 2008.

Heuser, Stefan. "The Public Witness of Good Works: Lutheran Impulses for Political Ethics." *Journal of Lutheran Ethics* 6, no. 7 (2006): http://www.elca.org/JLE/Articles/582 (accessed April 22, 2016).

Höppfl, Harro. *Luther and Calvin on Secular Authority.* Cambridge: Cambridge University Press, 1991.

Hubbard, Moyer V. *New Creation in Paul's Letters and Thought.* Cambridge: Cambridge University Press, 2004.

Hunsinger, George. "What Karl Barth Learned from Martin Luther." *Lutheran Quarterly*, (Summer 1999): 125–55.

Hütter, Reinhard. "The Church as Public: Dogma, Practice, and the Holy Spirit." *Pro Ecclesia* 3, no. 3 (Summer 1994): 334–61.

Hütter, Reinhard. "The Church: The Knowledge of the Triune God: Practices, Doctrine, Theology." In *Knowing the Triune God: The Work of the Spirit in the Practices of the Church.* Edited by James Joseph Buckley and David S. Yeago, 23–47. Cambridge: Eerdmans, 2001.

Hütter, Reinhard. "St. Thomas on Grace and Free Will in the *Initium Fidei*: The Surpassing Augustinian Synthesis." *Nova et Vetera* 5, no. 3 (2007): 521–54.

Hütter, Reinhard. *Suffering Divine Things: Theology as Church Practice.* Translated by Doug Stott. Grand Rapids, MI: Eerdmans, 2000.

Hütter, Reinhard. "The Twofold Center of Lutheran Ethics: Christian Freedom and God's Commandments." In *The Promise of Lutheran Ethics.* Edited by Karen L. Bloomquist and John R. Stumme, 31–54. Minneapolis: Fortress Press, 1998.

Hyman, Gavin. *The Predicament of Postmodern Theology: Radical Orthodoxy or Nihilist Textualism?* London: Westminster John Knox Press, 2001.

Ingold, Tim. "The Textility of Making." *Cambridge Journal of Economics* 34, no. 1 (January 2010): 91–102.

Insole, Christopher. "Against Radical Orthodoxy: The Dangers of Overcoming Political Liberalism." *Modern Theology* 10, no. 2 (April 2004): 213–41.

Jennings, Willie James. *The Christian Imagination: Theology and the Origins of Race.* New Haven: Yale University Press, 2010.

Jenson, Robert W. "The Hidden and Triune God." *International Journal of Systematic Theology* 2, no. 1 (March 2000): 5–12.

Jenson, Robert W. "Luther's Contemporary Theological Significance." In *The Cambridge Companion to Martin Luther.* Edited by Donald K. McKim, 272–88. Cambridge: Cambridge University Press, 2003.

Jenson, Robert W. "Response to Mark Seifrid, Paul Metzger, and Carl Trueman on Finnish Luther Research." *Westminster Theological Journal* 65 (2003): 245–50.

Jenson, Robert W. *Systematic Theology, Volume 2: The Works of God.* Oxford: Oxford University Press, 1999.

Jenson, Robert W. *Visible Words: The Interpretation and Practice of Christian Sacraments.* Philadelphia: Fortress Press, 1978.

Jorgenson, Allen G. "Luther on Ubiquity and a Theology of the Public." *International Journal of Systematic Theology* 6, no. 4 (October 2004): 351-68.

Juntunen, Sammeli. "Luther and Metaphysics: What Is the Structure of Being according to Luther?" In *Union with Christ: The New Finnish Interpretation of Luther*, 129-60. Grand Rapids, MI: Eerdmans, 1998.

Kärkkäinen, Velli-Matti. "'The Christian as Christ to the Neighbor': On Luther's Theology of Love." *International Journal of Systematic Theology* 6, no. 2 (April 2004): 101-17.

Kolakowski, Leszek. *Modernity on Endless Trial*. Chicago: University of Chicago Press, 1990.

Kolb, Robert, and Timothy J. Wengert, eds. *The Book of Concord: The Confessions of the Evangelical Lutheran Church*. Translated by Charles Arand et al. Minneapolis: Fortress Press, 2000.

Lash, Nicholas. "Not Exactly Politics or Power?" *Modern Theology* 20, no. 2 (October 1992): 353-64.

Lazareth, William. *Christians in Society: Luther, the Bible and Social Ethics*. Minneapolis: Fortress Press, 2001.

Lazareth, William. "Response to Antti Raunio, 'Natural Law and Faith.'" In *Union with Christ: The New Finnish Interpretation of Luther*. Edited by Carl E. Braaten and Robert W. Jenson, 125-8. Grand Rapids, MI: Eerdmans, 1998.

Lehmann, Paul. *The Decalogue and a Human Future: The Meaning of the Commandments for Making and Keeping Human Life Human*. Grand Rapids, MI: Eerdmans, 1995.

Leinhard, Marc. *Luther: Witness to Jesus Christ*. Minneapolis: Augsburg Publishing, 1982.

Lohse, Bernhard. *Martin Luther's Theology: Its Historical and Systematic Development*. Edinburgh: T&T Clark, 1999.

Long, D. Stephen. *Divine Economy: Theology and the Market*. London: Routledge, 2000.

Machiavelli, Niccolo. *Discourses on Livy*. Translated by Harvey C. Mansfield and Nathan Tarcov. Chicago: University of Chicago Press, 1996.

MacIntyre, Alasdair. *A Short History of Ethics: A History of Moral Philosophy from the Homeric Age to the Twentieth Century*. 2nd Edition. London: Routledge, 1998.

Malysz, Piotr. "Exchange and Ecstasy: Luther's Eucharistic Theology in the Light of Radical Orthodoxy's Critique of Gift and Sacrifice." *Scottish Journal of Theology* 60, no. 3 (2007): 294-308.

Malysz, Piotr. "*Nemo iudex in causa sua* as the Basis of Law, Justice, and Justification in Luther's Thought." *Harvard Theological Review* 100, no. 3 (2007): 363-86.

Mannerma, Tuomo. *Christ Present in Faith: Luther's View of Justification*. Edited and translated by Kirsi Stjerna. Minneapolis: Fortress Press, 2005.

Mannerma, Tuomo. *Two Kinds of Love: Martin Luther's Religious World*. Translated by Krisi I. Stjerna. Minneapolis: Fortress Press, 2010.

Mannerma, Tuomo. "Why Is Luther so Fascinating?" In *Union with Christ: The New Finnish Interpretation of Luther*. Edited by Carl E. Braaten and Robert W. Jenson, 1-20. Grand Rapids, MI: Eerdmans, 1998.

Mansfield, Harvey. "Introduction." In Niccolo Machiavelli. *Discourses on Livy*. Translated by Harvey C. Mansfield and Nathan Tarcov, xvii-xliii. Chicago: University of Chicago Press, 1996.

Mathewes, Charles. *A Theology of Public Life*. Cambridge: Cambridge University Press, 2007.

Maxfield, John A. *Luther's Lectures on Genesis and the Formation of Evangelical Identity*. Kirksville, MO: Truman State University Press, 2008.

McKim, Donald K., ed. *The Cambridge Companion to Martin Luther*. Cambridge: Cambridge University Press, 2003.
Meilaender, Gilbert. "Book Review." *Studies in Christian Ethics* 23, no. 1 (February 2010): 97–102.
Meilaender, Gilbert. *The Theory and Practice of Virtue*. Notre Dame: University of Notre Dame, 1984.
Milbank, John. "Alternative Protestantism: Radical Orthodoxy and the Reformed Tradition." In *Radical Orthodoxy and the Reformed Tradition: Creation, Covenant and Participation*. Edited by James K. A. Smith and James Olthuis, 25–41. Grand Rapids, MI: Baker Academic, 2005.
Milbank, John. *Being Reconciled: Ontology and Pardon*. Abingdon: Routledge, 2003.
Milbank, John. *Beyond Secular Order: The Representation of Being and the Representation of the People*. Chichester: Wiley-Blackwell, 2014.
Milbank, John. "Can a Gift be Given? Prolegomena to a Future Trinitarian Metaphysic." *Modern Theology* 11, no. 1 (January 1995): 119–61.
Milbank, John. "Enclaves, or Where Is the Church?" In *The Future of Love: Essays in Political Theology*, 133–44. London: SCM Press, 2009.
Milbank, John. "An Essay against Secular Order." *The Journal of Religious Ethics* 15, no. 2 (Fall 1987): 199–224.
Milbank, John. *The Future of Love: Essays in Political Theology*. London: SCM Press, 2009.
Milbank, John. "The Grandeur of Reason and the Perversity of Rationalism: Radical Orthodoxy's First Decade." In *The Radical Orthodoxy Reader*. Edited by John Milbank and Simon Oliver, 365–404. London: Routledge, 2009.
Milbank, John. "Knowledge: The Theological Critique of Philosophy in Hamann and Jacobi." In *Radical Orthodoxy: A New Theology*. Edited by John Milbank, Catherine Pickstock, and Graham Ward, 21–37. London: Routledge, 1998.
Milbank, John. "Liberality versus Liberalism." In *The Future of Love: Essays in Political Theology*, 242–63. London: SCM Press, 2009.
Milbank, John. "Postmodern Critical Augustinianism: A Short Summa in Forty-Two Responses to Unasked Questions." In *The Radical Orthodoxy Reader*. Edited by John Milbank and Simon Oliver, 49–61. London: Routledge, 2009.
Milbank, John. "Radical Orthodoxy: A Conversation." In *The Radical Orthodoxy Reader*. Edited by John Milbank and Simon Oliver, 28–48. London: Routledge, 2009.
Milbank, John. *Theology and Social Theory: Beyond Secular Reason*. 2nd Edition. Oxford: Blackwell Publishing, 2006.
Milbank, John. *The Word Made Strange*. Oxford: Blackwell Publishers, 1997.
Milbank, John and Simon Oliver. *The Radical Orthodoxy Reader*. London: Routledge, 2009.
Milbank, John, Catherine Pickstock, and Graham Ward. *Radical Orthodoxy: A New Theology*. London: Routledge, 1998.
Murphy, Debra Dean. "Power, Politics and Difference: A Feminist Response to John Milbank." *Modern Theology* 10, no. 2 (April 1994): 131–42.
Nestingen, James Arne. "The Two Kingdoms Distinction: An Analysis with Suggestion." *Word and World* 19, no. 3 (Summer 1999): 268–75.
Nietzsche, Friedrich. *The Birth of Tragedy*. Translated by Walter Kaufmann. New York: Vintage Books, 1967.
Nietzsche, Friedrich. *On the Genealogy of Morality*. Edited by Keith Ansell-Pearson. Translated by Carol Diethe. Cambridge: Cambridge University Press, 1997.
Nimmo, Paul. "The Orders of Creation in the Theological Ethics of Karl Barth." *Scottish Journal of Theology* 60, no. 1 (2007): 34–5.

Nygren, Anders. "Luther's Doctrine of the Two Kingdoms." *Ecumenical Review* 1, no. 3 (Spring 1949): 301–10.
Oberman, Heiko. *The Dawn of the Reformation: Essays in Late Medieval and Early Reformation Thought*. Edinburgh: T&T Clark, 1986.
Oberman, Heiko. *Forerunners of the Reformation: The Shape of Late Medieval Thought*. Translated by Paul L. Nyhus. Cambridge: James Clarke, 2002.
Oberman, Heiko. *The Harvest of Medieval Theology: Gabriel Biel and Late Medieval Nominalism*. Cambridge: Harvard University Press, 1963.
Oberman, Heiko. *Luther: Man between God and the Devil*. Translated by Eileen Walliser-Schwarzbart. New Haven: Yale University Press, 1989.
Oberman, Heiko. *The Two Reformations: The Journey from the Last Days to the New World*. Edited by Donald Weinstein. New Haven: Yale University Press, 2003.
O'Donovan, Oliver. *The Desire of the Nations: Rediscovering the Roots of Political Theology*. Cambridge: Cambridge University Press, 1996.
O'Donovan, Oliver. *Resurrection and Moral Order: An Outline for Evangelical Ethics*. 2nd Edition. Grand Rapids, MI: Eerdmans, 1992.
O'Donovan, Oliver and Joan Lockwood O'Donovan. *Bonds of Imperfection: Christian Politics, Past and Present*. Grand Rapids, MI: Eerdmans, 2004.
Pasewark, Kyle. "The Body in Ecstasy: Love, Difference, and the Social Organism in Luther's Theory of the Lord's Supper." *The Journal of Religion* 77, no. 4 (October 1997): 511–40.
Peknold, Chad. "Migrations of the Host: Fugitive Democracy and the Corpus Mysticum." *Political Theology* 11, no. 1 (January 2010): 77–101.
Pelikan, Jaroslav. *Luther's Works: Companion Volume: Luther the Expositor: Introduction to the Reformer's Exegetical Writings*. Saint Louis, MO: Concordia Publishing House, 1959.
Peters, Albrecht. *Commentary on Luther's Catechisms: Ten Commandments*. Translated by Holger K. Sonntag. Saint Louis, MO: Concordia Publishing House, 2009.
Peura, Simo. "Christ as Favor and Gift (donum): The Challenge of Luther's Understanding of Justification." In *Union with Christ: The New Finnish Interpretation of Luther*. Edited by Carl E. Braaten and Robert W. Jenson, 42–69. Grand Rapids, MI: Eerdmans, 1998.
Peura, Simo. "What God Gives Man Receives: Luther on Salvation." In *Union with Christ: The New Finnish Interpretation of Luther*. Edited by Carl E. Braaten and Robert W. Jenson, 76–94. Grand Rapids, MI: Eerdmans, 1998.
Placher, William. *The Domestication of Transcendence: How Modern Thinking about God Went Wrong*. Louisville, KY: Westminster John Knox Press, 1996.
Prenter, Regin. "Luther on Word and Sacrament." In *More about Luther: Martin Luther Lectures*. By Jaroslav J. Pelikan, Regin Prenter, and Herman A. Preus, 63–122. Decorah, IA: Luther College Press, 1958.
Prenter, Regin. *Spiritus Creator: Luther's Concept of the Holy Spirit*. Translated by John M. Jensen. Philadelphia: Muhlenberg Press, 1953.
Preus, James Samuel. *From Shadow to Promise: Old Testament Interpretation from Augustine to the Young Luther*. Cambridge: Harvard University Press, 1969.
Probst, Christopher J. *Demonizing the Jews: Luther and the Protestant Church in Nazi Germany*. Bloomington: Indiana University Press, 2012.
Roberts, Richard H. "Transcendental Sociology? A Critique of John Milbank's 'Theology and Social Theory beyond Secular Reason.'" *Scottish Journal of Theology* 46, no. 4 (November 1993): 527–35.

Rolf, Sibylle. "Luther's Understanding of Imputation in the Context of His Doctrine of Justification and Its Implication for the Preaching of the Gospel." *International Journal of Systematic Theology* 12, no. 4 (October 2010): 435–51.
Rousseau, Jean-Jacques. *On the Social Contract with Geneva Manuscript and Political Economy.* Edited by Roger D. Masters. Translated by Judith R. Masters. Boston: Bedford/St. Martins, 1978.
Russell, William R. "The Smalcald Articles, Luther's Theological Testament." *Lutheran Quarterly* 5, no. 3 (Autumn 1991): 277–96.
Ryan, Alan. *On Politics: A History of Political Thought from Herodotus to the Present.* London: Penguin, 2012.
Saarinen, Risto. "Ethics in Luther's Theology: The Three Orders." In *Moral Philosophy on the Threshold of Modernity*. Edited by Jill Kraye and Risto Saarinen, 195–215. Dordrecht: Springer, 2005.
Saarinen, Risto. "Forgiveness, the Gift, and Ecclesiology." *Dialog* 45, no. 1 (Spring 2006): 55–63.
Sasse, Herman. *This Is My Body: Luther's Contention for the Real Presence in the Sacrament of the Altar.* Adelaide: Lutheran Publishing House, 1977.
Sauter, Gerhard. "God Creating Faith. The Doctrine of Justification from the Reformation to the Present." *Lutheran Quarterly* 11, no. 1 (Spring 1997): 17–102.
Schaeffer, Hans. *Createdness and Ethics: The Doctrine of Creation and Theological Ethics in the Theology of Colin E. Gunton and Oswald Bayer.* Berlin: Walter de Gruyter, 2006.
Schwarz, Reinhard. "Luthers Lehre von den drei Ständen und die drei Dimensionen der Ethik." *Lutherjahrbuch* 45 (1978): 15–34.
Shakespeare, Stephen. *Radical Orthodoxy: A Critical Introduction.* London: SPCK, 2007.
Shults, F. LeRon, and Brent Waters. *Christology and Ethics.* Grand Rapids, MI: Eerdmans, 2010.
Sider, J. Alexander. *To See History Doxologically: History and Holiness in John Howard Yoder's Ecclesiology.* Grand Rapids, MI: Eerdmans, 2011.
Simon, Wolfgang. "Worship and Eucharist in Luther Studies." *Dialog* 47, no. 2 (Summer 2008): 143–56.
Skinner, Quentin. *The Foundations of Modern Political Thought: Vol. 1: The Renaissance.* Cambridge: Cambridge University Press, 1978.
Skinner, Quentin. *The Foundations of Modern Political Thought, Vol. 2: The Age of Reformation.* Cambridge: Cambridge University Press, 1978.
Smith, James K. A. and James Olthuis. *Radical Orthodoxy and the Reformed Tradition: Creation, Covenant and Participation.* Grand Rapids, MI: Baker Academic, 2005.
Smith, Ronald Gregor. *J.G. Hamann: A Study in Christian Existence.* London: Collins, 1960.
Stayer, James M. *Martin Luther: German Saviour: German Evangelical Theological Factions and the Interpretation of Luther, 1917–1933.* Montreal: McGill-Queen's University Press, 2000.
Stephenson, John R. "The Two Kingdoms and the Two Governments in Luther's Theology." *Scottish Journal of Theology* 34, no. 4 (August 1981): 321–37.
Stout, Jeffrey. *Democracy and Tradition.* Princeton: Princeton University Press, 2004.
Stout, Jeffrey. "The Spirit of Democracy and the Rhetoric of Excess." *Journal of Religious Ethics* 35, no. 1 (March 2007): 3–21.
Strassler, Robert B. *The Landmark Thucydides: A Comprehensive Guide to the Peloponnesian War.* Translated by Richard Crawley. New York: Touchstone, 1996.

Tanner, Kathryn. *Christ the Key.* Cambridge: Cambridge University Press, 2010.
Tanner, Kathryn. *God and Creation in Christian Theology: Tyranny or Empowerment.* Oxford: Blackwell Publishers, 1988.
Taylor, Charles. *Sources of the Self: The Making of the Modern Identity.* Cambridge: Harvard University Press, 1989.
Thompson, W. D. J. Carghill. *The Political Thought of Martin Luther.* Brighton, Sussex: Harvester Press, 1984.
Trueman, Carl. "Is the Finnish Line a New Beginning? A Critical Assessment of the Reading of Luther Offered by the Helsinki Circle." *Westminster Theological Journal* 65 (2003): 231–44.
Ulrich, Hans G. "Bodily Life as Creaturely Life: The Ethical Coexistence of Human Beings with Disabilities and Its Fulfillment." *Journal of Religion, Disability and Health* 15, no. 1 (2011): 42–56.
Ulrich, Hans G. "God's Commandments and Their Political Presence: Notes of a Tradition on the 'Ground' of Ethics." *Studies in Christian Ethics* 23, no. 1 (2010): 42–58.
Ulrich, Hans G. "On the Grammar of Lutheran Ethics." In *Lutheran Ethics at the Intersection of God's One World.* Edited by Karen L. Bloomquist, 27–48. Geneva: The Lutheran World Federation, 2005.
Ulrich, Hans G. "Stations on the Way to Freedom: The Presence of God—the Freedom of Disciples." In *Who Am I? Bonhoeffer's Theology through His Poetry.* Edited by Bernd Wannenwetsch, 147–74. London: T&T Clark, 2009.
Ulrich, Hans G. "Waiting for the Other Word—God's Advent in Human Preaching: Considerations for a Theology of Preaching." Paper delivered to the Society for the Study of Theology, 2007.
Ulrich, Hans G. *Wie Geschöpfe leben: Konturen evangelischer Ethik.* 2nd Edition. Berlin: Lit Verlag, 2007.
Voegelin, Eric. *History of Political Ideas, Vol. IV: Renaissance and Reformation.* The Collected Works of Eric Vogelin, Volume 22. Edited by David L. Morse and William M. Thompson. Columbia: University of Missouri Press, 1998.
Wannenwetsch, Bernd. "*Caritas fide formata.* 'Herz und Affekte' als Schlüssel zu 'Glaube und Liebe.'" *Kerygma and Dogma* 45 (2000): 205–24.
Wannenwetsch, Bernd. "'Christians and Pagans': Towards a Trans-Religious Second Naïveté or How to be a Christological Creature." In *Who Am I? Bonhoeffer's Theology through His Poetry,* Edited by Bernd Wannenwetsch, 175–96. London: T&T Clark, 2009.
Wannenwetsch, Bernd. "Ecclesiology and Ethics." In *The Oxford Handbook of Theological Ethics.* Edited by Gilbert Meilaender and William Werpehowski, 57–73. Oxford: Oxford University Press, 2005.
Wannenwetsch, Bernd. "For in its welfare you will find your welfare: Political Realism and the Limits of the Augustinian Framework." *Political Theology* 12, no. 3 (June 2011): 457–65.
Wannenwetsch, Bernd. "'Hier Liegt Ihr Auf Dem Altar'. Darbringung Der Gaben Und Die Konsekration Der Gemeinde." In *Gottesdienst Der Kirche. Handbuch der Liturgiewissenschaft.* Edited by Martin Klöckener, Angelus A. Häußling, and Reinhard Messner, 393–4. Regensberg: Verlag Friedrich Pustet, 2008.
Wannenwetsch, Bernd. "The Liturgical Origin of the Christian Politeia: Overcoming the 'Weberian' Temptation." In *Church as Politeia: The Political Self-Understanding of Christianity.* Edited by Christoph Stumpf and Holger Zaborowski, 322–40. Berlin: Walter de Gruyter, 2004.

Wannenwetsch, Bernd. "Luther's Moral Theology." In *The Cambridge Companion to Martin Luther*. Edited by Donald K. McKim, 134–45. Cambridge: Cambridge University Press, 2003.

Wannenwetsch, Bernd. "'Members of One Another': Charis, Ministry and Representation: A Politico-Ecclesial Reading of Romans 12." In *A Royal Priesthood? The Use of the Bible Ethically and Politically: A Dialogue with Oliver O'Donovan*. Edited by Craig Bartholomew, Jonathan Chaplin, Robert Song, and Al Wolters, 196–219. Grand Rapids, MI: Zondervan, 2002.

Wannenwetsch, Bernd. "Political Love." In *'You Have the Words of Eternal Life': Transformative Readings of the Gospel of John from a Lutheran Perspective*. Edited by Kenneth Mtata, 93–105. Geneva: The Lutheran World Federation, 2012.

Wannenwetsch, Bernd. *Political Worship*. Translated by Margaret Kohl. Oxford: Oxford University Press, 2004.

Wannenwetsch, Bernd. "The Political Worship of the Church: A Critical and Empowering Practice." *Modern Theology* 12, no. 3 (July 1996): 269–99.

Wannenwetsch, Bernd. "Representing the Absent in the City: Prolegomena to a Negative Political Theology according to Revelation 21." In *God, Truth, and Witness: Engaging Stanley Hauerwas*. Edited by L. Gregory Jones, Reinhard Hütter, and C. Rosalee Velloso Ewell, 167–92. Grand Rapids, MI: Brazos Press, 2005.

Wannenwetsch, Bernd. "Ruled by the Spirit: Hans Ulrich's Understanding of Political Existence." *Studies in Christian Ethics* 20, no. 2 (2007): 257–72.

Wannenwetsch, Bernd, ed. *Who Am I? Bonhoeffer's Theology through His Poetry*. London: T&T Clark, 2009.

Wannenwetsch, Bernd. "The Whole Christ and the Whole Human Being: Dietrich Bonhoeffer's Inspiration for the 'Christology and Ethics' Discourse." In *Christology and Ethics*. Edited by F. LeRon Shults and Brent Waters, 75–98. Grand Rapids, MI: Eerdmans, 2010.

Wannenwetsch, Bernd. "Wovon handelt die 'material Ethik'? Oder: warum die Ethik der elementaren Lebensformen ('Stände') einer 'Bereichsethik' vorzuziehen ist Oswald Bayer zum sechzigsten Geburtstag." In *Kirche(n) und Gesellschaft*. Edited by Andrease Fritzsche and Manfred Kwiran, 95–136. Munich: Bernward, 2000.

Wannenwetsch, Bernd. "Zwischen Schindmähre und Wildpferd: Luthers Reittier-Metapher ethisch betrachtet." *Zeitschrift der Luther-Gesellschaft* 65, no. 1 (1994): 22–33.

Ward, Graham. *Cities of the Good*. London: Routledge, 2000.

Weber, Max. *The Vocation Lectures: "Science as Vocation," "Politics as Vocation."* Edited by David Owen and Tracy B. Strong. Translated by Rodney Livingstone. Indianapolis: Hackett Publishing, 2004.

Webster, John. *Word and Church: Essays in Christian Dogmatics*. Edinburgh: T&T Clark, 2001.

Westhelle, Vito. "The Word and the Mask: Revisiting the Two-Kingdoms Doctrine." In *The Gift of Grace: The Future of Lutheran Theology*. Edited by Niels Henrik Gregersen, 167–78. Minneapolis: Fortress Press, 2005.

White, Graham. *Luther as Nominalist: A Study of the Logical Methods Used in Martin Luther's Disputations in Light of Their Medieval Background*. Helsinki: Luther-Agricola-Society, 1994.

Whitford, David M. "'Cura Religionis' or Two Kingdoms: The Late Luther on Religion and the State in the 'Lectures on Genesis.'" *Church History* 73, no. 1 (March 2004): 41–62.

Wingren, Gustav. *The Christian's Calling: Luther on Vocation*. Translated by Carl C. Rasmussen. Philadelphia: Muhlenburg Press, 1957.

Wolf, Ernst. "Die Institutionen als von Gott angebotener Ort der Bewährung in Verantwortung." In *Sozialethik: Theologische Grundlagen*, 168–77. Göttingen: Vandenhoeck & Ruprecht, 1975.

Wolin, Sheldon. *Politics and Vision: Continuity and Innovation in Western Political Thought*. Expanded Edition. Princeton: Princeton University Press, 2004.

Wright, William J. *Martin Luther's Understanding of God's Two Kingdoms: A Response to the Challenge of Scepticism*. Grand Rapids, MI: Baker, 2010.

Yeago, David. "'A Christian Holy People': Martin Luther on Salvation and the Church." *Modern Theology* 13, no. 1 (January 1997): 101–20.

Yeago, David. "Gnosticism, Antinomianism, and Reformation Theology: Reflections on the Cost of a Construal." *Pro Ecclesia* 2, no. 1 (1993): 37–49.

Yeago, David. "Martin Luther on Grace, Law and Moral Life: Prolegomena to an Ecumenical Discussion of 'Veritatis Splendor.'" *The Thomist* 62, no. 2 (1998): 163–91.

Yoder, John Howard. *The Politics of Jesus*. 2nd Edition. Grand Rapids, MI: Eerdmans, 1994.

Zachman, Randall. *The Assurance of Faith: Conscience in the Theology of Martin Luther and John Calvin*. Minneapolis: Fortress Press, 1993.

INDEX

Abelard, Peter 52
Althaus, Paul 108–9, 147 n.131, 155, 162 n.43, 173, 183
Aquinas, Thomas 20, 34, 40 n.47, 53 n.95, 92 n.24, 118, 121, 136 n.92, 186 n.170
Arendt, Hannah 93–7
Aristotle 8, 62, 92 n.4, 94–5, 97, 117–18, 128, 135, 150, 180
Augustine of Hippo 16–17, 20–1, 40, 43 n.58, 47, 87–93, 104 n.89, 105, 110–11, 115, 117–20, 127, 183–4

Barth, Karl 43 n.58, 106 n.97, 122 n.34, 151 n.139, 155–62
Bayer, Oswald 21, 39 n.43, 40, 41 n.51, 46 n.73, 59 n.6, 61–3, 66 n.39, 78 n.92, 132 n.78, 133 n.81, 144 n.121, 145, 147 n.132, 148 n.134, 150–1, 163, 170 n.80, 173, 175, 179–81, 183–7, 189
Beiner, Ronald 4 n.12
Benne, Robert 173 n.95
Biel, Gregory 11, 31, 38, 53 n.95
Bonhoeffer, Dietrich 2–3, 67 n.43, 146 n.129, 147 n.131, 148 n.134, 158 n.25, 173–4, 179 n.138, 182, 193 n.198
Bornkamm, Heinrich 183
Bourdieu, Pierre 77–9
Bretherton, Luke 17 n.70, 20, 114 n.3, 128 n.66
Breyfogle, Todd 36 n.25
Brian, Rustin 10 n.32
Brock, Brian 21, 64 n.34, 138 n.102, 148, 164, 174, 177, 182 n.150
Brunner, Emil 122 n.34, 156–60, 162

Cain 98–103, 135, 173, 179, 188–90, 193
Calvin, John 32–5, 38, 122 n.34, 158
Cavanaugh, William 60, 77, 79–85, 89 n.10
Chambers, Katherine 90 n.14
Chester, Stephen 41 n.51

Clairvaux, Bernard 52
collect 84–5
communicatio idiomatum 41 n.51, 46, 84, 171
Connolly, William 9 n.31
Cranz, F. Edward 108–9
creation 3, 15, 27, 43, 59, 62, 67–70, 92, 109, 113–15, 140–6, 149–51, 157–9, 175–9, 181

Derrida, Jacques 77–9
Diem, Harald 183 n.152
Duchrow, Ulrich 106 n.97, 109 n.110

Ebeling, Gerhard 71–2, 109 n.109, 185
ecclesia 4, 7–8, 15–16, 25–7, 30, 56, 58, 60, 74, 76, 80, 86–7, 90, 98–106, 108, 109 n.9, 110–11, 113, 115, 133, 153, 162–3, 165, 167–8, 178–81, 188–9, 192
ecclesiology of Luther 11–14, 19, 57, 59–60, 73–6, 98–106
Elert, Werner 183 n.152
Elshtain, Jean Bethke 6–7, 20
Erasmus 120–4, 126, 129, 139
Estes, James 16 n.67, 108 n.108
eudaimonism 115–17, 119–20, 126

faith and love 34–5, 42–3, 46–56, 150, 153
Figgis, J. N. 5, 14, 19 n.79
Forell, George 183–4, 188 n.187
fortunate exchange 41 n.51, 44–6, 83

gift exchange 18–19, 77–8
Gregersen, Niels Henrik 68 n.46, 69–70
Gregory, Eric 17 n.70, 20, 22 n.88, 114 n.3, 128 n.66

habituation gap 116, 124
Hagen, Kenneth 53 n.96
Hamann, J. G. 148 n.134, 163, 181 n.148

Hamm, Berndt 51–4
Hauerwas, Stanley 9 n.31, 20–1, 57 n.2, 128, 130, 147
Heckel, Johannes 182, n.152
Hegel, G. W. F. 34, 151 n.139
Heuser, Stefan 133 n.82
Hobbes, Thomas 36–7, 110
Höppfl, Harro 9 n.31
Hubbard, Moyer 146 n.130
Hunsinger, George 160 n.33
Hütter, Reinhard 21, 122 n.31, 133, 162

individualism 5, 60, 64, 83
Ingold, Tim 136
institutions 4 n.13, 7–8, 14–15, 19–20, 25–8, 58–9, 99–103, 110, 113–15, 130, 132, 148, 150, 153–94

Jenson, Robert 40 n.43, 42, 47 n.74, 62–3, 67 n.44, 76 n.82, 81 n.102, 140, 166 n.60
Jorgenson, Allen G. 67 n.43
Juntunen, Sammeli 39–40
justification 24–7, 30, 32–5, 37, 39–44, 48–9, 51–6, 60, 76–7, 79–82, 115 n.4, 123–5, 128 n.66, 129–30, 132–4, 137, 140, 144, 149–51, 153, 171–3, 193

Lash, Nicholas 93
Lau, Franz 183 n.152
law/gospel distinction 154, 156–62
Lazareth, William 26 n.92, 156–7, 161
Lehmann, Paul 181 n.147
Leinhard, Marc 12 n.29, 21, 57 n.2
Lohse, Bernhard 41 n.51, 163

Machiavelli, Niccolo 1, 4, 7–8
MacIntyre, Alasdair 5–6, 7 n.24, 14, 21
McGrath, Alister 124 n.45
Malysz, Piotr 80 n.98, 82 n.103, 110 n.113, 167 n.67
Mannermaa, Tuomo 30, 39, 41–2, 47 n.74, 50 n.87
Mansfeld, Harvey 7–8
Mathewes, Charles 17 n.70, 20, 114 n.3, 128 n.66
Meilaender, Gilbert 116 n.5, 127 n.62
Melanchthon, Philip 38, 41, 103, 108 n.108
Metzger, Mark Louis 55 n.107
mimesis 120–3, 125, 128–9, 145

nature/grace distinction 119 n.17, 121, 127–30, 139–40, 170–1
Nietzsche, Friedrich 1–2, 5
Nimmo, Paul 160 n.31
nominalism 9, 11, 19, 31–5, 37, 38–41, 57, 59, 67–8, 74 n.78, 114, 122, 129
Nygren, Anders 78, 188

Oberman, Heiko 38, 52 n.95, 53 n.97
Ockham, William 5, 10–11, 31–2, 34, 38, 52
O'Donovan, Oliver 20, 87, 89 n.10, 90 n.14, 92 n.26, 185 n.162
oeconomia 7, 27, 76 n.4, 99 n.60, 101–3, 153, 163, 165, 168, 174, 176, 180–2, 185, 189–90, 192
orders of creation 155–60, 162, 164, 173, 175
otherworldly/worldly 1–5, 187

Pasewark, Kyle 76 n.84, 80
Pelikan, Jaroslav 70–1
Peters, Albrecht 162 n.45
Peura, Simo 41 n.48, 42 n.53, 125–6
Placher, William 136 n.92
polis (see *politia*)
politia 7–8, 25–7, 56, 58, 74, 89 n.9, 90 n.16, 93–7, 99 n.60, 101–7, 110–11, 113, 115, 130, 153, 155, 163, 165, 168–9, 176, 183–90, 192
Prenter, Regin 134 n.85, 147 n.131
Preus, James Samuel 71 n.62

redemption 10, 23, 25, 52, 55, 70–1, 89 n.9, 92 n.28, 111, 113–14, 130, 132 n.78, 137, 140–6, 149–50, 155, 157–8
Rousseau, Jean-Jacques 1–5
Russell, William R. 175 n.107

Saarinen, Risto 163 n.47
sacraments 3, 13, 16, 24, 33, 43, 58 n.2, 59–60, 65, 67–70, 75–86, 100–1, 125–6, 143, 146–9, 164, 169–73, 180, 190 n.187, 192
sanctification 25–6, 33 n.15, 39–41, 51–2, 115, 123–5, 129–30, 132–4, 140, 143, 149–51, 153–4, 171–3
Schaeffer, Hans 62
Schwarz, Reinhard 163 n.47

Index

Scotus, John Duns 10–11, 31, 32 n.10, 33, 53 n.95, 122
Shakespeare, Steven 75 n.81
Simon, Wolfgang 82
Skinner, Quentin 7 n.24, 9–13
sola scriptura 6, 24, 36–7, 59–60, 64, 71–3, 86
Spinoza, Baruch 36–7
Stayer, James 155 n.5, Stout, Jeffery 9 n.31, 17 n.70, 20, 128

Tanner, Kathryn 36 n.25
Taylor, Charles 30 n.2, 119
Thompson, W. D. J Carghill 183
three estates
  see institutions
Törnvall, Gustav 183 n.152
Trueman, Carl 43
two *civitates* 15, 22, 25, 30, 88–93, 102–10
two *ecclesiae* 4, 15–16, 24–7, 30, 87–8, 98–106, 108–11
two kingdoms 5, 12, 14, 26 n.92, 36–7, 87–93, 102–8, 115 n.15, 188
two *regiments* 16, 22, 25–7, 87–8, 106–11, 175

Ulrich, Hans 21, 58 n.5, 95, 134, 145 n.125, 162 n.43, 164, 171 n.85, 172 n.91, 178, 180, 181 n.149, 191–2
union with Christ 24, 39–41, 42–6, 49–50, 55–6, 57, 60, 81, 83, 123–4, 138, 149

VanHoozer, Kevin 128 n.67
virtue, acquired 118–19
virtue, infused 118–19, 126, 143
Voegelin, Eric 6, 47–8, 51 n.91, 79 n.94
voluntarism 9, 11, 18, 24–5, 31–2, 35–7, 60, 74 n.78, 86, 119, 122, 129

Wannenwetsch, Bernd 8 n.29, 21, 47 n.74, 50 n.87, 51 n.91, 66, 73 n.70, 74 n.75, 79 n.94, 85 n.118, 97 n.51, 104 n.89, 137–8, 153, 160 n.33, 162, 169–70, 176, 179 n.138, 183 n.153, 191
Weber, Max 10, 14 n.51, 32, 94–5
Webster, John 74 n.78
Wells, Samuel 128 n.67
Westhelle, Vitor 87 n.2
Whitford, David M. 108 n.108
Wolf, Ernst 174 n.102
Wolin, Sheldon 9–10, 13–16, 19–20
words of institution 59 n.6, 70, 82, 85 n.118, 170, 173, 178, 180
Wright, William J. 106 n.97

Yeago, David 21, 60, 161–2, 184
Yoder, John Howard 9 n.31, 90 n.16

Zachman, Randall 123 n.39